A Student's Guide to the Plays of Samuel Beckett

by Samuel Beckett

published by Faber and Faber

COLLECTED SHORTER PLAYS
ENDGAME: A Play in One Act *and* ACT WITHOUT WORDS
HAPPY DAYS: A Play in Two Acts
WAITING FOR GODOT: A Tragicomedy in Two Acts

published by John Calder Publishers Ltd

COLLECTED POEMS IN ENGLISH AND FRENCH
COME AND GO
COMPANY
FIRST LOVE
FOR TO END YET AGAIN *and* OTHER FIZZLES
FOUR NOVELLAS
HOW IT IS
ILL SEEN ILL SAID
IMAGINATION DEAD IMAGINE
MALONE DIES
MERCIER AND CAMIER
MOLLOY
MORE PRICKS THAN KICKS
MURPHY
NO'S KNIFE
POEMS IN ENGLISH
PROUST *and*
THREE DIALOGUES WITH GEORGES DUTHUIT
SIX RESIDUA
STILLS
TEXTS FOR NOTHING
THE UNNAMABLE
WATT
WORSTWORD HO

A Student's Guide to the Plays of
SAMUEL BECKETT

BERYL S. FLETCHER
and
JOHN FLETCHER

faber and faber
LONDON · BOSTON

First published in 1978
by Faber and Faber Limited
3 Queen Square London WC1N 3AU
Second edition, revised and expanded, 1985

Photoset and printed in Great Britain by
Redwood Burn Limited
Trowbridge Wiltshire
All rights reserved

British Library Cataloguing in Publication Data

A student's guide to the plays of Samuel
Beckett.—2nd ed.
1. Beckett, Samuel—Criticism and interpretation
I. Fletcher, Beryl S.
822'.912   PR6003.E282Z/
ISBN 0–571–13418–1
ISBN 0–571–13419–X Pbk

Library of Congress Cataloging in Publication Data

Fletcher, John, 1937–
A student's guide to the plays of Samuel Beckett.
Rev. ed. of: A student's guide to the plays of Samuel
Beckett/Beryl S. Fletcher. 1978.
1. Beckett, Samuel, 1906–   —Criticism and
interpretation. I. Fletcher, Beryl S. Student's guide
to the plays of Samuel Beckett.   II. Title.
PR6003.E282Z6647 1985   822'.912   85–1538
ISBN 0–571–13418–1
ISBN 0–571–13419–X (pbk.)

To the memory of Roger Blin

CONTENTS

Contents

PREFACE AND ACKNOWLEDGEMENTS

This *Guide* has an overriding aim: to offer as much help as possible to its users, students and general readers alike. As the Select Bibliography shows, it digests a great deal of material and seeks to provide a complete short guide to all Beckett's published plays and to the criticism that has been devoted to them.

All the published drama is discussed in approximate order of original composition in so far as this can be ascertained at the present time. The text used is the English one, although reference is occasionally made to the French where this offers some illumination. Unusual words are glossed unless they are adequately defined for our purpose in the Concise Oxford Dictionary. As many as possible of Beckett's quotations are identified, although it is often futile to attempt to track down to their source all the echoes heard in texts composed by a writer who is steeped in the classics (especially the King James Bible, Dante, Shakespeare and Milton).

The pattern of the *Guide* is straightforward. After an introductory essay, which attempts to set Beckett's drama in the general cultural and aesthetic context from which it springs, to trace its development, and to deal with the vexed problem of what the plays are intended to 'mean', the sections on individual works are for the most part laid out as follows:

Details of composition and publication, and of first performance
Reception (i.e. how the critics greeted the play when it was first produced)
Décor (details of staging, props, etc.)
Dramatis personae (the characters)
Structure (the shape and form of the work)
Language and dramatic expression (especially aspects of dialogue)
Notes on the text

References to critical essays or articles published in periodicals are given in full in the text, but for bibliographical details about books cited the reader should refer to the Select Bibliography.

Finally, while we have tried to provide as much useful objective information as possible, we have also not hesitated to give some kind of evaluation of the different plays. We consider Beckett a great dramatist, but not all his works (as he would be the first to agree) are of equal merit or interest; and where we feel they are not, we have not hesitated to say so.

Among the many people who have helped us we should especially like to thank Samuel Beckett himself for putting us right over several questions of fact, Professor James Knowlson (whose knowledge in this field is unrivalled), Barry Smith (who contributed valuable material on some of the plays), Peter Aston, Walter Bachem, Pierre Chabert, Julian Elloway, Martin Esslin, Michael Hayes, Martin Hollis, Richard Leah, John Spurling, David Warrilow, R. B. Woodings and participants in John Fletcher's Beckett seminars at Konstanz University and the University of East Anglia. We are also grateful for the co-operation of the BBC Sound Archives and BBC Television, and to the publishers of the following works in which some of our material appeared in a different form: *Beckett the Playwright*, by John Fletcher and John Spurling (Methuen); *Fin de partie* by Samuel Beckett, edited by John and Beryl S. Fletcher (Methuen Educational); *Waiting for Godot* by Samuel Beckett, edited by John Fletcher (Faber Educational Books); *Modernism 1890–1930*, edited by Malcolm Bradbury and James McFarlane (Penguin Books); and *Themes in Drama, 4*, edited by James Redmond (Cambridge University Press).

Norwich
September 1984

BSF
JWF

EDITIONS OF SAMUEL BECKETT'S WORKS REFERRED TO IN THE TEXT

PLAYS

Collected Shorter Plays (for all the plays except those listed immediately below). Faber and Faber, 1984, and Grove Press, 1984.

Endgame. Faber Paperback Edition (1982 reprint).

Happy Days. Faber Paperback Edition (1981 reprint).

Waiting for Godot. Faber Paperback Edition (1981 reprint).

OTHER WORKS

More Pricks than Kicks. Calder & Boyars, 1970.

Murphy. Routledge, 1938.

No's Knife. Calder & Boyars, 1967.

Poems in English. John Calder, 1961.

Proust. Chatto & Windus, 1931.

[Three Novels] *Molloy, Malone Dies, The Unnamable*. John Calder, 1959.

Watt. Paris, Olympia Press, 1958.

ABBREVIATIONS USED IN THE TEXT

B&B	*Beckett and Broadcasting* Clas Zilliacus
EAG	*En attendant Godot* Colin Duckworth (ed.)
Frescoes	*Frescoes of the Skull* James Knowlson and John Pilling
IDE	*The Irish Drama of Europe from Yeats to Beckett* Katharine Worth
KTWB	*Krapp's Last Tape: A Theatre Workbook* James Knowlson (ed.)
SBaE	*Samuel Beckett: An Exhibition* James Knowlson
SDR	Süddeutscher Rundfunk [South German Broadcasting Corporation]
STB	Schiller Theater Berlin *Warten auf Godot* (directed by Samuel Beckett)
COED	Concise Oxford [English] Dictionary
SOED	Shorter Oxford English Dictionary
Sc.	'Understand' or 'supply'

BIOGRAPHICAL TABLE

1906 Samuel Barclay Beckett born at Foxrock near Dublin on 13 April (Good Friday), second son of William Frank Beckett, a quantity surveyor, and his wife Mary, née Roe. Middle-class Protestant family, comfortably off. Kindergarten: Miss Ida Elsner's Academy, Stillorgan. Prep school: Earlsfort School, Dublin. Public school: Portora Royal, Enniskillen; excellent academic and sporting record.

1923–7 Trinity College, Dublin, first as pensioner, then as foundation scholar. In BA examinations placed first in first class in Modern Literature (French and Italian); awarded large gold medal and Moderatorship prize. Active in Modern Languages Society, Cricket Club, Golf Club; keen chess player. Summer 1926: first contact with France (bicycle tour of the châteaux of the Loire).

1928 Spends first two terms teaching at Campbell College, Belfast.

1928–30 Exchange *Lecteur* at École Normale Supérieure in Paris; meets James Joyce. Summer 1930: Beckett's first separately published work, the poem *Whoroscope*, issued by Nancy Cunard's Hours Press in Paris.

1930–2 Assistant Lecturer in French, Trinity College, Dublin. Resigns after four terms. 19–21 February 1931: performance of Beckett's first dramatic work, *Le Kid*, a parody sketch after Corneille written in collaboration with Georges Pelorson, French *Lecteur* at Trinity.

1931 *Proust*, his first and last major piece of literary criticism, published by Chatto & Windus.

1932–7 *Wanderjahre* culminating in the decision to settle permanently in Paris.

1933 Death of his father, who leaves him an annuity,

13

which forms the bulk of his slender income until the royalties from *Waiting for Godot* twenty years later.

1934   Chatto & Windus publish *More Pricks than Kicks* (short stories).

1935   *Echo's Bones and Other Precipitates* (first collection of verse) published in Paris.

1937   Begins (and abandons after writing part of one scene) a play called *Human Wishes* about the relationship between Dr Johnson and Mrs Thrale, the widow whom Johnson wanted to marry but who after dallying for four years married another man.

1938   *Murphy*, his first novel, published by Routledge. An Oxford undergraduate, Iris Murdoch, deeply influenced by the book.

1942   Resistance group in which Beckett is active is betrayed to the Gestapo; he escapes to the unoccupied southern zone with only minutes to spare.

1942–5   Helps out as an agricultural labourer not far from Avignon ('we were there together, I could swear to it! Picking grapes . . .', *Waiting for Godot*, p. 62). Writes *Watt*, his last English novel.

1945   Returns at Easter to Ireland to see his family; then, in order to get back to France, accepts in August a post as interpreter and storekeeper at the Irish Red Cross hospital in Saint-Lô, Normandy.

1946–50   Back in Paris, burst of creative activity. Writes in French the essential works of the canon, the trilogy of novels (*Molloy, Malone Dies, The Unnamable*) and the play *Waiting for Godot*, which was preceded by *Eleuthéria* (unpublished).

1950   Mother dies.

1951   *Molloy* and *Malone Dies* published in Paris ('getting known', *Krapp's Last Tape*, p. 62).

1952   *Waiting for Godot* published in Paris.

1953   World première of *Waiting for Godot* in Paris, 5 January, director Roger Blin.

1954   Beckett's English translation of *Godot* published in New York.

1955	World première of the English *Godot* in London, 3 August.
1957	First broadcast of *All That Fall* by BBC, 13 January, director Donald McWhinnie. Creation of *Endgame* (French text, with *Act Without Words I*) in London, 3 April, director Roger Blin.
1958	World première of *Krapp's Last Tape* in London, 28 October, director Donald McWhinnie.
1959	Hon.D.Litt., Dublin University. *Embers* wins Italia Prize.
1961	World première of *Happy Days* in New York, 17 September, director Alan Schneider. International Publishers' Prize, shared with Jorge Luís Borges.
1962	First broadcast of *Words and Music* by BBC, 13 November.
1963	Creation of *Play* (in German translation) at Ulm, 14 June, director Deryk Mendel. First broadcast of *Cascando* by RTF, 13 October, director Roger Blin.
1964	*Film* made in New York, director Alan Schneider.
1966	Creation of *Come and Go* (in German translation) in Berlin, January, director Deryk Mendel. *Eh Joe* televised by BBC, 4 July, production by Alan Gibson and Samuel Beckett.
1969	Nobel Prize for Literature. First independent production of *Breath* (originally incorporated by Kenneth Tynan as the opening sketch in *Oh! Calcutta!*), Glasgow, October, director Geoffrey Gilham.
1972	World première of *Not I* at the Lincoln Center in the Forum (Vivian Beaumont Theater Building), New York, 22 November, with Jessica Tandy as Mouth and Henderson Forsythe as Auditor, directed by Alan Schneider.
1976	In celebration of Beckett's seventieth birthday, first broadcast by BBC Radio 3 of *Rough for Radio*, and world première of *That Time* and *Footfalls* at the Royal Court Theatre, London; *Footfalls* was directed by Beckett himself.

1977   *Ghost Trio* and . . . *but the clouds* . . . televised by the BBC, 17 April, with Billie Whitelaw and Ronald Pickup, directed by Donald McWhinnie.

1979   *A Piece of Monologue* performed by David Warrilow at La Mama Theater, New York, 14 December.

1981   *Rockaby* performed by Billie Whitelaw (directed by Alan Schneider) at the Center for Theater Research, State University of New York at Buffalo, 8 April; *Ohio Impromptu* performed by David Warrilow and Rand Mitchell, directed by Alan Schneider, at Ohio State University, Columbus, 9 May – both premières in honour of Beckett's 75th birthday. *Quad* televised by SDR, 8 October; direction by Samuel Beckett.

1982   World première of *Catastrophe* at the Avignon Festival, 21 July; director Stephan Meldbegg.

1983   *Nacht und Träume* transmitted by SDR, 19 May; direction by Samuel Beckett. World première of *What Where* at the Graz Festival.

INTRODUCTION

THE CONTEXT OF MODERNISM AND OF THE 'THEATRE OF THE ABSURD'

One of the greatest successes of the London stage in recent years was Tom Stoppard's play *Rosencrantz and Guildenstern Are Dead*. Rosencrantz and Guildenstern, of course, are two courtiers, minor characters in *Hamlet*. In Shakespeare's play they very much occupy a rear seat, but are brought to the front of the stage in Stoppard's contemporary rewrite. His play impinges on *Hamlet* at several points, not least at the end, where Horatio's sombre words bring the action of both plays to a close:

> so shall you hear
> Of carnal, bloody and unnatural acts,
> Of accidental judgments, casual slaughters,
> Of deaths put on by cunning and forced cause,
> And, in this upshot, purposes mistook
> Fallen on the inventors' heads: all this can I
> Truly deliver.

Stoppard is not producing here a mere trick or a literary parody: his play is an interpretation of Shakespeare, a development of its inner potentialities. *Hamlet* has an element of the derisory about it, of the absurd: as the player puts it in *Rosencrantz and Guildenstern Are Dead*, it's 'a slaughterhouse – eight corpses all told'. But, as he is careful to add, this 'brings out the best in us'. Unlike *King Lear*, *Hamlet* does not end with a sense of universal waste and desolation: the conclusion of *Hamlet* is more 'modern'. The death of Rosencrantz and Guildenstern was not willed by the King, but happened by a grotesque turn of events. Stoppard at one point wonders whether they were really 'traitors hoist by their own petard' at all, or merely 'victims of the Gods'. He thinks that 'we shall never know'. Shakespeare's world is already one of 'accidental judgments' and

17

'casual slaughters'; Stoppard merely underlines the casualness and the accidentalness of it all. He also speaks up for the little people in life and in drama, those who have little more than walk-on parts. 'Who are we that so much should converge on our little deaths?' Guildenstern asks towards the end of Stoppard's play; 'who are *we*?' The Player replies: 'You are Rosencrantz and Guildenstern. That's enough.' To this Guildenstern answers: 'No, it is not enough. To be told so little – to such an end – still, to be denied an explanation...' They overtly question, in other words, the absurdity of existence: they are not Hamlet, and yet their death is as real, final and definitive as his, although they are not princes and therefore not graced with tragic virtues.

We have mentioned *Rosencrantz and Guildenstern Are Dead* not only because it is an entertaining contemporary play, nor merely because it is an interesting modern reading of a classic. We do so chiefly because it reveals qualities that are characteristic of modern drama since Ibsen and Strindberg. Its ironic, seemingly flippant tone, its up-to-date colloquial language, can be heard in a number of modern plays. And yet it is not iconoclastic: there is genuine reverence for the great classic work that it reinterprets for us. And so, like much modern drama, it is both contemporary and timeless; unmistakably modern in its manner, it none the less wrestles with the same theme as Shakespeare does: lack of meaning in a life that can so abruptly and, it seems, randomly end in 'casual slaughter'. Stoppard may have been the first playwright to put a pair of attendant lords in the lead; but he writes deliberately in the shadow of what he calls 'the great homicidal classics', the ancient tradition of which goes back to the Greeks, and was renewed in recent times by the Norwegian dramatist, Henrik Ibsen. For Ibsen yields nothing to Euripides or Shakespeare in violence: his Hedda Gabler shoots herself (at the end of the play of that title) in a gesture worthy of Antigone.

In stressing that modern drama is not as dissimilar as is often thought from the great classics of European theatre, we do not wish to suggest that no change of any particular significance occurred around 1900, the beginning of the modern era. Quite the contrary. There is a self-awareness, a sophistication in the kind of drama that Ibsen inaugurated that is not found in precisely the same form in any previous work. What, then, are the principal features of modern as opposed to classical drama? It has something to do with the serious levity one finds as the dominant tone of Stoppard's play, as we shall see if we turn to other modern playwrights – notably Samuel Beckett, of course – in an attempt to pinpoint the major characteristics of the modern movement.

Beckett is widely recognized – on the basis of a surprisingly slight corpus of plays – to be one of the world's foremost living dramatists. This is something rather new in the history of the theatre. Shakespeare, Molière and Ibsen, three great masters of the European stage, have all left a substantial opus. To date, Beckett has written getting on for three dozen plays, but a high proportion of these can count only as playlets or what an earlier generation would have called 'curtain-raisers', short pieces that might have come in useful to a theatre manager wishing to fill out a particular programme. Of his full-length plays the first and the most elaborate, *Eleuthéria*, remains unperformed and unpublished; and of the others normally only *Waiting for Godot* is considered able to stand comfortably on its own in an evening programme.

Slight as some of the 'dramaticules' and occasional pieces that are discussed towards the end of this *Guide* undoubtedly are, they do reveal a remarkably restless and fertile talent, albeit one that is now able to operate only in a small and restricted compass. It is not only Beckett's age that prevents him tackling full-length plays any longer: he has deliberately written himself out of the normal form. When it was first produced, *Breath* seemed like a joke, a spoof, a *canard*, and it was all those things, to some extent; but it was also prophetic of things to come. Beckett has been getting inexorably shorter all the time. *Human Wishes*, his first attempt at playwriting, begun and abandoned in 1937, was planned to use four acts; *Eleuthéria* is in three, and *Godot* in two – 'One act would have been too little', Beckett said apologetically, 'and three would have been too much'; how astute, how apt, that remark now sounds. *Endgame* began as a two-act play but Beckett sensibly dropped the interval when it became clear to him that it could not be structurally justified.

Since *Krapp's Last Tape*, with the exception of *Happy Days* (which needs an interval for a purely technical reason, the time required to plant Winnie deeper in the ground), all his plays have been one-act, even one-scene, affairs.

There is no intrinsic reason why plays should take two or three hours to perform, of course; the fact that most do is attributable to sociological factors. Until the advent of mass-audience movies and then home-based television, the theatre and the opera were the standard forms of public entertainment. Since these art forms, unlike the cinema or television, came relatively expensive to the individual consumer – and now usually require state subsidy to function at all – the audience expected value for money in the shape of a full evening's entertainment as a return for the outlay on the ticket price. Elaborate evening dress and expensive suppers after the show all added to the sense of occasion but also to the cost. Plays and operas were therefore created to satisfy the demand for agreeably distracting ways of filling the time between dinner and supper. Hence the rise and fall of the so-called 'well-made play': it survived just so long as did the leisured classes who were able to pay for it. When their importance and their influence on the leisure market declined, it fell into desuetude, after a short time lag, as well.

What makes Beckett one of the greatest dramatists, not only of our century but of all time, is that his contribution is fundamental and original in a way few others' have been. Like Molière in the seventeenth century and Ibsen in the nineteenth, he perceived instinctively the way things were going and helped them along. Such prescience involves technical innovation, of course, but is not limited to it. That is why Beckett is greater than Pirandello or Brecht, both of whom were in some ways more inventive theatrically than he has been. His importance is in fact more akin to Molière's. Beckett tried to write traditional historical drama in *Human Wishes*, but found that his natural dramatic manner subverted the genre so destructively that he had to abandon the play after a few pages. Molière did write a few traditional plays – in his case, knockabout, vulgar farces – until his own particular genius for the more serious and socially aware sort of comedy (which he largely invented) took over.

The Misanthrope still retains elements of farce, but they are subordinated to the portrayal of a man, who obstinately maintains that complete candour is not only feasible but desirable, at odds with a society that knows that neither is the case. Likewise, *Waiting for Godot* has traditional elements (derived mainly, it is true, from popular forms like the circus) but these are transcended in a play that stands, thirty years after its first production, as the most apt dramatic image yet created of our situation in a world without God, deprived of the transcendent confidence that belief in the existence of God confers.

Having broken the mould with *Endgame* – after being trapped in it in *Human Wishes* and to a lesser extent in *Eleuthéria* – Beckett was freed of the compulsion to write full-length works. His statements could just as effectively – even more effectively – be made in tauter, tighter, more polyphonic dramatic structures. The breakthrough came with *Krapp's Last Tape*, perhaps his most perfect theatre piece. In *Krapp* a single character is doubled, then trebled, by the use of a timely mechanical invention, the magnetic tape recorder, thus making possible a dialogue between an old man and his middle-aged earlier self, via prerecorded tape, and their shared sarcastic jokes about the young man they both once were. And the technical innovation made possible the frame that keeps real experience at the necessary emotional distance. So that few sensations are more poignant in the modern theatre than the sight of that dirty, drink-sodden old wreck listening forlornly to his earlier self asking rhetorically on the tape, 'What remains of all that misery? A girl in a shabby green coat, on a railway-station platform?' (p. 58), and offering with a bravado that conceals deeply felt regret the opinion that he was 'well out of that, Jesus yes! Hopeless business', that he was right to break with a lover because 'it was hopeless and no good going on' (pp. 58, 61). Perfect dramatic form, beautifully crafted, and totally convincing in its effortless modernity: that is what strikes us now about *Krapp's Last Tape*.

Few critics and theatre people would therefore be surprised if Beckett is considered by posterity to rank in importance with the three masters we mentioned just now, Shakespeare, Molière and Ibsen. It is still too early to say, of course; but it *is* clear that Beckett has done as much as any dramatist in this century to extend and modify the resources of the stage, to adapt its millennial arts to the expression of the concerns and anxieties of the present age. Just as Shakespeare explored the political and moral dilemmas of the Renaissance, or Molière adjusted the anarchic world of comedy to neo-classical and rationalistic norms, or Ibsen created and transformed patterns of naturalism to give perfect expression to the psychological ghosts that haunted the bourgeoisie in the age of imperialism and high capitalism, so Beckett has found the means of setting out the metaphysical doubts that torment us now in forms that, like all radical innovations, surprise at first and then in a short space of time begin to seem natural and inevitable. Brecht and Pirandello in this century have also, as we have acknowledged, achieved major theatrical revolutions, but it is arguable that the changes they brought about have not been as far-reaching, nor are they likely to be as long-lasting, as those Beckett has provoked. It would be difficult to name a single important playwright of the younger generation – from Albee to Stoppard – be it in Britain, America, France or Germany, who has not been deeply affected by Beckett's example or influenced by his practice. Whatever posterity's verdict about his intrinsic worth and stature as a dramatist, there is no doubt that it will concede, at the very least, that he is one of the most important innovators in the history of the modern stage. This is to some extent because his contribution came at precisely the right moment; as one contemporary playwright, John Spurling, put it, 'Samuel Beckett was waiting for the theatre as the theatre was waiting for Samuel Beckett.'

That moment – now over thirty years ago – was also a moment of crisis in modernism, the great literary and artistic movement that began in the closing years of the last century, reached its finest flowering in the early decades of this, and went into decline in the 1930s and 1940s. Economic and political upheaval lasting roughly from the rise of Hitler to the death of Stalin forced the movement into abeyance; but it was to experience a second and probably a final flowering in the 1950s, 1960s and early 1970s. There are unmistakable signs at the time of writing that the period of relative peace and prosperity that the developed countries enjoyed for over thirty years from the end of World War II is now at an end, and that there is likely to be another protracted era of strife, conflict and instability, which will have, as in the 1930s, a profound impact on the arts. It has probably already put an end to the second phase of modernism, known to critics and cultural historians as either neo-modernism or post-modernism. But even if the modern movement is finally doomed – and it is one that has produced such giants as Joyce, Picasso and Schoenberg in its time – Beckett will have had an undisputed and major role in revitalizing it in the early 1950s, and in enabling it to survive for two further impressive decades.

Modernism proper runs from about 1890 to about 1930, and includes among its varied manifestations literary symbolism and surrealism, cubism and abstract painting, twelve-tone music, and expressionism in the cinema; post-modernism, being closer to us, shows less clearly marked temporal and aesthetic contours, but it obviously includes the *nouveau roman* or 'new novel' in France, abstract expressionism in painting, electronic music, the films of the French *nouvelle vague* and those of Ingmar Bergman in Sweden and Michelangelo Antonioni in Italy, and the so-called 'theatre of the absurd'. It is this theatrical movement that concerns us here, since it is in the context of the response the stage has made to the post-modernist revival that we must view Beckett's importance as a playwright; and that response has been given the convenient if somewhat restrictive label of the 'theatre of the absurd'. This has been defined by its leading theorist, Martin Esslin, as tending 'toward a radical devaluation of language, toward a poetry that is to emerge from the concrete and objectified images of the stage itself'; the element of language, Esslin explains, 'still plays an important part in this conception, but what *happens* on the stage transcends, and often contradicts, the *words* spoken by the characters' (*The Theatre of the Absurd*, p. 26). Esslin's point is well illustrated in a fine example of the new theatre, Harold Pinter's play *The Homecoming*, in which the banality of North London speech – 'Where's my cheese roll?' is is a not untypical line from the play – masks a complex power struggle between different members of the same family which leads the wife of one of them to desert her husband and accept the role of call-girl in their employ. Likewise the same author's first play, *The Room*, begins with chat about damp in the basement and ends with a murder and blinding of almost Sophoclean proportions; what we see in this work is a characteristically modernist shift, from metaphor in the early scenes (where one of the characters says 'It's very cold out . . . It's murder') to realism in the last episode, in which a particularly brutal killing is enacted before our very eyes. The language here, as Martin Esslin would say, is transcended by the action, and the mythic quality of the most everyday utterances brought astonishingly to life.

On the other hand, seldom has language been used more effectively in the theatre. As Dina Sherzer observes,

> Beckett is a great manipulator of, exploiter of, and performer with the manifold resources and possibilities of language. For are not the passages borrowed from other literary texts, the use of banal, everyday conversations mixed with literary language, the slang, puns, and modified clichés, the importance granted to talking (to torment the other or to make time pass), and the careful creation of rhythms and use of repetitions all ways of demonstrating the exuberance of language and Beckett's ability to play with it and to manipulate it, resulting in a new and powerful dramatic expressiveness?
>
> (*French Review*, 1979, pp. 307–8)

In ways like these, modernism raises, for the first time in the history of drama, the issue of *metatheatre* in an acute manner. Lionel Abel has defined this concept as resting upon two basic postulates: (1) that the world is a stage, and (2) that life is a dream. Neither of these two notions originated at all recently. 'Life is a dream' is the literal translation of the title of a play by the Spanish dramatist Calderón (1600–1681), and 'the world's a stage' (or, in Latin, *theatrum mundi*) was a cliché long before Shakespeare and other Renaissance dramatists took it up. As Elizabeth Burns comments in her book *Theatricality* (Longman, 1972), 'The *theatrum mundi* metaphor was derived from the idea that God was the sole spectator of man's actions on the stage of life' (p. 143). What modernism did with the life-a-dream and all-the-world-a-stage metaphors was this: it caused them to transcend the purely ethical plane that they occupied in the Renaissance synthesis, a sphere and context in which moral observations on the transitoriness of life, the shallowness of human endeavour and so on held pride of place, and in which men and women were viewed as mere actors in an absurd play, making their entrances and exits upon the stage of life and mouthing there (in the words of Shakespeare in *As You Like It* and *Macbeth*) tales 'full of sound and fury' signifying nothing. Modernism took these notions and transferred them to the realm of aesthetics, where the real was opposed to the illusory, the mask to the face, the stage to the auditorium, and above all the smile was opposed to the tear in that characteristically modernist phenomenon, the grimace of tragicomedy. This mixed genre, which Bernard Shaw defined as being both 'deeper and grimmer' than tragedy, is in fact the modernist mode *par excellence*. It encapsulates a great deal in the modernist aesthetic of drama, from Ibsen's *The Wild Duck* to Beckett's *Waiting for Godot* (which is not subtitled 'a tragicomedy' by accident).

Tragicomedy is generally considered to be marked by an air of tentativeness, but it is in reality distinguished by a confident stance and an assured knowingness, a knowingness shared with and by the spectator, who becomes for the first time genuinely implicated in the construction of a drama, indeed of an entire spectacle. In Ibsen's *The Wild Duck* this spectacle is that of Hjalmar's pretended 'nobility in the presence of death' which we, like one of the other characters, Dr Relling, know to be a sham, because within a year he will be offering maudlin eloquence upon young Hedvig's suicide. It is also the spectacle of those clownish intellectuals in their down-at-heel togs playing histrionically to the gallery as they fill in the empty time waiting for Godot. In both cases the tone is ambiguous: Hjalmar's situation is heart-breaking, and Estragon's is desperate; but the manner in which these situations are presented suffices to make them comical. The end of Beckett's play, which has throughout balanced existential anguish against bowler-hatted slapstick straight out of Laurel and Hardy, offers the ultimate in this mode. The two men have just botched an attempt at suicide:

their hanging rope has snapped. Unfortunately the rope that was supposed to put an end to them also serves as the belt holding up Estragon's trousers. At one of the most sombre moments in the history of drama in this century, at a time when all hope, even of easeful death, has evaporated: at that precise point the victim's trousers concertina around his ankles. (Stoppard imitates the same gesture at a critical moment in *Rosencrantz and Guildenstern Are Dead* too, incidentally.) 'Pull on your trousers,' Estragon's comrade tells him. But even this is not the whole joke, because Estragon, in fine music-hall style, gets it all wrong. 'You want me to pull off my trousers?' he asks with comic oafishness. Astonishingly, we are within minutes only of the final curtain, of the unbearable poignancy of that last silence ('Let's go' – *They do not move*) on which the play ends.

Beckett is one of the few dramatists to have adapted popular forms of entertainment, like the music-hall in this example, to 'serious' drama. His intention throughout is comic: it cannot be emphasized enough that *Waiting for Godot* is, properly performed, a very funny play. As Roger Blin, Beckett's first director, has said, 'He is unique in his ability to blend derision, humour and comedy with tragedy: his words are simultaneously tragic and comic.' There is no conflict between the circus fun of the dropping of Estragon's trousers and the intense sadness of the end of the play: in a less sophisticated way the circus, and then the masters of the silent film, Buster Keaton and Charlie Chaplin, achieved a similar harmony between laughter and tears. That is what Nell means in *Endgame* when she says, in words that are cynical only in appearance, 'Nothing is funnier than unhappiness . . . It's the most comical thing in the world.' One day, in childhood, we all of us learn to laugh through our tears – 'All that matters,' Beckett said once, 'is the laugh and the tear' – and in that moment we experience a great truth: to be able to laugh at our condition is the only way to set about the necessary business of bearing it. Beckett's great achievement is to have cast this simple intuition in the form of a witty and moving dramatic symbol: that of two clowns waiting on a country road for someone who fails to keep the appointment.

Ibsen and Beckett thus represent the poles of modernism: in

time, of course, but also in spirit; modernism tends to be symbolic, post-modernism to repudiate symbolism. This is the measure of the difficulty. How is one to define an aesthetic of modern drama that needs to embrace two such disparate figures, two giants (in their very different ways) of modern dramaturgy?

There are a few indicators, which the very 'metatheatrical' aspect of modernism implies. One might, for instance, if with some exaggeration, attach to modernist dramaturgy the label of 'the aesthetics of silence'. Never before had the fragmentary, the low-key, the inarticulate, even the incoherent and the frankly non-verbal tendencies of theatrical intercourse been so extensively developed. There are, of course, instances in plays dating from earlier periods of characters falling silent, aghast, amazed or terrified; but such moments remain theatrical, within the context of the play; they do not serve as a comment upon it. The silences in Strindberg, in Pinter or in Beckett are equally justified dramatically within the play, but they also serve as a reflection upon it: in Beckett's case, quite explicitly so. 'This is deadly,' Hamm comments to the audience in *Endgame* when he (and we) have been exasperated by a particularly tedious piece of 'time-wasting' business from Clov. Or in *Godot*, after the dialogue has once again run away into the sand, the characters sigh, waiting for someone to start things off once more. As bored and clumsy as an office boy taking sherry with the boss, Estragon is the first to break the silence through the straightforward device of simply drawing attention to it:

ESTRAGON: In the meantime nothing happens.
POZZO: You find it tedious?
ESTRAGON: Somewhat.
POZZO: (*To* VLADIMIR) And you, sir?
VLADIMIR: I've been better entertained.
    (*Silence.*)

(*Waiting for Godot*, p. 38)

In spite of this tendency to lapse into wordlessness, Beckett's characters are very literate. The speakers know their classics, and quote from them liberally (Estragon from Shelley's 'To the Moon', Winnie – with a fine sense of irony – from *Romeo and*

Juliet, while Hamm sardonically distorts Baudelaire's sublime line 'Tu réclamais le Soir; il descend; le voici' as the evening of his life draws in). The inarticulacy, in other words, is in the medium as much as it is part of the message.

It is rather different with Harold Pinter, who has always countered journalistic clichés about his work with the statement that he is not concerned with the so-called impossibility of communication, but with the fear of it; people instinctively take refuge in evasions, he believes, rather than run the risk of having to articulate what is really bothering them. Silence or digression are after all a much safer refuge than discursive and explicit statements. The *locus classicus* of this is the seemingly astounding irrelevance of Aston's account (in Pinter's *The Caretaker*) of his inability to drink Guinness from a thick mug, whereas what really troubles him is the haunting dread of another mental breakdown, which would mean undergoing electroshock treatment again. In Eugène Ionesco, likewise, language serves rather to mask than to reveal tensions and conflicts: *The Lesson* is a perfect exposition of how to project fantasies of rape and murder under a comically parodic form of academic discourse. But the unveiling of erotic tensions through a language to which they bear little apparent relation was certainly not invented by Ionesco: Ibsen does it superbly in *Hedda Gabler*, and so do Chekhov in *Ivanov* and Strindberg in *Miss Julie*. Likewise Pinter is not the first playwright to show characters evading a realization of their plight: Chekhov's Gayev takes refuge from his embarrassments in *The Cherry Orchard* by imagining himself playing billiards, 'potting into the corner pocket', as he exclaims, or 'cannoning off the cushions'. The spectacle of language breaking down, the explosion of the hysteria underlying the polite banalities of social intercourse, and violence resulting from quite trivial provocations: all this forms the basis of Chekhov's drama, just as it does of Pinter's. There is a marked difference in setting, of course: the estates of the declining nobility in pre-Revolutionary Russia are a far cry from the seedy bed-and-breakfasts or the trendy modernized farmhouses in which Pinter's characters, from *The Birthday Party* (1958) to *Old Times* (1971), tear each other apart, but both are the authentic locales of their respective periods. Long after the last derelict Victorian pile has disappeared under the developer's bulldozer as irrevocably as Madame Ranyevskaia's cherry orchard under the axe, Pinter's people, like Chekhov's, will still be probing the resources of speech in order to find loopholes through which to escape from their truths, signalling messages as they go of hostility and repressed antagonism, either by the use of irrelevant language (like Mick's assertion in *The Caretaker*, 'I understood you were an experienced first-class professional interior and exterior decorator... You mean you wouldn't know how to fit teal-blue, copper and parchment linoleum squares and have those colours re-echoed in the walls?... You're a bloody imposter, mate!), or by non-verbal means, as when in the same play the Buddha is smashed against the gas stove.

In pursuing further this theme of metatheatre as the one possible unifying characteristic of modernist drama, we cannot fail to note the 'life is a dream' motif that runs through so much of it. Central to the theatre of Pirandello (1867–1936) is the ambiguous interrelation of the 'fictive' and the 'real', but this derives in its turn from Strindberg's *Dream Play* (1901), a work of profound and revolutionary originality, and leads on afterwards to one of the most perfect works thrown up in the post-1950 renascence of modernism, Arthur Adamov's *Professor Taranne* (1951), in which an eminent academic finds himself accused of a list of offences of ever-increasing gravity, ranging from lack of courtesy towards colleagues and students, to plagiarizing the work of another scholar, and finally to indecent exposure. It is impossible to be sure, within the terms set by the play itself, whether or not the professor is the victim of a concerted campaign of defamation and distortion, or genuinely guilty of the offences alleged against him. When, on being told the contents of the Belgian vice-chancellor's letter explaining why he is not being invited to lecture again, Professor Taranne slowly starts taking his clothes off as the curtain falls, the audience is unsure if he is merely conforming to the nightmare, or confirming its truth. The success of this play lies in the fact that its ambiguity remains entire. Is Taranne's dignity a mask for paranoia and deviant behaviour? What is the reality, and what the illusion? These are questions modernism is adept at posing, undermining our categories and destroying our confidence in familiar things and places: such as a middle-class flat, a safe enough place, one might have thought, until Eugène Ionesco in *Amédée* peopled it with an expanding corpse and covered its carpets in mushrooms, or until Pinter in *The Room* made it the scene of the Sophoclean ritual murder and blinding we referred to earlier. Life is here implicated with art, and art with life: when tragedies are enacted in the drawing room, when – as in Pinter's *The Homecoming* – Iphigenia is sacrificed in North London, or when *The Taming of the Shrew* is sardonically rewritten by Edward Albee as *Who's Afraid of Virginia Woolf*, we return by another route to that essential tragicomedy that is, as we have seen, so inseparable from modernism.

Equally characteristic is an attitude to the theatrical space that either divides it somewhere across the middle, or throws the barrier around the playhouse altogether. Drama before modernism sought to foster the illusion that the audience was eavesdropping, that a 'fourth wall' had fallen away unbeknown to the characters and that the spectators were looking straight in. Ibsen does not disdain this trick, since trick is what it is: *The Wild Duck* begins in the most conventional manner imaginable, with the family servant explaining to the hired waiter the situation from which the drama is to spring. It is a very obvious device, since the playwright has engineered, by this simple artifice, for the audience to be 'put in the picture' and the action meaningfully started. This awkward but essential phase once past, the play is performed just as if an audience were not watching; indeed, it needs to be so performed if the tension is going to be effectively created. The actors have to concentrate hard on the situation; any hint of a gesture to the gallery would destroy the illusion. Yet it is precisely this illusion – the illusion of realist drama, symbolized by the juxtaposition of a darkened, hushed auditorium and a brightly lit busy stage – that Bertolt Brecht sought to abolish. This did not entail removing the footlights and making the stage and the auditorium continuous. On the contrary: to do that would have been to create another illusion, just as totalitarian, that the world *within* the theatre walls is a real world, the only genuine one.

The purpose behind Brecht's rejection of the theatrical illusion was a didactic and political one; but his innovation has opened the way to much else that is vital in contemporary theatre, not least the works of Samuel Beckett, which self-consciously play 'across' the footlights. In *Waiting for Godot* the emptiness of the auditorium is humorously commented upon by the actor/characters; in *Endgame*, Hamm (like the 'ham actor' he is) plays to the stalls, and when Clov asks what there is to keep him there, replies, truthfully enough, 'the dialogue'; and in *Happy Days* Winnie 'begins her day' like an old pro, summoned by the peremptory bell, limbering up for another canter through the familiar material. Likewise Ionesco never wearies of reminding the audience that they are sitting in a playhouse, watching a game the rules of which may be modified but still need to be respected; in such stage discussions Ionesco is not above puckishly referring to himself by name.

It is evident that these and other features can, in default of a single and consistent aesthetic, be seen as helping to make up the modernist synthesis. Some of the other features (ritual and fairy tale, mask and dance, stylization and formalization, relativity and flux) could be examined in detail, but they all derive essentially from the major traits that have been identified here. Many of these aspects can, naturally enough, be observed operating in parallel in other performing arts in this century, such as the ballet, the cinema or, more recently, television.

The principal characteristics of drama since Ibsen and Strindberg can be summarized as follows:

1 A tone of 'serious levity' towards drama, and particularly towards the classics of the medium, as we saw at the beginning when we looked briefly at Stoppard's play about Hamlet.
2 The exploration of antagonism and violence, particularly on a psychological plane.
3 'Metatheatre' (founded, as we saw, on two basic postulates, (a) that the world is a stage, and (b) that life is a dream), signifying a medium totally aware of itself and involving the spectator in an equally searching act of self-awareness.

4 A preference for tragicomedy rather than the genres most favoured by classical theatre, tragedy or comedy.

5 A movement – sponsored particularly by Brecht – away from the picture-frame stage towards a tendency to play 'across' the footlights.

If all this seems confusing, it is because modern drama since the turn of the century has been one of the most bewilderingly lively and inventive of European art forms. There is no simple pattern, but rather a tension and a continual dialectic. The twin forces pulling in different directions in Beckett's dramaturgy – those of rigour and of feeling – are a case in point. It is such interaction, not only within modern drama, but also between contemporary plays and the classics of the past, that makes the theatre of today in general, and its leading exponent Beckett in particular, such a fascinating object of study.

BECKETT'S DRAMATIC DEVELOPMENT

In a career spanning six decades, it is not surprising that Beckett has developed considerably as a dramatist over these years. His evolution can be traced in six broad phases (see also the Biographical Table above). The first represents the apprentice years during the 1930s, in which he wrote a college sketch (*Le Kid*, a parody of Corneille's drama *Le Cid*) and began an ambitious four-act play, *Human Wishes*, about the relationship between Dr Johnson and his benefactress Mrs Thrale, of which only part of one scene was ever completed. Then came the forced interruption of the war years, after which Beckett wrote two full-length plays, *Eleuthéria* (still unpublished and unperformed) and *Waiting for Godot*. These represent his second phase, in which he was finding his own distinctive voice as a playwright; neither work is however fully mature as first written. *Eleuthéria* Beckett was content to abandon once it became clear that *Godot*, with only five characters as opposed to over three times that number, would be cheaper and easier to put on than the first play. *Waiting for Godot* then developed considerably in production. The differences between the first published text in French (1952), and the version Beckett uses in productions in which he himself is now from time to time involved, are considerable; as our detailed notes on the play point out, the current text is both shorter and tauter, much more an acting script, than the often rather self-indulgently literary version that a less experienced playwright handed to his publisher shortly after it was written. The remarkable thing is the originality of the basic conception, which Beckett has needed only to refine and sharpen over the years; even if he was not always sure about details, he never had any doubts about the essential shape and intention of this play.

He abandoned the stage for some years after completing *Godot* in 1949 and spent much time translating his French works into English. But the notoriety of that play put pressure on him to write another. The BBC suggested he try his hand at radio drama, and *All That Fall* was the result. At the same time he was struggling with another stage play, and finally produced *Endgame*. These two works, plus the *Acts Without Words*, the fragments (or 'roughs') for theatre, and *Krapp's Last Tape* constitute, in the late 1950s, a third phase.

All That Fall was for Beckett a new departure, in that he moved into a different medium, radio; but in itself it is a relatively traditional work with a naturalistic setting and everyday characters. *Endgame*, on the other hand, is a radically experimental work by any standard. The claustrophobic set, the terminal situation and the characters without identifiable origins that characterize *Endgame* made *Godot* seem a work almost of social realism in comparison. The harsh and unremitting nature of this play, its refusal to make any concessions to the audience's hunger for progression or development of the situation on stage, link it with the remorseless monologues of the Unnamable or of the voice in *Texts for Nothing* (1950); whereas as Beckett himself said, the tone of *Godot* is closer to that of *Murphy* (1938). *Krapp's Last Tape* is equally radical, a monodrama in which the characters are reduced to one, an old man communing with an earlier self via the tape recorder that brings back voices from his past. Although at first sight the dramatic situation appears dangerously compressed, the play succeeds brilliantly in conveying the agonizing poignancy of Krapp's loss. No spectator who has ever seen a competent production can forget the intense emotion felt when decrepit old Krapp listens helplessly to his middle-aged predecessor waxing lyrical about 'the fire in me now' (p. 63), a fire that, all too obviously, was long ago extinguished in the decayed geriatric we see before us.

A fourth phase opens in 1959 with *Embers*, a radio play as radical in conception as *All That Fall* is traditional. This time Beckett seizes on the fact that the origin of a sound on the radio is essentially ambiguous, uncertain: is it meant to be live, prerecorded, or imagined? Is it inside the protagonist's head or has it some independent source? In the other radio plays of this period he exploited this discovery to the full, and indeed worked it through so that, after *Cascando*, he found no further challenge in this medium. He was already moving into film (with *Film*) and television (with *Eh Joe*). He discovered a particular affinity with the intimate, small-scale possibilities of television, the reduced sets, the limited number of actors, the concentration and informality of the small screen, and above all the feasibility of using the camera as a character in its own right. This was encouraged by the interest of the South German Broadcasting Corporation (Süddeutscher Rundfunk, Stuttgart), which invited him to direct *Eh Joe* himself. The resulting production was in fact transmitted by SDR before the BBC, for whom it was written, got their version on the air. Since then Beckett has returned several times to Stuttgart to direct works for television he has written with this enlightened patron specifically in mind.

But this phase is equally rich in stage plays of great originality. From *Happy Days*, through *Play* and *Come and Go* to *Breath*, Beckett continually invented new ways of using the theatrical space. In *Happy Days* the protagonist is imprisoned in the earth surrounded by her meagre possessions, and is forced to act, to play, by the peremptory ringing of a harsh bell. 'Begin your day, Winnie' she tells herself, and gallantly takes up the challenge like the seasoned trouper she is. In *Play* three individuals, barely recognizable as human beings, retell at the behest of an inquisitorial beam of light as domineering as Winnie's bell a sadly comic tale of adultery. The innovation here is to have them repeat the play they have just run through so that two acts, as it were, are squeezed out of one. *Come and Go* and *Breath* reduce drama to the briefest statement possible; *Breath*, in particular, is just that, an inhalation and an exhalation heard as an amplified recording on a stage empty of everything except rubbish.

Many thought Beckett had written his last play in *Breath*, seen in 1966 as the culmination of his entire development as a dramatist to that day. They were wrong. He did not write another play for some years, admittedly. He spent much time in the late 1960s directing his own plays in Paris and Berlin. But a fifth phase began in 1972 with *Not I*, an excruciatingly difficult work for an actress to perform, since her delivery must be carefully articulated but so rapid as to be barely comprehensible. Then followed two further explorations of extreme theatre, *That Time* with nothing but a lit face and three monologues prerecorded by the same actor, and *Footfalls* with low and slow voices conducting a ghostly dialogue, as an old woman shuffles slowly to and fro. Two further and even more reduced experiments in television, *Ghost Trio* and *... but the clouds...*, belong to this phase of the mid-1970s.

The sixth phase begins in 1979 after another busy interval of self-direction in London, Paris and Berlin. All the pieces of this most recent period are short, even 'occasional', in the sense of having been written for a specific event, such as a benefit night for a persecuted fellow dramatist, or conceived for a particular performer whose work had impressed Beckett. Thus *Catastrophe* was written to support the Czech dissident Vaclav Havel, and *A Piece of Monologue* for David Warrilow to act. Slight as some of these works written more or less to order are, they have their moments of dramatic intensity, and they all show that even in old age Beckett remains theatrically as inventive and unpredictable as ever.

PROBLEMS OF INTERPRETATION

When *Waiting for Godot* was first staged in London, a flurry of articles and letters to editors attempted to answer the question: 'What does the play mean?' It is now clear, after the passage of several years, that the answer is simply, 'It means what it says.' There are two reasons for this. Firstly, none of the 'interpretations' offered, Christian or otherwise, fitted all the facts, and most were obliged, in order to put forward a coherent view, to ignore passages that did not square with that view. Secondly, Beckett's other works have become more widely known since 1955, and they show clearly that he is not a didactic author concerned to put across a 'message' in literary form. Such 'truths' as he does enunciate are the simple observations about the human condition that have been common coin since Job and Sophocles. It is an undeniable fact, for instance, that we must sooner or later die, and many people today are doubtful whether anything lies beyond death. Beckett's works however are not statements of this theme, but *meditations* upon it, and early critics mistook the latter for the former. They were to some extent misled by the Christian echoes that abound in this play. For example, when Vladimir asks, 'We are not saints, but we have kept our appointment. How many people can boast as much?' (p. 80), the spectator who knows his Bible can answer, 'the Wise Virgins' (cf. Matt. 24, 25). Some writers, such as William Golding, might incorporate an allusion like that into a complex, but coherent, religious statement. Not so Beckett. The reason for the presence of Christian elements in his works is simple: 'Christianity', he told Professor Duckworth, 'is a mythology with which I am familiar, so I naturally use it.' In other words, he is interested in mythologies for their own sake, without any commitment to them whatsoever. As he put it to another interviewer: 'I'm not interested in any system. I can't see any trace of any system anywhere.'

In fact, Beckett is the complete agnostic: he is simply not interested in whether the Christian Church is telling fairy stories or not. Even were God to exist, he would, says Beckett, make no difference: he would be as lonely, and as enslaved, as the voice in *The Unnamable*, and as isolated and ridiculous as man is, in a cold, silent, indifferent universe. If *Waiting for Godot* can be called religious at all, it is a poem on a world without any divinity but a kind of malignant fate, a world in which man waits and hopes for something to give a meaning to his life, and relieve him of the absurdity of a death that irrevocably terminates all. But he waits in vain, and so our life is as meaningless as our death. Between man's life and a mayfly's there is, in the last analysis, little to choose: hence Pozzo's remark, 'the light gleams an instant' (p. 89), an instant only. It is, after all, a monstrous paradox that, for the individual, life is an eternity while it lasts, but that it is less than an instant in regard to cosmic time, just as a man's six foot is nothing compared with the immense distances between the galaxies. Consciousness, of course, is all, but the consciousness by which man is aware of his individual existence is continually at risk from heart failure or mental breakdown.

Man in any case is held in a two-dimensional prison: time. In this prison, only forward motion is possible; but man deludes himself that he is progressing of his own free will to some sort of goal. As Beckett put it in *Proust*, 'We are rather in the position of Tantalus, with this difference, that we allow ourselves to be tantalized'; little wonder, then, that 'We are disappointed at the nullity of what we are pleased to call attainment' (p. 3). In Beckett's best-known play, that nullity is named 'Godot'. Birth, for him, is a 'calamity' because it launches us on our one-dimensional way (see Act I, p. 11), from which the only release is death. *Waiting for Godot* is therefore, quite simply, a picture of the antics of man as he tries to distract himself until 'Godot' comes. But Godot is only death. He is not, however, seen as death, because man flatters himself with groundless hopes; thus Godot becomes anything the expectation of which helps man to bear his existence. Or as Estragon puts it, 'We always find something, eh Didi, to give us the impression we exist?' (p. 69).

It is therefore evident that a Christian interpretation, which would see some hope of salvation, in spite of all, in the arrival of Pozzo or the messenger, is as unhelpful to an understanding of this play as a Marxist reading, which would see it as an indictment of the alienation of man under capitalism. Both these and other exegeses – even those that see it as an 'anti-Christian' play – make the mistake of assuming that the work must have a *positive* meaning; whereas its whole manner eschews the positive and the definite like the plague. It operates exclusively by hint and understatement; it has, in fact, been most aptly termed 'drama of the non-specific' (Alec Reid). To look for a 'specific' message in such drama is like seeing the magnetic pole at the Antarctic. Beckett's art avoids definition because he believes passionately that 'art has nothing to do with clarity, does not dabble in the clear and does not make clear'. The writer is no 'magus' possessing privileged insight or knowledge not vouchsafed to other mortals; all he can do is to distil in words, however imperfect, a vision or experience of the misery and desperateness of life. That, for Beckett, is 'poetry' broadly defined, and it is for him the only thing that ultimately has any value.

He has, of course, a 'philosophy of life' like anyone else, but it is an intuition rather than a systematic set of beliefs. Like the German thinker Schopenhauer (1788–1860), whom he greatly admires, he feels that Will is evil, and that desire is the source of our misery: such happiness as there is, therefore, can only be obtained by the 'ablation' of all desire. This, he says in *Proust*, is 'the wisdom of all the sages, from Brahma to Leopardi', the nineteenth-century Italian poet whose words he quotes frequently:

> Now be for ever still,
> Weary my heart. For the last cheat is dead,
> I thought eternal. Dead. For us, I know
> Not only the dear hope
> Of being deluded gone, but the desire.
> Rest still for ever. You
> Have beaten long enough. And to no purpose
> Were all your stirrings; earth not worth your sighs.
> Boredom and bitterness
> Is life; and the rest, nothing; the world is dirt.
> Lie quiet now. Despair
> For the last time. Fate granted to our kind
> Only to die. And now you may despise
> Yourself, nature, the brute
> Power which, hidden, ordains the common doom,
> And all the immeasurable emptiness of things.
>
> (translated by John Heath-Stubbs)

Beckett feels a deep kinship with such writers as Schopenhauer and Leopardi, and shares their repudiation of happy optimism, but this does not lead him to quietist renunciation. Like his character Bom in *Murphy*, no doubt, he hears 'Pilate's hands rustling in his mind' (p. 170), but he does not give up on that account. He writes novels that tell of man's derisory, but heroic, attempts to conquer the 'silence of which the universe is made', and plays that portray man's doomed efforts to master time. The two things are closely related in his mind. Of *Waiting for Godot* he says, 'Silence is pouring into this play like water into a sinking ship': the characters are terrified of silence because silence threatens cessation. The fall (in Act II) symbolizes this.

As a director of his own plays, Beckett maintains an emphasis on the symmetries of speech and on action punctuated by stylized gesture; tempo and manner alike make few concessions to verisimilitude. In his 1979 London production of *Happy Days* with Billie Whitelaw at the Royal Court Theatre, for instance, he safeguarded, over Willie's intentions at the end of the play, the carefully structured ambiguities of the text; is Willie wearily struggling uphill to touch Winnie, or the revolver, and if the weapon, for what, one wondered: to keep it from Winnie, or to use it on her? Or on himself? The curtain fell on Willie reaching out still.

For the 1975 Berlin Schiller Theater production of the German translation (by Elmar Tophoven) of *Waiting for Godot* (*Warten auf Godot*), the text was amended and corrected by Beckett himself (often extensively, since his German is excellent), with greater stress on fidelity to the French original and on the network of motif words. Beckett has a long and intimate connection with the Schiller: *Endgame*, *Krapp's Last Tape*, *Happy Days*, *Play*, *That Time* and *Footfalls* have all been directed by him there. In the Schiller *Warten auf Godot* production (abbreviated STB) the major symbolic function was the costuming of Vladimir and Estragon. They each wore half of the other's suit, that is to say Estragon wore a blue-grey jacket with black trousers in Act I and the opposite (black jacket and blue-grey trousers) in Act II, while Vladimir's costume was identical but exactly the inverse of Estragon's in both acts, as if to underline, Irving Wardle said, that they were inseparable.

The result, for Wardle, was 'one of the most superbly balanced double acts I have seen': Estragon was a 'frisky troll' and Vladimir a 'knock-kneed, shambling and blank-faced' clown. (Wardle noted too Estragon's 'nautical roll' and Vladimir's 'splay-footed shuffle' (*The Times*, 26 April 1976). Actually, Vladimir's toes turned in and Estragon's pointed out.) Clearly Beckett intended to emphasize that if Estragon's physical resources are greater than his companion's, Vladimir's linguistic reserves are more remarkable. As Hilary Spurling commented in the *Observer* (25 April 1976), 'Beckett's exhilaratingly precise orchestration brings out the play's plastic and above all musical qualities to a miraculous degree.' Beckett himself refers to this characteristic as 'ballet-like' (*Theatre Quarterly*, vol. v, no. 19 (September–November 1975), p. 26). Verbal repetitions are reflected in similar repetitions of physical movements. For example, when Pozzo in Act I lights his pipe, takes a puff and says 'Ah! Jetzt geht's mir besser' ('Ah! That's better'), he is echoed a few minutes later by Estragon, having gnawed the discarded chicken bones, burping heavily (the burp is not indicated in the printed text), and saying, 'Ah! Jetzt geht's mir besser' (pp. 26, 28). This is all the more pointedly comic in that Estragon, unlike Pozzo, has not had the benefit of a full meal. 'In Beckett's ambiguous "tragicomedy" the clown is a figure who embodies [the] inscrutability of existence. He creates laughter out of failure, irresolution and frustration; his is not a comedy of affirmation, but the bitter half-laugh of a "perhaps",' writes Elizabeth Winkler.

Beckett's manuscript production notebooks, now in the Samuel Beckett Archive at Reading University (MS 1396/4/ 3 and 4), show extremely detailed annotations of stage movements in relation to the German text, with diagrams by Beckett himself, and offer a thorough and minute design of the play. They reveal a strong interest in pattern, shape and the return of motifs (doubts, sleepiness, recollection, the sky, and so on), as well as in lighting and in the principal prop (the tree). Throughout, Estragon and Vladimir's close relationship is stressed, for instance by their whispering in unison 'Wollen Sie ihn loswerden?' ('You want to get rid of him?') – again not in the published text (p. 32) – from their shared position left, or by their superbly choreographed saunter down imaginary boulevards as they exchange thoughts about Godot's need to consult his agents, his correspondents, his books and his bank account before taking a decision (pp. 18–19); this is deftly paralleled in Act II after Vladimir says, 'Let us not waste our time in idle discourse!' and, taking Estragon's arm, walks him round the stage (p. 79). Other examples will be found in the detailed notes to *Waiting for Godot* below.

In view of what has been said, this play (or indeed any of the others) should present few difficulties of interpretation, despite the many erudite analyses and attempts at critical elucidation that bewilder the theatregoer; he experiences on stage a clear and intelligible, if admittedly complex, metaphor about the nature of existence. We know that the tree (like the dance) is a common image for the isolation and majesty of the artist, and in *Waiting for Godot* Beckett's tree, no exception, shares in the aura of the archetype; but at the same time we should bear in mind that the changes in the tree, like the sudden rising of the moon, 'are stage facts, important only in the way in which the protagonists react to them. Of themselves they have no other meaning or significance and Beckett has no other interest in them' (Alec Reid). In brief, this play can no more easily be reduced to a formula than can any other work of art worthy of the name. Some may say it means 'where there's life there's hope'; others may retort that it says rather 'life is hope and hope is life'. Both assertions have some truth in them – Beckett's characters indulge in a kind of existential Micawberism – but neither does more than touch the surface of this extraordinary work. Our guide begins, appropriately, with a detailed consideration of it.

WAITING FOR GODOT

Written in French during the winter of 1948–9 as a diversion from the writing of the trilogy of novels. (It comes between *Malone meurt* [*Malone Dies*] and *L'Innommable* [*The Unnamable*].)

First publication   Les Editions de Minuit, Paris, 1952
First publication in English   Grove Press, New York, 1954
First performance   5 January 1953, Paris
First British performance   3 August 1955, Arts Theatre Club, London

RECEPTION

The reactions of the Paris audience were mixed but the play immediately gained distinguished supporters. Jean Anouilh (*Arts*, 27 February 1953) saw the opening of *Godot* as being as important as the first production of a Pirandello play in Paris forty years earlier. Jacques Audiberti wrote in *Arts* on 16 January 1953 that Godot seemed 'a perfect work which deserves a triumph', and Armand Salacrou claimed in the same magazine on 27 February that they had all been waiting 'for this play of our time'. Alain Robbe-Grillet, writing in *Critique* in February 1953, expressed his enthusiasm in spite of misgivings over Beckett's 'dangerously contagious regression'.

At its first London production the play was treated with bafflement or derision by the daily papers but two important reviews in the *Sunday Times* and the *Observer*, the one by Harold Hobson and the other by Kenneth Tynan, started the flow of enthusiasm, speculation and controversy that has surrounded *Godot* ever since. After the publication of the text by Faber in 1956, a review by G. S. Fraser in the *Times Literary Supplement* provoked a correspondence lasting several weeks about the meaning of the play. Since then each new production has attracted attention and *Godot* has become a classic of the stage over which, in the face of a silent author, literary critics never tire of speculating.

The BBC has produced a documentary on the first London production and subsequent provincial tour of *Godot*, entitled *Waiting for What?* The actors recall that the initial critical reaction – 'We felt like highbrow aunt-sallies' – led them to use excessive 'stage-manship' to popularize the jokes, double-takes and throwaway lines. They also recall cutting the running time by twenty minutes by missing out the pauses on one occasion, in order to catch the train out of Blackpool, presumably for safety's sake!

DÉCOR

Beckett sets his characters in a dream landscape: a bare road with a single tree, a flat terrain reminiscent of Yves Tanguy paintings, which stretch to infinity. To choose a road as a meeting place for Vladimir and Estragon is a brilliant dramatic device: it can be seen as an emblem of movement, future and progress but it also suggests that other people might 'come along'.

Perhaps the most striking décor was that of the May 1961 production at the Odéon, Théâtre de France in Paris. The play was performed on almost empty boards with a slender tree designed by Giacometti. Others have been tempted to go beyond Beckett's indications, as did for instance Peter Hall in the first British production: he added a dustbin and miscellaneous rubbish to the required tree.

DRAMATIS PERSONAE

In this dream landscape two men, half tramp, half clown (according to Harold Hobson, Beckett originally saw them as circus clowns and it was Peter Hall, in the first British production, who thought of them as tramps; see Duckworth, p. viii), wait for a Mr Godot, who never turns up. Pozzo and Lucky arrive instead. Each character, though distinct, now and then drops his individuality and speaks in the 'impersonal' voice that can be heard from *Murphy* to *The Unnamable*. Pozzo's speech ('They give birth astride of a grave...', p. 89) and Vladimir's ('We have time to grow old...', p. 91) are examples of this 'impersonal' vein: the sentiment expressed is universal and takes its origin remote from the individual situation (which can also, of course, give rise to a personal lament, like Estragon's 'God have pity on me!', p. 77). For Beckett, the only real brotherhood of man lies in his grief and loneliness: in the cry of distress we are all one, Estragon, Vladimir, Pozzo, so different in appearance, yet so similar in spiritual condition, within the mind. For mind, in Beckett's world, is universal, impersonal and timeless.

Early on in the play the different characters of the two friends manifest themselves. Vladimir is intellectual, rational, loquacious and has a more 'feminine' personality. He is on the whole good-humoured and tolerant, but he is excitable. Estragon is intuitive and creative, rather taciturn, and has the more 'masculine' personality. He is brusque and quick-tempered, and the more complaining of the two. One has the impression that he tends to stoutness, whereas Vladimir seems thin; Beckett gives no directions on this point, but they are usually cast in this way, and Vladimir's fidgets beside Estragon's laziness seem to justify this interpretation. Their tics are characteristic: Estragon plays with his boots, and Vladimir with his hat. It is interesting to note that only in the list of characters are they named as Estragon and Vladimir. They call each other Gogo and Didi and the boy (p. 49) addresses Vladimir as Mr Albert.

Pozzo treats Lucky brutally and is obeyed at once, if not always correctly. Relations are based on mutual need: Vladimir and Estragon need someone to break the monotony of their waiting and Pozzo needs an audience; Pozzo, furthermore, needs Lucky's menial services and Lucky needs a master to guide him. Ruby Cohn (*Samuel Beckett*, pp. 213–14) notes the dramatic contrast between Vladimir and Estragon, the former representing the intellect, the latter physical man. For instance, Vladimir stinks from his feet, Estragon from his mouth: Estragon on two occasions mimes a scene while Vladimir's tendency is to rhetoric. This carries through into their relationship with Lucky and Pozzo. The two pairs split into other pairs with Vladimir and Lucky representing the intellect (the emphasis is on their hats and on Lucky's hair and it is Vladimir who wants Lucky to think) and Estragon and Pozzo the lower nature

(Estragon's preoccupation with his boots and Pozzo's baldness symbolize this, and Estragon requires Lucky to dance). Instinctively, Vladimir feels drawn to Lucky, and Estragon senses a kinship with Pozzo. The pairs thus divide and regroup, as their names dictate they must:

VLADIMIR ——————————— LUCKY
ESTRAGON ——————————— POZZO

The eight-letter names are destined to remain together, and the five-letter names likewise, but because of their contrasted natures, they can do so only in uneasy harmony. Thus Estragon and Vladimir bicker and squabble like an old married couple; they have been together so long ('half a century') that they know one another's weak spots thoroughly. Pozzo bullies Lucky, but is also made to weep by him: theirs is a more subtle sado-masochistic relationship than the semi-conjugal ties between the other two, but in both cases the links are by no means entirely amicable. As Martin Esslin points out: 'The opposition of their temperaments is the cause of endless bickering between them and often leads to the suggestion that they should part. Yet, being complementary natures, they also are dependent on each other and have to stay together' (*The Theatre of the Absurd*, p. 47). Ultimately, however, Vladimir and Estragon must be seen as the superior couple since they are not as naive and have fewer illusions about life.

STRUCTURE

The play is in two acts of unequal length, both of which are set in the same place and begin at the same time (early evening), and night falls at the close of each. In both acts Pozzo and Lucky appear, but their passage occurs later, comparatively speaking, in Act II, and then is sooner over. Both acts, towards the end, see the entrance of a boy, a messenger from Godot; and in both, his message is the same, that Godot will not come that evening but 'surely tomorrow'. In Act I, however, he delivers this message 'in a rush'; in Act II Vladimir drags it out of him. This is one instance among many of the play's asymmetry: Act II is a development, and not a simple repeat, of Act I.

The dynamic between the four individuals helps to give the

play its underlying unity and its unique quality of uneasy equi-librium: everything balances out, but only just. At the extremes of the poised poles are Vladimir and Pozzo, who are divided both by their name-lengths and their temperaments, and the same applies to Lucky and Estragon, who even do each other physical injury (pp. 32 and 88). Estragon's fear of 'being tied' (pp. 19 and 69) is reflected by Lucky's being tied in real fact. This kind of balance is characteristic of the play. As Beckett once said, 'It is the shape that matters.' He was referring to a remark of St Augustine's ('Do not despair – one of the thieves was saved; do not presume – one of the thieves was damned') but it applies to his own work even more aptly. He is an artist for whom the shape is all-important, and the 'shape' of the re-lationships in *Waiting for Godot* between the four main charac-ters is of more interest to him than the characters themselves. That is why the question, 'Why did Pozzo leave home?' (*No's Knife*, p. 92), is an 'insidious question', a red herring which, by ascribing a past and a present situation to Pozzo, diverts atten-tion from the real issue: his role in the play. And that role is pri-marily to counterbalance Estragon and link up with Lucky.

The characters interlock, in fact, with almost Racinian pre-cision, but in other ways Beckett's dramatic method is totally unlike that of neo-classical tragedy. The latter is based on an in-itial exposition of the situation, developments and peripeteia, conflict and catastrophe, all in a rigorous and meticulous order. Beckett gives only minimal information at the beginning (we learn merely that the two men have been together for a long time, have an appointment with Godot, and tend to get separ-ated at night); what action there is, such as the arrival of Pozzo and Lucky, comes to nothing; and there is no conflict and no conclusion – everything continues as in the past. Tragedy raises hopes only to dash them all the more effectively; *Waiting for Godot* never really implies that Godot will come, so that although the end of the second act is much sadder than the first, it lacks tragic finality. Beckett considered that the term 'tragi-comedy' fitted this sort of drama, but its analogues lie further back than the tragicomedies of the Renaissance and Baroque periods. *Waiting for Godot*, indeed, has more in common with the medieval mystery play or the Japanese Noh than it has with

46

the mainstream of modern European drama. Its structure is not dynamic, but static; it does not rise and fall ballistically, but meanders and coils on itself. Its fundamental mode is not revelation, as in classic Western drama, but repetition, or rather repetition-with-a-difference; asymmetry rather than symmetry. Because of this it disconcerted its early audiences, who kept hoping that something was going to happen; but they failed to perceive that the play relies for its structural cohesion not on a forward movement but on the return of leitmotifs that weave in and out through the work. The most obvious of these is the phrase 'We're waiting for Godot', which recurs in different guises a dozen times, but there are others, like 'Nothing to be done'.

Apart from the leitmotifs, Beckett also relies on an elaborate system of counterpoint between the two acts. Nearly everything in Act I can be shown to have its echo or parallel somewhere in Act II, as the attentive reader will notice readily enough. In the theatre, of course, the spectator cannot be expected to pick up all these repeats, just as he will not hear every note in a symphony, but there are so many of them that, provided he is not expecting a quite differently constructed play, he will sense the unity of this one before long.

Nevertheless, the very fact of repetition accounts largely for the more sombre tone of Act II: we have been through all this before, if a little differently, and can expect the situation to reproduce itself to infinity with only slight modifications, and this in itself makes a point about the expectation of Estragon and Vladimir. It is essential, in fact, that the producer bring out what Beckett himself has called the 'stylized movement that's in the play': the pauses and silences specified in the stage directions must be scrupulously respected. If this is done, the play's characteristic rhythm, which consists of the alternation between a burst of speech and activity on the one hand and a period of motionless silence on the other, comes forcibly across. Far from boring the audience, the production that conveys this rhythm generates a palpable tension in the spectator. The best illustration of how Beckett's words should be played is the closing sequence of each act. The reader will notice that although the words are identical in both cases, the punctuation is modified at the end of Act II ('Well? Shall we go?') in order to slow down the delivery, and the roles are inverted (Vladimir speaks the last sentence of Act I, and Estragon of Act II). This inversion is made in accordance with the principle of asymmetry already referred to. The vital thing for the director to achieve, however, is a distinct difference between the tone of the ends of the two acts, and he should do this by allowing the first to be delivered with normal pauses between the exchanges and the curtain, and the second as follows:

VLADIMIR: Well? (*Three seconds.*) Shall we go? (*Six seconds.*)
ESTRAGON: Yes, (*three seconds*) let's go. (*Nine seconds.*)

The stage-manager should then contrive to close the curtain at half the normal speed.

When all this is done, the emotion in the auditorium is so intense one should be able to hear a pin drop. Timing, here and everywhere else in the play, is all. Once again the musical analogy holds good: just as a conductor can spoil one's enjoyment of a symphonic movement by taking it too fast or too slow, the producer can ruin *Waiting for Godot* by taking the fast sections (such as the hat swapping, pp. 71–2) too slowly, and the slow passages too fast. Tight control must be exercised over the timing of every utterance and every movement in this play, and the actors, like well-trained acrobats, must rehearse each gesture until it is perfectly smooth and precise. No one, in fact, should be under any illusion that this is an easy work to perform properly: Beckett demands top fitness of the men who play his decrepits, and also thorough rehearsal, for as Peter Bull, the first London Pozzo, has remarked, one of the main difficulties for the actor is that identical cues recur every few pages, so that it is 'remarkably easy to leave out whole chunks of the play'.

Our analogy with acrobatics is intentional, for it has escaped no one that *Waiting for Godot* owes a great deal to the circus. Pozzo is a kind of ringmaster who cracks his whip and commands the show while he is 'on', and Estragon's dropping of his trousers (p. 93) is pure clowning. The multiple tumble in Act II may disconcert the seasoned theatregoer, but it would be familiar to any circus fan, for whom the 'cussedness of the inanimate', it has been said, 'is overcome by the perfection of the juggler'; Vladimir's 'spavined gait' would likewise strike a chord. Other popular forms of entertainment, too, are affectionately alluded to in this play. The silent film comedy, which so delighted Beckett's generation, has bequeathed its bowler hats to the actors: that Laurel and Hardy lie to some extent behind Vladimir and Estragon is certain. And that late-Victorian phenomenon, the music-hall, which declined only with the advent of talking movies, has suggested the pattern, so characteristic of *Waiting for Godot*, of individual turns interspersed with double acts: Pozzo, in his 'solo' moments, is like the sentimental singer who so delighted our great-grandparents, or the conjurer who would come and perform in front of the curtain while scenery was shifted behind it. Lucky's speech, too, is set in the play like the star 'number' of an Edwardian evening, and the banter of Estragon and Vladimir frequently takes on the aspect of 'cross-talk' in which two comedians swap gags or fail comically to understand each other. In Britain, Morecambe and Wise continued the tradition of cross-talk, but it is no longer a really living form of entertainment: today's audiences find it too unsophisticated, for the changes were rung on a limited repertoire of material: mothers-in-law, obese beach beauties, seaside landladies, and so on. A slightly more subtle form of humour lay in having comedian A play a 'straight' man trying, for instance, to explain to comedian B, the 'funny' man, the complexities of the traffic system or income-tax rules, and feign exasperation at B's comic propensity for getting the wrong end of the stick. An echo of this sort of comedy can be heard frequently in the quick-fire exchanges between the two friends in this play.

A more difficult concept to embrace than either characters or structure as manipulated 'object rules' in *Waiting for Godot* is the notion that 'time' too becomes an object which the dramatist manipulates. At its most simple this is the reason why *Waiting for Godot* seemed 'boring' to its first audiences – 'Nothing happens, nobody comes, nobody goes, it's awful' – and in contrast the reason why its first British director found the play so exciting 'in its ability to make dramatic use of boredom to create tension' (Peter Hall, *Waiting for What?* BBC, 9 April 1961). We can see that such features as the humour and the

49

carefully controlled length of the respective acts ('One would have been too little and three too much'; see Ruby Cohn, *Samuel Beckett*, p. 212) attempt to avoid the imitative fallacy of presenting boredom by boring the audience – but we must also see that the lack of development insists on the play being always *present, now.* Richard Schechner ('There's Lots of Time in *Godot*', *Modern Drama*, vol. ix, no. 3, pp. 268–76) suggests that this is dramatically achieved by the pairings, which create what he calls 'discontinuous co-ordinates'. 'This peculiar sense of time and place', he writes, 'is not centred in the characters, but *between* them. Just as it takes two lines to fix a point in space, so it takes two characters to *unfix* our normal expectations of time, place and being' (p. 269). This is the reason why the play seems to bleed the same blood wherever it is cut, though Robbe-Grillet points out that this feature is highlighted by certain episodes, and in particular by Estragon's insistent question 'Why doesn't he put down his bags?' becoming nullified and meaningless through the fact that Lucky has, eventually, put them down: 'Since he has put down his bags it is impossible we should have asked why he did not do so' ('Samuel Beckett, or "Presence" in the Theatre', in *Samuel Beckett*, ed. Esslin, p. 112).

From this perspective, *Waiting for Godot* becomes akin to a game of manipulations of constants, similar to Pozzo's belief that 'the tears of the world are a constant quantity. For each one who begins to weep, somewhere else another stops. The same is true of the laugh' (p. 33). Jacques Guicharnaud has commented, 'When all of life is a game, theatre, the game *par excellence*, has the last word' (*Modern French Theatre*, 1967, p. 258), and this seems to be the case *par excellence* in the play *Waiting for Godot*. Lucky's speech encapsulates this system of manipulation of givens: given God, given man, given earth (the three basic assumptions of his discourse), he manipulates each without any movement towards a satisfactory or meaningful conclusion. There is no conclusion that can be reached: every moment of endurance declares its own autonomy, every moment *is* presence, *is* situation, every particle static and of the same substance as the whole. In its production the audience too become part of this presence (hence the explicit references to them in the play). But never more than 'is'. As Vladimir remarks of the tree when he realizes he cannot even hide himself behind it: 'Decidedly this tree will not have been of the slightest use to us' (p. 74) – but it has been there all the time, as constant, endurable, and meaningless as Estragon and Vladimir themselves.

LANGUAGE AND DRAMATIC EXPRESSION

The dialogue ranges from the earthy and realistic to the mysterious and disturbing:

VLADIMIR: There's man all over for you, blaming on his boots the faults of his feet. This is getting alarming. One of the thieves was saved. It's a reasonable percentage.

The movement in these few words of Vladimir's (p. 11), from the banal to the bizarre and back to the comforting, is characteristic of the whole play, which modulates continually from one tone to another. Pozzo's declamation on the night (pp. 37–8) shifts violently from the false sublime to the prosaically ridiculous, and after rising to 'vibrant' heights sinks to 'gloomy' depths and silence. After a long pause, the other two strike up, like the strings when the sound of the brass has faded away, and swap vaudeville remarks. The transition is almost musical in its subtlety.

The language of the play is marked by several Irishisms which are pointed out in the *Notes on the Text* below. These are understandably common in Beckett's work and occur in later plays also.

The disintegration of language is central in Beckett's drama and there is a steady progression until in a play such as *Not I* the audience is fortunate to be able to make out anything of what is said on stage. Lights and bells take on the force of a character. In *Waiting for Godot*, however, we are only at the beginning of this process, taking up dramatic language on the brink of disintegration, where most traditional playwrights would end their experiments. Niklaus Gessner has listed ten different modes of disintegration of language to be found in the play. They include misunderstandings, *double entendre*, monologues, clichés, repetition, inability to find the right word, and telegraphic style, culminating in Lucky's speech. As Martin Esslin points out, 'In a purposeless world that has lost its ultimate objectives, dialogue, like all action, becomes a mere game to pass the time' (*The Theatre of the Absurd*, p. 86).

NOTES ON THE TEXT

p. 3

(*A tragicomedy in two acts.*) 'A play, combining the qualities of a tragedy and a comedy, or containing both tragic and comic elements; a play mainly of tragic character, but with a happy ending' (SOED). The play is called a 'tragicomedy' in the English translation only.

In directing the work for the Schiller Theater, Berlin (STB), Beckett divided the two acts up into sections that form natural units, and in a different sort of play would be scenes. They are:

A1 pp. 9–13 ('bloody ignorant apes')
A2 pp. 13–21 ('Like to finish it?')
A3 pp. 21–8 (Vladimir's second, vehement 'Let's go!')
A4 pp. 28–38 ('You see my memory is defective' – *Silence*)
A5 pp. 38–48 ('Adieu!' – *Long silence*)
A6 p. 48 to the end of Act I
B1 pp. 57–65 ('Ah! que voulez-vous. Exactly' – *Silence*)
B2 pp. 65–77 ('Pity! On me!')
B3 pp. 77–82 ('We are men' – *Silence*)
B4 pp. 82–9 ('They give birth astride of a grave . . . On!')
B5 p. 89 to the end of the play

Note that there are five sections in Act II as against six in the longer Act I.

p. 6

(*Characters.*) Listed in order of first appearance; Pozzo is pronounced Po'dzo. According to Beckett, no significance attaches to the choice of names: there is no intention on his part, for instance, to 'internationalize' the play by giving the characters French, Russian, English and Italian names. In any case the latter are not fixed: if Vladimir calls himself 'Vladimir', for instance, on p. 9, he is addressed as 'Mister Albert' by the boy on p. 49; and Estragon gives his name as 'Catullus' in the first Faber edition, and as 'Adam' in the definitive edition (see p. 37). In his introduction to the French text (Harrap, 1966), Colin Duckworth reveals that in the manuscript of the play Estragon is named as 'Lévy' throughout the first act, and when questioned by Pozzo gives his name without hesitation as 'Magrégor, André', thus making himself, says Professor Duckworth, 'one of the great family of Beckett's M's' (p. lxiii).

p. 7

(*A tree*.) Beckett sees this tree as simple and bare, like the rest of the set. In a production in Paris in 1961 the tree was designed, appropriately, by Giacometti.

p. 9

Nothing to be done. In translating '*Rien à faire*' Beckett deliberately avoided 'Nothing doing', which he regards as a 'facile colloquialism'. The first words spoken should introduce the theme of the play, he believes, and 'nothing doing' would not achieve this. Cf. 'There's nothing we can do' (p. 68), and 'There's nothing to do' (p. 74).

(*legs wide apart*.) Vladimir suffers from enlargement of the prostate gland, a painful complaint not uncommon in old men, which accounts both for his gait and his sudden urges to pass water. Cf. 'the last moment' (p. 10).

(*musing on the struggle*.) Note here and elsewhere a puckish element in some of Beckett's stage directions.

Get up till I embrace you. An Irishism. As for this whole dialogue, it is clear that it recurs in much the same terms every evening, and has become a kind of litany between the two men.

p. 10

On the other hand. Vladimir is always the more resilient character of the two.

who said that? Prov. 13: 12: 'Hope deferred maketh the heart sick.' The French original was a colloquial remark overheard in the street, but Beckett is fond of rendering his demotic French by quotations from the Bible or Shakespeare (cf. 'Our revels now are ended' for '*Finie la rigolade*' in *Endgame*). Beyond the fact that the words of the quotation fit the situation of the two men aptly enough, no particular significance attaches to them. Beckett may have remembered their being used by Dickens in *Bleak House* (Oxford edition, 1962, p. 344) to describe the misery inflicted on the suitors by the delays and complexities of the legal process.

I feel it coming. Vladimir is still musing about his prostate complaint and its idiosyncrasies.

(*feels about inside it.*) For fleas; cf. 'It itched me', p. 72.

p. 11

One of the thieves was saved. Up till now, the play has been fairly light in mood: this remark introduces the first serious and more sombre note. It follows closely on chatter about boots and feet, but is closely connected with it in Beckett's mind. He has, he says, always been impressed by the symmetry of Augustine's words already quoted, 'Do not despair – one of the thieves was saved; do not presume – one of the thieves was damned', even though he does not believe in them. The same symmetry affects Estragon's feet, one of which is 'saved', the other 'damned', so that the boot will go on one foot, but not the other. The situation is not a particularly enviable one, but it could be worse – after all, adds Vladimir, resilient as ever, 'it's a reasonable percentage'.

Gogo. It is natural that these two old companions should address each other with nicknames, and 'Gogo' and 'Didi' are obvious diminutives for them to adopt. It is unlikely that they have any other significance.

Our being born? In *Proust* (1931) Beckett quoted Calderón, 'Man's greatest sin is to have been born', and Schopenhauer

(1788–1860) used the same quotation again, before Beckett did. There is no doubt that it represents one of his most deeply felt convictions; that is why it is no laughing matter, as Vladimir finds when he forgets his malady for a moment.

(*ceases as suddenly.*) Note the clownish humour of Vladimir's instant Cheshire-cat grin.

p. 12

I must have taken a look at it. It is characteristic of Estragon's inconsistency that later on he should affirm that all his life he has compared himself to Christ. Compare Vladimir's denial on p. 13 that he said 'from hell' on p. 12.

only one speaks of a thief being saved. Luke 23: 43. The same idea was used by Beckett in *Murphy*, where Neary says, 'Do not despair . . . Remember also one thief was saved' (p. 213).

p. 13

both of them abused him. From here to the end of A1 the two actors spoke face-to-face, close to each other, and very fast, in a bickering tone (STB).

the third. Matt. 27: 44 states: 'The thieves also, which were crucified with him, cast the same in his teeth.' Such blatant inconsistency worries the more intellectual Vladimir; for Estragon there is no problem, and people merely show their 'bloody ignorance' in believing the kindlier version. His savage outburst puts a temporary halt to the flow of Vladimir's chatter.

p. 14

(*facing auditorium.*) Thereby bringing the latter ironically into the global situation. Cf. 'that bog', p. 15.

We're waiting for Godot. This is the first intimation of what has brought these two together again this evening, and the first occurrence of the leitmotif that threads through the play and helps to give it cohesion. In the manuscript, Professor Duckworth tells us (pp. l–li), the two men have a *written* assignation with Godot for 'Saturday evening and subsequent evenings', which does not help them much since they aren't sure which day it is (see p. 15). But a written note, however unhelpful, makes Godot's existence too definite, and Beckett therefore dropped this from the published versions. As for the name of Godot, Beckett told his first producer Roger Blin that it was suggested to him by *godillots* and *godasses*, French slang words for boots.

(*despairingly*.) This significant stage direction does not occur before the definitive edition.

I don't know. A willow. This is a characteristic example of annulment, a common habit with Beckett's characters. In the novels, too, assertions made with some confidence are liable to be qualified or even contradicted by the narrator soon afterwards; cf. 'a pomeranian I think, but I don't think so' (*Three Novels*, p. 12). It is by such means that the narrative undermines itself in the process of narration. (See also p. 93.)

p. 15
I must have made a note of it. Beckett changed the initial subject of the sentence ('He' in his draft) to 'I', which withdraws the suggestion of a concrete, physical and active Godot in favour of a more shadowy figure. (See note above to p. 14: *We're waiting for Godot.*)

(*very insidious*.) Long familiarity has taught Estragon subtle methods of needling the neurotic Vladimir, but he soon tires of this piece of the old fun, as of everything else. On the other hand this may be an indication that dramatic stress should be laid on the uncertainty of the friends' situation.

p. 16
Don't tell me! Here and elsewhere, the intellectual, rational mind recoils in horror from the lucubrations of the creative intelligence.

The English. The first British edition had 'All the best people'.

In making the change Beckett has brought the text into line with the French and American editions, perhaps because he wishes to leave Estragon's nationality vague. (The original British formulation would imply that Estragon is himself English.)

An Englishman having drunk a little more than usual ... An obscene French joke that turns on the alleged preference of the English for sodomy. Ruby Cohn gives it in full in *Journal of Beckett Studies*, I (Winter 1976), p. 42, note 2.

p. 17
mandrakes. An ancient fertility symbol, mandrakes were believed to grow below gibbets for the reason that Vladimir, ever a fund of useless knowledge, gives here. Cf. James Joyce's:

- God's truth, says Alf. I heard ... from the head warder that was in Kilmainham when they hanged Joe Brady, the invincible. He told me when they cut him down after the drop it was standing up in their faces like a poker.
- Ruling passion strong in death, says Joe, as someone said.
- That can be explained by science, says Bloom. It's only a natural phenomenon ...

(*Ulysses*, The Bodley Head, 1955, p. 289)

p. 18
an even chance. As in the discussion about 'a reasonable percentage' (p. 11), they are content to opt for less than perfection – until it comes to doing something positive.

before it freezes. A characteristically Beckettian twist on a popular cliché.

p. 19
I think so too. This concludes the first example of music-hall cross-talk that is such a characteristic feature of the dialogue. Exhausted by their little 'canter' (see p. 65), they now sink again into temporary silence.

Take your time. As in 'Use your intelligence, can't you?' (p. 17),

57

Estragon, who possesses the quicker intuitive intellect, is irritated by Vladimir's slowness in making connective associations. His remark is also characteristic of the 'straight man' in a music-hall double act.

(*They remain motionless.*) In a good production the actors refrain from fidgeting in the long pauses indicated '*silence*', and remain frozen in the attitudes they have adopted as the last words were being spoken. Where this is done (as it was at the Royal Court Theatre in 1965), the powerful rhythm in the play between bursts of activity and dialogue on the one hand, and periods of motionless silence on the other, comes forcibly across. Together with the return of leitmotifs already referred to, this recurrent rhythmical pattern gives the play its cohesion.

(*totters.*) The first of many pratfalls that go to make up the play's circus character.

p. 20

(*violently.*) Another stage direction that does not occur in the first edition. Immediately preceding this, there is in the original French an exchange in which Estragon suggests they leave, and Vladimir answers (our translation): 'Where? Tonight we'll probably sleep at his place, warm and dry, our bellies full, on the straw. That's worth waiting for, isn't it?' Estragon says, 'Not all night,' and Vladimir answers, 'It's still day.' Beckett's reason for dropping this can only be guessed at, but it probably has something to do with his wish to make Godot's 'promises' as nebulous as possible.

I asked you a question. I.e. 'We're not tied?', interrupted by Vladimir's 'Listen!' (p. 19). The way things get dropped, and then either lost sight of completely (e.g. 'Like to finish it?' on p. 21) or picked up again later (like the question, 'You want to get rid of him?' on p. 31), is characteristic of the random inconsequentiality of everyday conversation that Beckett surely imitates.

p. 21

(*before Pozzo appears.*) Beckett's so-called 'drama of inaction' turns out, on closer inspection, to be by no means lacking in action and suspense. The audience, at this point, is wondering, like the two men, whether this isn't Godot at last. According to Professor Duckworth (pp. lx–lxi), Beckett himself once toyed with this possibility: on the manuscript he scribbled, 'Suggest that Pozzo is perhaps Godot after all, come to the assignation, and that he doesn't know that Vladimir and Estragon are Vladimir and Estragon. But the messenger?'

(*Pozzo a whip*.) Pozzo figures recur frequently in Beckett's *oeuvre*. 'The fool [Lucky] in league with the knave [Pozzo] against himself is a combination that none may withstand' (*Murphy*, p. 170); in the French novel of 1946, *Mercier et Camier*, a character named Conaire uncovers his bald pate and asks people to guess his age, and he behaves and is dressed like the Pozzo we are familiar with from productions of the play. In *Molloy*, Moran rubs up against 'a big ruddy farmer. He was wearing an oilskin, a bowler hat and wellingtons. His chubby cheeks were streaming, the water was dripping from his bushy moustache' (p. 173); and Malone says of a visitor, 'Tomorrow perhaps he will be wearing leggings, riding-breeches and a check cap, with a whip in his hand to make up for the umbrella and a horse-shoe in his button-hole' (*Three Novels*, p. 274).

It is of interest that Roger Blin considered that Charles Laughton would have made the ideal Pozzo.

In most productions Lucky is dressed in frayed livery, but Professor Knowlson tells us that Beckett originally envisaged him dressed as a station porter.

p. 22

(*assistance*.) The original stage direction here was more explicit: 'divided between the wish to go to his assistance and the fear of not minding their own business'.

Does that name mean nothing to you? Pozzo, being a local landowner of some substance, is astonished to find that his name does not strike a chord.

p. 23

(*He puts on his glasses.*) Compare the comedy of this with 'looks at the two likes' on p. 24. Note how rapidly through his language and dramatically obvious loud voice and gestures, Pozzo's pompous, bullying and conceited character is established. For an actor with the right voice and physique the part holds out great opportunities (see for example the series of actions detailed on p. 24).

p. 24

(*looks at the two likes.*) Vladimir enfolds Estragon protectively in his arms as Pozzo inspects them closely with his spectacles; he repeats the same gesture (p. 74), when Estragon recoils in horror from the audience (STB).

p. 25

Why doesn't he put down his bags? It is typical of the meandering dialogue and also a source of humour that Estragon's question is not answered, despite being asked repeatedly, until p. 31.

p. 27

but in theory the bones go to the carrier. Professor Duckworth makes two suggestions about the source of Lucky's name. Either he is lucky because he gets the bones or, as Beckett suggested in conversation with him, he is lucky to have no more expectations (*EAG*, p. lxiii).

the bones. The first edition had 'will you be wanting the bones?' Similarly, a few lines further on, 'What age are you?' reads 'How old are you?'

p. 28

(*He puts the bones in his pocket.*) The French, less graphic, has him throw them away.

Done it! On his next two risings, he has Estragon, comically, beg him to regain his seat.

(*vehemently.*) Another new stage direction, made more necessary by the shortening of Vladimir's plea from 'Let's get out of here.'

p. 29

Who told you? Who, indeed? Pozzo shows uncharacteristic perspicacity in deducing, from what he was told on p. 23, that the two men need Godot, as Vladimir is not slow to notice.

I too would be happy to meet him. Godot, of course. The humour of this passage lies in the fact that Pozzo and Estragon are each pursuing their own separate line of thought, while Vladimir tries to mediate.

p. 30

(*sprays his throat.*) An old trouper's trick. The famous singer Melba used a 'Melba mixture' in a similar way before going on stage.

p. 31

Ah! Why couldn't you say so before? Note that Estragon is successful in conveying the meaning of their question.

He wants to cod me. 'Fool me', an Irishism.

Atlas, son of Jupiter! Pozzo is mistaken: Atlas, in Greek mythology, was the son of a Titan, Iapetus. For his part in the revolt of the Titans he was condemned to support the heavens on his head and hands.

p. 32

waagerrim. At the fifth time of asking, because his question is slurred by repetition, Vladimir succeeds in attracting Pozzo's attention.

before he stops. Something of the original French punning on *pleurer* (to weep) and *pleuvoir* (to rain) survives here.

It's a good sign. I.e. of a healthy wound that is cleansing itself. In Act II (p. 67), however, the wound has begun to fester.

p. 33

a constant quantity. Cf. 'the syndrome known as life is too diffuse to admit of palliation. For every symptom that is eased, another is made worse' (*Murphy*, p. 57). In both contexts, Beckett was thinking of the analogy of physical energy.

knook. This word was invented by Beckett, and was suggested to him by the word for a Russian whip, *knout*. Pozzo's claim that he learned 'all these beautiful things' from his 'knook' is borne out by the similarity between his purple prose and Lucky's speech later.

(*he consults his watch.*) This is, of course, an obvious vaudeville gag. But all the same, like Vladimir's 'looking wildly about him, as though the date was inscribed in the landscape' (p. 15), it is a comment on human time.

(*He puts his hat under his arm.*) In fact holds it in his right hand, with the suitcase (STB).

(*He is completely bald.*) In unpublished lectures on 'The Godot Tradition' delivered at Cambridge University during the Long Vacation Term, 1961, Dr J. R. Northam argued that the intellectual barrenness of Pozzo was symbolized by his baldness, in contrast to Lucky's abundant white hair. (See also *Dramatis personae* above.)

p. 34

How dare you! Vladimir's rapid about-face is comically typical of the mercurial person he is, and his word 'crucify' is an Irishism, like 'dudeen' on p. 35.

What have I done with my pipe? The answer is that he put it in his pocket (p. 30). 'Kapp and Peterson' is a famous Irish make of briar pipe.

p. 36

Pan sleeps. In this, the second of his mythological references (the only words spoken by Schumann in the course of a long walk in the country with a friend), Pozzo alludes to the Greek god of flocks and shepherds.

Will night never come? Shouted, each word separated (STB).

p. 37
(*witticism.*) I.e. that Vladimir had longed for the sky to be black ('Will night never come?' on p. 36). The French makes this clear by adding, 'Patience, it's coming.'

p. 38
night is charging and will burst upon us. Cf. *Aeneid* 8: 369: 'night fell, and embraced the earth in her dark wings'.

Oh tray bong. In Berlin, this was dropped. Instead, Estragon repeated (but more perfunctorily) the thumbs-up gesture with which Vladimir had said, 'Oh very good, very very good' (STB). It is natural that Beckett, steeped in two cultures, should go in for the bilingual joke. Cf. 'Que voulez-vous?' (p. 65).

You see my memory is defective. Sc. 'of the classics'. Pozzo attributes the relative weakness of his performance to his declining powers of allusion.

p. 39
That's enough! This has, of course, no connection with Pozzo's 'enough', but means 'shut up', as the French ('*tais-toi*') makes clear; Estragon, however, interprets it to mean that five francs would be sufficient, and is quick to reply to Vladimir that he will settle for five but won't go below that.

I'd like well to hear him think. The construction is an Irishism, and of course the remark is typical of the more 'intellectual' Vladimir.

p. 40
(*He laughs briefly.*) At his own joke, once again.

He refused once. The greater menace of the English here (the French has simply, 'I'll explain that in a moment') is deliberate.

The Hard Stool. A phrase meaning constipation. Beckett deleted this whole passage in the 1964–5 London revival at the Royal Court Theatre because it 'dragged', replacing it with Pozzo, Vladimir and Estragon asking themselves in turn 'Where were we?' (See Knowlson, *SBaE*, p. 70.)

(*squirming like an aesthete*.) Vladimir feels called upon to make some critical comment; Estragon attempts a more practical form of criticism; both fail. Vladimir reveals his pretentiousness, Estragon his tendency to make a fool of himself by rushing headlong into action that he should have thought better of.

What have I done with my spray? The last we heard of this was on p. 37.

p. 41
Why doesn't he put down his bags? Correctly timed and delivered, this should bring the house down. The question was answered, of course, on p. 31.

Stoutly reasoned! The fallacy in Vladimir's reasoning is obvious, but not to Pozzo. It is correct that Lucky put down his bags in order to dance, but this means he held them before that, and thus provoked the query, as Vladimir inconsistently concedes in saying that Pozzo has already explained why Lucky does not put them down.

True! After this exclamation there is a long passage in the original French that has not been translated; the burden of it is that Lucky doesn't refuse (Estragon's question) because he wants to make Pozzo feel sorry for him, and therefore keep him. This was cut at the first production of the play because Blin felt that it was unactable and made for a sort of hiatus in the action. The passage is indeed rather feeble, but at least it provides an answer to Estragon's question, albeit one very similar to the answer to his first question, about why Lucky doesn't put down his bags.

He can't think without his hat. This is comic, because we have just seen that the other three can't think *with* their hats. Note how his thinking is abruptly terminated by the removal of his hat (p. 45), as if a part has been removed from a piece of machinery.

p. 42

I'll put it on his head. These words terminate a sequence in which every ounce of verbiage has been pressed from the situation, in a typically vaudeville manner.

Think! In spite of the apparent unintelligibility and lack of structure of Lucky's speech, on stage at any rate, the tirade does fall into three parts, formal and thematic. Anselm Atkins, writing in *Modern Drama* (vol. ix no. 3, p. 309), sees the formal structure thus: (a) unfinished protasis of a theological or philosophical argument, (b) an incomplete fragment of a rational argument that is the last half of an objection to the unfinished demonstration in the first; (c) a second objection parallel to the earlier one, which lapses into aphasia. The German critic Horst Breuer sees the thematic breakdown as follows: (a) Absence of God; (b) Shrinking of man; (c) World as chaos. He also notes three subordinate clauses that pretend to launch off an essential message, which is, of course, cunningly held back. It is, however, sensible perhaps to remember Colin Duckworth's caveat: 'By reducing Lucky's "think" to a semblance of coherence, one destroys the parodic effect, the pathos, the growing tension, and the brilliance of the speech which demands an equal brilliance in performance' (*EAG*, pp. cviii–ix). It is, after all, Lucky's only opportunity to fly away beyond the constraints and limitations of his condition. Beckett's own summary of the monologue's theme is characteristically terse: 'to shrink on an impossible earth under an indifferent heaven' (Kristin Morrison, *Canters and Chronicles*, p. 24n).

Puncher and Wattmann. Lit. 'ticket-puncher' and 'tram-driver'.

quaquaquaqua. Beckett comments: 'quaquaversal: divine attribute'. (See COED.) Cf. the closing words of Shem the Penman's section in *Finnegans Wake* by James Joyce:

> He lifts the lifewand and the dumb speak.
> – Quoiquoiquoiquoiquoiquoiquoiq!

(p. 195)

p. 43

apathia ... athambia ... aphasia. Respectively, 'freedom from, or insensibility to, suffering'; 'imperturbability'; 'muteness, inability to communicate'.

Miranda. In Shakespeare's *The Tempest*, Prospero's gentle daughter; cf. I. ii, 421.

so blue ... so calm. A quotation from Verlaine's 'Le Ciel', in *Sagesse*. Later, Lucky refers to Hölderlin's poem 'Hyperions Schicksalslied'.

crowned. '*Couronnées*' is a French academic cliché for the attribution of a prize, and '*caca*' and '*popo*' childish words for excrement and chamberpot respectively.

Testew, Cunard, Fartov, Belcher. Invented names of vulgar origin. 'Public works' (Fr. *travaux publics*) is a more respectable pun, like Essy-in-Possy (Lat. *esse*, to be, and *posse*, to be able).

conating, camogie. The first is not a sport, but the act of willing and desiring (philos.); the second an Irish form of women's hockey.

shrink and dwindle. This (the sort of observation an Academy of Anthropometry could be expected to 'crown') is the crux of Lucky's speech, which is far from being gibberish. In an admittedly blurred and pedantically repetitious manner, Lucky, senile professor, decayed scholar and degraded man of reason, makes a kind of statement: that in spite of the existence of a loving God (of sorts) and progress of various kinds, man is in

66

full decline. Less forcefully put than Pozzo's declaration on p. 89, it makes a similar point.

p. 44

Feckham. An invented place name. (The other three are real.)

Bishop Berkeley. An Irish philosopher (1685–1753) for whose writings Beckett has a high regard; he was at once one of the great British empiricists and a leading representative of the brand of philosophy known as idealism. (See below, note to p. 91.)

Steinweg and Peterman. Two invented names that pun on words for 'stone'; cf. 'abode of stones' below. 'Labours lost', of course, is Shakespeare.

the skull in Connemara. Cf. 'Thelma née bboggs [wife of Beckett's first fictional hero Belacqua] perished of sunset and honeymoon that time in Connemara' (*More Pricks than Kicks*, p. 189).

p. 45

Avenged! For the kick, of course (p. 32).

p. 46

what have I done with my watch? The last was heard of this on p. 37; 'I must have left it at the manor' (below) is obviously wrong. Pozzo thus loses three things during his halt; where they went is a mystery to all, and one best left so. There is no authority anywhere in the play to justify a producer having Estragon steal them.

I must have left it at the manor. Cf. 'Why did Pozzo leave home, he had a castle and retainers. Insidious question to remind me I'm in the dock' ('Text for Nothing, V', in *No's Knife*, p. 92).

p. 48

Adieu! In Berlin, Beckett stressed the comic aspect of this episode. 'Adieu' is yelled nine times in all by the three actors, and (as in a music-hall turn) Vladimir and Estragon raise their hats twice in unison (STB).

You forget everything. For Vladimir, this encounter has happened before, as it will happen again in Act II, when the two travellers will be even more 'changed'.

It's the other foot! Estragon has only one boot on, but on the foot that is 'damned' – hence the bad fit, and the pain. The stage direction 'boots' on p. 50 should therefore read 'boot', as in the first edition.

p. 49
Off we go again. The two men turn together, Vladimir erect at the rear, Estragon seated on his stone, and face the boy; pause (STB).

Mister Albert . . . ? In *L'Avant-Scène* (June 1964, p. 8), Paul-Louis Mignon records that Beckett told him that the dialogue between Vladimir and the boy has its origins in a dialogue between a glazier and his apprentice in his first (unpublished) play *Eleuthéria*.

p. 51
He minds the sheep, sir. Cf. 'And Abel was a keeper of sheep' (Gen. 4: 2); it is characteristic of Beckett's world that it should be the Abel figure who is not respected. For the boy, cf. Charlie Chaplin's 'kid', Jackie Coogan.

p. 52
(*In a moment it is night.*) Beckett is not interested in naturalism.

At last! Sc. 'night has come'.

Of climbing heaven and gazing on the likes of us. From Shelley's 'To the Moon' ('Art thou pale for weariness / Of climbing heaven and gazing on the earth . . .'). Estragon, the poet, naturally quotes poetry when appropriate.

And they crucified quick. This bathos strikes a facile note in the play that is regrettable.

p. 57

(*The tree has four or five leaves*.) Cf. Dante, *Purgatorio*, XXXII, 59–60: 'The tree renewed itself, which before had its boughs so naked'; but where Dante the Christian optimist sees the tree as representing the possibility of renewal for mankind through God's grace, Beckett the agnostic pessimist sees the tree only as an isolated phenomenon, inexplicable, a deceitful mirage like Godot himself, holding out no genuine promise or significance. At the end the tree mockingly remains ('Everything's dead but the tree', p. 93), not even of any use for hanging oneself on.

And dug the dog a tomb. This is a German round song, translated by Beckett, and an appropriate choice for a play based on cycles and the return of leitmotifs.

p. 58

Come here till I embrace you. This play is asymmetrical throughout. In Act I, Estragon was joined on stage by Vladimir: vice versa here. Vladimir's invitation to embrace is slightly different in wording (see p. 9). It would not be possible to note here all the repeats, but it is their existence that gives the play its unique structure, as the perceptive reader will not be slow to notice.

p. 60

It's never the same pus. A sour twist on the saw of Heraclitus to the effect that we never step twice into the same stream (i.e. all is continually changing, and time is irreversible).

p. 62

In the Cackon country! Another pun on the French child's word for excrement, *caca*. It was Estragon, of course, who brought up the Rhône episode on p. 53.

Picking grapes for a man called . . . Bonnelly, in the original French version, of Roussillon, in the *département* of the Vaucluse in south-east France. Beckett hid there during the latter part of the German occupation, and used to buy his wine from M. Bonnelly.

But down there everything is red! An allusion to the colour of the soil at Roussillon.

The best thing would be to kill me, like the other. Lucky (cf. p. 32, 'The best thing would be to kill them'). Estragon's memory is not as defective as he claims.

p. 63

Like leaves. These lines were intoned, with Vladimir and Estragon facing the audience (STB). A. J. Leventhal notes in the *Dublin Magazine* (vol. xxx, April–June 1954, pp. 11–16) an interesting point about the meaning of this passage, which Beckett sees as 'cross-talk on a lyrical level': 'Death then is as inadequate as life.' Is this an early suggestion of the notion of interminable voices in the present employed in later works such as *Embers, Cascando* and *Not I*? Notice that the two friends' immediate reaction is to fall back on Godot.

p. 65

That wasn't such a bad little canter. One more markedly 'intellectual' in tone than those of Act I.

p. 67

You see, all that's a lot of bloody – Probably 'lies' (cf. 'a pack of lies', p. 50). Note that throughout this exchange Vladimir has been patiently leading his friend towards what he hopes (vainly, as it turns out) will be an incontrovertible demonstration of the fact that they were in very truth at the same spot on the previous evening.

p. 68

What'll we do, what'll we do! This was shouted, as if the question were being flung accusingly at the malign fate or divinity that controlled their existence (STB).

p. 69

They're too big. Beckett wrote Professor Duckworth the following comment on this: 'The second day boots are no doubt same as first and Estragon's feet wasted, pined, shrunk and dwindled in interval', as Lucky's speech had warned. Lest we take the author too seriously, he added: 'There's exegesis for you!' For Estragon's dread of laces, cf. 'We're not tied?' (p. 19).

p. 70

(*Vladimir . . . takes off his coat.*) Contrast Pozzo's selfish bellow 'Coat!' (p. 24).

(*Walks him up and down.*) Humming 'Death and the Maiden' (STB; cf. *All That Fall*, p. 12).

p. 71

(*Estragon takes Vladimir's hat.*) This 'three hats for two heads' routine is one used by the Marx Brothers in the film *Duck Soup* and also by Laurel and Hardy. (See Knowlson, *SBaE*, p. 70.)

p. 73

Gonococcus! Spirochaete! Respectively, the micrococcus found in gonorrhoea discharge, and the germ associated with syphilis.

p. 74

There's no way out there. The fact of being in a theatre is humorously exploited in Vladimir's suggestions to Estragon at this point.

p. 76

Off we go! They begin to waltz, humming 'The Merry Widow' (STB; cf. *Happy Days*, p. 30).

Let's just do the tree. A gymnastic exercise that involves standing on tiptoe with outstretched arms.

p. 77

(*Enter Pozzo and Lucky.*) From the opposite side to the one used by them in Act I. Although this is not specified in the stage directions, Beckett wrote us as follows: 'In all productions of *Godot* I have had anything to do with P. and L. in Act II come in from the opposite side. This for me is correct. They go to and fro.' (In conversation he elaborated on this by saying that they were returning from the fair, and added half jokingly that Pozzo hadn't been able to find a buyer for Lucky.) The detail is characteristic of the visual exactitude of Beckett's dramaturgy, like Lucky's hideous neck sore caused by Pozzo's thoughtless jerking on the rope, and the bags held painfully a few inches above the ground – this is an ungentle milieu, and the audience is made acutely aware of the fact when, for instance, the rope brings Lucky down offstage (p. 47). In his callous indifference to Lucky's physical well-being Pozzo stands condemned, but by visual, not verbal, means.

(*Pozzo is blind.*) Vladimir and Estragon's doubt over this question (p. 90) has led to speculation among critics, both about the truth of the statement and the implications if it is untrue and Pozzo is simulating blindness. For comment on these speculations see Duckworth, *EAG*, pp. ciii–civ. Professor Duckworth tells us that in his manuscript Beckett initially suggested that Pozzo may only be pretending (p. lxii).

Poor Pozzo! I knew it was him. Who? Godot. Not only the assonance suggests the link between the two. In his manuscript Beckett toyed with the idea that Pozzo might be Godot but with each production the possibility has become more remote and this interpretation should not now seem possible. (See note to p. 21.)

p. 79
all mankind is us. They stand in a Laurel and Hardy pose (STB).

p. 80
(*aphoristic for once.*) These two last words are a significant addition in the definitive text. As for Vladimir's eloquence, he owes it, no doubt, to Lucky's hat, which he adopted on pp. 71–2.

p. 82
(*Estragon pulls, stumbles, falls.*) This multiple fall Beckett sees as 'the visual expression of their common situation' and as

being 'related to the threat in the play of everything falling'. The four bodies must form an intersection, thus:

In this diagram, made by Beckett himself, Pozzo lies at right-angles across Lucky in the direction in which he is to crawl, and Vladimir lies diagonally across Pozzo to form a kind of arm-chair into which Estragon fits. It must not, Beckett says, 'be an untidy heap, but has to function'. Such multiple tumbles are common in children's theatre, circus acts and variety shows.

p. 83
Pozzo! Pozzo! They discord, i.e. one uses an ascending tone, the other a descending tone (STB).

p. 84
Perhaps he can see into the future. The blind were once supposed to have the gift of prophecy; cf. Tiresias, the seer of Greek mythology. In Berlin, great stress was laid on the word 'blind', which was twice repeated, to stress how worrying Vladimir finds this change in Pozzo's circumstances (STB).

pp. 85–6
night is drawing nigh. Vladimir is quoting from the same hymn that Krapp sings (*Krapp's Last Tape*, p. 59).

p. 86
Memoria praeteritorum bonorum. Intoned, as if in church (STB). Means 'memory of past happiness'. Note that Estragon understands this Latin tag.

It isn't by any chance the place known as the Board? Another humorous reference to theatre.

p. 87

Yes yes, let your friend go, he stinks so. There is a fairly long passage omitted here from the original French, which contains further discussion between Vladimir and Estragon about the people he thought he saw on pp. 73–4. Beckett evidently felt that the presence of others should be left as uncertain as possible.

p. 89

Dumb! Note the repetition of this word, to balance with 'blind', pp. 84–5 (STB).

I'm going. In Act I it was Pozzo who hesitated to leave.

When! When! One day, is that not enough for you. This easily comprehensible metaphysical statement is often overlooked in contrast to Lucky's speech, which, because of its obscurity and obvious need for exegesis, seems to attract more of the critics' attention and enthusiasm.

p. 91

At me too someone is looking. Cf. 'Do you think God sees me?' (p. 76). According to Berkeley, that which is not perceived cannot be held to exist; God however perceives everything and thus ensures its existence.

p. 92

I think it's white, sir. According to Beckett, the whiteness shows Vladimir that Godot is very old: 'If he were less experienced there might be some hope.'

What am I to tell Mr Godot, sir? The first edition had 'say to', as in Act I (p. 52). In accordance with the principle of asymmetry, the definitive text has been modified.

(*exit running.*) In Berlin, in both acts he was directed by Beckett to walk slowly backwards away; cp. *Ghost Trio*, p. 254.

p. 93

Ah! He didn't come? The 'ah' was whispered, in a tone of weary annoyance (STB).

(*Estragon loosens the cord that holds up his trousers which fall about his ankles.*) Even at this desperate juncture the clowning goes on. But Vladimir's reaction is not comic; he doggedly faces the audience as he tells Estragon to pull up his trousers (STB).

ALL THAT FALL

Written in English, July–September 1956. The play was written at the suggestion of the BBC, mainly because they had been impressed by *Waiting for Godot* in 1955. Although Beckett took some time to act on the suggestion, he wrote quickly once he had the idea that led to this play. On 18 July 1956 John Morris, then Controller of the Third Programme, wrote to Val Gielgud, Head of Drama: 'I saw Samuel Beckett in Paris this morning. He is extremely keen to write an original work for the Third Programme ... I got the impression that he has a very sound idea of the problems of writing for radio and I expect something pretty good.' For further discussion of the original production of *All That Fall*, see Martin Esslin's interesting article in *Encounter* (September 1975, pp. 38–46), entitled 'Samuel Beckett and the Art of Broadcasting', which is also the source of the letter quoted above.

First publication   Grove Press, New York, 1957
First British edition   Faber and Faber, London, 1957. This
    edition contains a small number of textual deletions, no
    doubt made after the first recording.
First broadcast   13 January 1957, BBC Third Programme,
    directed by Donald McWhinnie

RECEPTION
Critics immediately recognized the affinity between the works of Beckett and the medium of radio. In the *Listener*, 24 January 1957, Roy Walker proclaimed the play a 'radio classic', saying that it was even better as such than *Under Milk Wood*. Christopher Logue called it 'radio triumphant' (*New Statesman*, 14 September 1957) but another poet, Donald Davie, although he applauded Beckett's originality in inducing syntax to 'parody itself', none the less found fault with the play as a whole because of its 'derivative slapstick' and 'trick ending' ('Kinds of Comedy: All That Fall', *Spectrum*, Winter 1958). Hugh

Kenner made perhaps the most exact comment when he said that 'radio proves to be the perfect medium for Beckett's primary concern: the relationship between words, silence and existence' (*Spectrum*, Spring 1961).

In France the impact of the radio play was not as great as that of the television production in January 1963. 'Ce fut admirable,' exclaimed François Mauriac in the *Figaro Littéraire* (2 February), but Beckett did not agree and has not been happy with either this production or with a German stage presentation given at the Schiller-Theater Werkstatt, Berlin, in January 1966.

DÉCOR

This is the only play set in a named location, that of Boghill, an Irish suburb. There is, of course, no décor as such except that evoked with a precision unusual in a Beckett play by Mrs Rooney, as on p. 25, but there is an outstanding aural décor. Beckett comments: 'It is a text written to come out of the dark' (Reid, *All I Can Manage*, p. 68), but when he sent his manuscript to John Morris at the BBC, he already included a note about the special quality of 'bruitage' (sound effects) that might be necessary. Martin Esslin (*Encounter*, September 1975, pp. 39–40) tells us that the experiments with sound for *All That Fall* led directly to the establishment of the BBC's Radiophonic Workshop. These experiments, in which Beckett took a close interest, were directed by the play's producer, Donald McWhinnie, who saw from the start what was necessary: 'I do feel that without being extreme we need, in this particular case, to get away from standard realism,' he wrote to Beckett, explaining that he preferred animal noises imitated by humans rather than any taken from the BBC's effects library. The various other sounds needed were processed in order to rid them of excessive naturalism and to make it possible to create 'the enclosed, subjective universe' of *All That Fall*. For the most part Beckett's text reinforces the unreal realism. Notice for instance that Maddy tends to call up the sounds by her own comments (see especially p. 32), instead of commenting on them after she has heard them.

77

DRAMATIS PERSONAE

The lack of the usual austerity of décor is complemented by the presence of at least double the usual number of actors. Beckett seems to have allowed himself to be tempted by the possibilities of radio, whereas his only stage play with so many characters, *Eleuthéria*, has never been staged. The minor figures are minimally sketched but assume a natural and vivid identity, perhaps because we experience them all through Mrs Rooney's subjective consciousness and our own reactions are based on her previous knowledge of and familiarity with these people. The bigotry of the ironically named Miss Fitt and the tyrannical manner of the stationmaster, Mr Barrell, whose attempts to slink away are rapidly detected, the bawdiness of Mr Tyler, all these slip easily into the setting of an Irish suburb that Mrs Rooney has skilfully created for us. But this lady, of course, dominates. Even her husband Dan is there only to serve her purpose, both to bring into relief her morbid preoccupations and to demand explanations that she would not have to give to a man with normal sight. He is also able to tell the listener about her physical state because of his own need to depend upon such indications; cf. 'You are quivering like a blancmange' (p. 29).

Maddy is otherwise not unusual as a Beckett heroine. She is noticeably Irish and has an extensive knowledge of Dublin Protestantism, even to the extent of being on easy terms with the Regius Professor of Divinity. She gives us the following description of herself: 'Oh I am just a hysterical old hag I know, destroyed with sorrow and pining and gentility and churchgoing and fat and rheumatism and childlessness' (p. 14). Her gentility, however, does not prevent a suggestion to Mr Tyler that he should unlace her corset behind the hedge nor various salacious remarks to Mr Slocum, her old admirer and to Dan, her husband. The latter comes over as a testy individual, with an abrasive humour that controls some of his wife's worst self-indulgence. For Maddy is dominated by sadness, grief over her dead child, and is interested almost exclusively in death and decay and in others' misfortunes. In the first part of the play, her journey to the railway station, she indulges herself almost totally. Each person is greeted ('How is your poor wife? . . .

78

What news of your poor daughter?') with an inquiry after a sick relative, but her attempts to obtain sympathy for her own plight result in failure, perhaps because of the excessive lugubriousness of it all. Or is it because the others cannot accept the bathos as she switches from tears to humour: 'Can't you see I'm in trouble? . . . Have you no respect for misery? . . . Minnie! . . . In her forties now she'd be . . . girding up her lovely little loins, getting ready for the change' (p. 16). She is fully aware of her inability to communicate her sorrows to others and ponders on this (p. 22). And it is this that sustains tension between her and Dan, a man who jokes about his blindness: 'The loss of my sight was a great fillip. If I could go deaf and dumb I think I might pant on to be a hundred' (p. 32). His very different attitude to children ('Did you ever wish to kill a child? Nip some young doom in the bud' (p. 31)) seems closely linked with her pain, either as a defence against being absorbed into her sorrow and the ensuing view of life, or perhaps as the real cause for her obsession, in that he has never really been willing to procreate. But there are times when his sympathy for her seems genuine enough, particularly when she tells of the little girl who had never really been born (pp. 35–6); overall we are left with the impression of a couple, like Estragon and Vladimir, who have learnt to live together and have evolved a close relationship in spite of all.

STRUCTURE

The play, like much of Beckett's work, has an almost musical structure. 'Not only is *All That Fall* very clearly a three-movement structure (Maddy Rooney's anabasis, her wait at the station, her and Dan's katabasis), but it has also a very complex pattern of small-scale rhythms – the footsteps of the anabasis, the doubled footsteps and the thumping of Dan's stick in the katabasis, the rhythmic panting, etc.' (Martin Esslin, *Encounter*, September 1975, p. 41). Similarly there is a pattern of suspense, which dominates the first and final parts. The first (and shortest) part is composed of rapid scenes that are lively and picturesque; the final (and longest) one is slow, with psychological analyses and a mysterious end. The weather changes from 'Nice day for the races' (p. 12) via 'the clouding blue' (p. 25) to 'Curse that sun, it has gone in' (p. 29) and rain (p. 36).

All through the play we are given ominous hints that are not so evident on first reading or hearing as when one rereads with the knowledge of the surprise ending. Not only is there an obsession with death – Schubert's music, the various moribund relatives, the rotting leaves in the ditch, the squashed hen and even Mr Slocum's car – but we also find specific hints about railway accidents such as the female voice warning her little girl against being sucked under the train (p. 25). The whole thing is beautifully orchestrated until the last few pages with its shock ending, and it is this that has most troubled critics. They have made various reproaches, labelling it as 'confusing', 'faintly irritating', a 'trick ending', but few seem to see the problem as clearly as John Spurling. He suggests that in Beckett's writings people are represented as being victims of an inexorable and completely depersonalized fate and are not responsible for other people's woes. The suggestion, therefore, that Mr Rooney might deliberately have caused the child to fall out of the railway carriage raises all sorts of questions that Beckett leaves himself no time to answer in this play. Mr Rooney might certainly have allowed the child to die but if he pushes him out of the train, then he dethrones fate, a thing nobody is allowed to do in Beckett's world since it runs counter to its quietist ethic. Apart from this problem the manner of the revelation has been questioned since the object that Jerry brings to Mr Rooney is an enigma. Is it a child's ball? Is it symbolic of a child's head? One critic has even suggested that it is Mr Rooney's testicle that he tries to reject and leave behind in the gents. All in all it is tempting to wish that the play had ended with 'Hold me tighter, Dan! Oh yes!' on p. 38, before it poses metaphysical problems in 'whodunnit' terms, disturbs the whole carefully structured balance, and raises (as Spurling says) more questions than it settles.

LANGUAGE

The role of Mrs Rooney has been played in BBC productions by two great Irish actresses, Mary O'Farrell and Marie Kean, and all characters spoke with colourful Irish accents. In a way,

Beckett had already written a dramatic scene in an Irish station: in the closing pages of *Watt* the railway staff and early morning travellers exchange ribaldries at Watt's expense, calling him 'the long wet dream with the hat and bags' (p. 271). Even to read, the dialogue in *All That Fall* is noticeably Irish with specific references to Ireland (such as the twenty-six counties on p. 24). The play is dominated, though, by Mrs Rooney's rather florid language with its exaggerations and lyrical effusions that contrast with her husband's more 'frigid rhetoric', as Kenner has put it. For Maddy is very conscious of her difficulties with language and its restrictions. As Donald Davie has said: 'She speaks by formula, but she does not live and feel by formula – or she strives not to, though her language continually traps her into it' (*Spectrum*, Winter 1958, p. 26). Notice that Mrs Rooney's comment on p. 13 about finding her way of speaking 'bizarre' is complemented on the return journey by the exchange between her and Dan about her struggle with a 'dead language' (p. 34).

NOTES ON THE TEXT

[Title.] See note to p. 38 below.

p. 12

(*Rural sounds.*) These sounds, the instructions for which were not strictly adhered to in the first production, are rather like the sounds of an orchestra tuning up.

(*Silence.*) This instruction was not followed in the first production and several other silences were omitted.

('*Death and the Maiden*'.) The title of a song by Schubert, the sad melody of which provides the theme of the same composer's String Quartet in D minor (D. 810), the *Andante* of which the 'poor woman' is playing on the gramophone. This is appropriate music for Maddy to hear since we soon learn that her own daughter died in childhood.

(*Sound of approaching cartwheels*.) In the first production cartwheels were not heard at first. Echoing hoofbeats overlapped
with Mrs Rooney's dying murmur and then cartwheels were
heard.

How is your poor wife? The first of many inquiries concerning ill
or dying people. See introduction to this play, *Dramatis personae*.

Nice day for the races, Ma'am. Most likely at the Leopardstown
course. Much of the setting of this play can be related to the
Dublin suburbs of Beckett's youth.

p. 13

Mercy! What was that? Notice that no sound is indicated. We do
not hear the horse neigh and paw the ground.

p. 14

Sigh out a something something tale of things. John Ford, *The
Lover's Melancholy*, IV, ii, the words of Meleander. For 'something something' read 'lamentable'; otherwise the quotation is
accurate.

they would have to scoop me up with a shovel. Like horse dung, of
course.

There is that lovely laburnum again. Compare p. 36. This is only
one of the many echoes and contrasts between the outward and
return journey.

(*Dragging feet*.) These were omitted in the first BBC production, and the bicycle bell echoed.

the whole ... er ... bag of tricks. A coy euphemism for hysterec-
tomy, reinforcing the general theme of sterility that runs
through the play. See also *Embers*, p. 103.

p. 15

I was merely cursing ... the wet Saturday afternoon of my concep-

tion. Various Beckett characters, including Murphy, Molloy and Krapp, utter similar curses concerning their conception.

p. 16

girding up her lovely little loins. A common biblical expression. See, for instance, Luke 12:35.

p. 17

Venus birds! Doves are traditionally associated with love.

these new balloon tyres I presume. Balloon tyres (which ran at lower pressure) replaced an earlier form of pneumatic tyre around 1933; this dates the action of the play in the mid-thirties, therefore.

p. 20

Pity! In the BBC production the vulgar French expletive '*Merde*' was used.

What are you doing stravaging. The Oxford English Dictionary gives 'stravaging' as a Scots and Northern dialect word for 'to wander about aimlessly'.

p. 23

I would soon be flown . . . home. She would be in heaven.

p. 24

the encircling gloo-oom. From 'Lead, kindly light', by Cardinal Newman (1801–1890). The words of this hymn are for the most part appropriate to Mrs Rooney's situation.

Wasn't it that they sung on the Lusitania? . . . *Or was it the* Titanic? Both major maritime disasters, the first off the coast of Ireland in 1915 in which 1,200 people died, the latter in 1912 in which 1,500 people drowned. 'Rock of Ages' is another popular hymn.

p. 25

I am sorry for all this ramdam. A French word meaning the 'row' or 'din' that is traditionally associated with festivities occurring during the nocturnal hours of the Muslim Ramadan fast. No wonder Miss Fitt (Mr Tyler in the first edition) 'marvels' at Mrs Rooney's erudite vocabulary: the word is not common even in French.

Give me your hand and hold me tight, one can be sucked under. A strong hint of what is to come. See also the reactions of Mr Barrell and Tommy, p. 27.

p. 27
(*'Boghill! Boghill!'*) A possibly bawdy name; but cf. Bally-boghill, a place north of Dublin.

p. 29
I think Effie is going to commit adultery with the Major. Theodor Fontane's great German novel *Effi Briest* (1895) is one of Beckett's favourites. It tells how the young wife of a Prussian civil servant, stationed on the Baltic coast, takes to meeting her officer lover in the sand dunes, and how she later comes to a tragic end. Mr Rooney's comment is remarkably astute, since the treatment of the young wife's transgression is so discreetly oblique in the novel that most readers miss it altogether on first reading. (See also note to p. 62 of *Krapp's Last Tape*.)

I have been up and down these steps five thousand times. Compare this with the beginning of Beckett's short story 'The Expelled'.

p. 30
One of the few satisfactions in life! Cf. Descartes, *Discourse on Method*: 'The child . . . who has been instructed in the elements of arithmetic, and has made a particular addition, according to rule, may be assured that he has found, with respect to the sum of the numbers before him, all that in this instance is within the reach of human genius' (p. 17).

p. 31
Nip some young doom in the bud. An apt and pithy phrase, giving sombre meaning to a cliché ('young bloom').

What restrained me then? A very ambiguous *then*. Does it confirm Dan's guilt in the present death of the child on the line?

Like Dante's damned, with their faces arsy-versy. See Dante, *Inferno*, XX, especially verses 23–4. The Diviners, Augurs and Sorcerers who in life attempted to see into the future have their faces twisted front to back. Mr Rooney manages as usual to find a picturesque expression of his own for this.

p. 32
Are we afraid we should never rise again? Unlike Christ on the third day.

p. 33
On the other hand, I said, there are the horrors of home life. Notice how Beckett slips in extraneous words, e.g. 'waning', 'scuffling', 'tearing'.

p. 34
Our own poor dear Gaelic. 'This is a joke that would have appealed to Synge (with his sardonic views on the life expectancy of Gaelic) and looks like a sly aside to his memory' (Worth, *IDE*, p. 250).

p. 35
Jerry led me to the men's, or Fir as they call it now. An allusion to the labelling of public lavatories in Ireland as a result of the attempt to revive the use of Gaelic in the 1920s; *'Fir'* is the 'Gents', *'Mna'* the 'Ladies'. Mr Rooney may be correctly quoting Grimm's Law, but the Gaelic *'fir'* is not likely to *derive* from a Latin word, even though *'vir'* does mean 'man' in Latin. At best, as Jakob Grimm (1785–1863) demonstrated in his *Deutsche Grammatik* (1822), there can be regularity of *correspondence* in the initial consonants, both Latin and Gaelic being Indo-European languages.

p. 36
The trouble with her was she had never really been born! This is something of a preoccupation with Beckett; the phrase recurs

in *Watt*, p. 274, almost word for word. In his discussion of *Waiting for Godot*, Niklaus Gessner draws our attention to C. G. Jung, who regarded socially 'unsituated' people as not really born. Jung, one of 'these new mind doctors', impressed Beckett when he attended one of his lectures in London in the 1930s.

Golden drizzle. Mrs Rooney's musings on the laburnum, coupled with the weather, seem to lead her to think of 'golden rain' fireworks, though this may be a classical allusion, to Zeus' shower of gold, the form he adopted to father Perseus on Danaë.

p. 37

It's like the sparrows. See Matt. 10: 31 and Luke 12: 6–7. Beckett is fascinated by discrepancies in the Scriptures. Cf. the discussion about the two thieves in *Waiting for Godot*, pp. 12–13.

All day the same old record. There is a disguised reference here to Foxrock, where Beckett was born and lived as a boy. In notes sent to Professor Duckworth and published by him in the *New Zealand Journal of French Studies* (vol. i no. 2), a childhood friend of Beckett's, Dorothy Coote, recalled that a local family had a son who was 'a bit mental' and played 'the same tune on his piano all day long' (p. 62). Miss Coote's recollections confirm that 'Boghill' is a thinly veiled description of Foxrock, from which the train service to Dublin was about hourly.

p. 38

Hardy. Presumably the friend that Mr Tyler was going to meet and whose life he once saved (p. 15).

'*The Lord upholdeth all that fall and raiseth up all those that be bowed down.*' This text, which of course supplies the play with its title, is cruelly ironic in the circumstances; hence the Rooneys' 'wild laughter'. It comes from Ps. 145.

p. 39

(MR ROONEY *groans*.) There are two ready explanations for this. Either Mr Rooney finds confirmed his fears that he may *unwittingly* have killed a child, or he fears Mrs Rooney's reactions at the failure of his attempt to hide what he did *knowingly*. One should perhaps also wonder at this point why 'Death and the Maiden' should make Mr Rooney weep on p. 37.

On to the line, Ma'am. . . . (JERRY *runs off.*) This remark and the instruction were omitted in the first BBC production.

(*They move on.*) The end of the play is mystifying but not violent. While the listener is left wondering what happened and how this fits in with the rest of the play, Maddy and Dan move off, receiving the news in a Beckettian way, seemingly unaware of the contrast between the shocking information and the resumption of their monotonous dragging walk. One thing is definite: Beckett did not intend to solve the mystery for us.

ENDGAME

Written in French between December 1955 and October 1956, from an idea that was already in Beckett's mind in 1953–4. The play caused him a lot of difficulty. In April 1956 he wrote to his friend, the American director Alan Schneider, 'I did finish another [play], but don't like it. It has turned out a three-legged giraffe, to mention only the architectonics, and leaves me in doubt whether to take a leg off or add one on.' By June he had reduced it to one act. In October when the play went into rehearsal Beckett commented to Schneider: 'I am panting to see the realization and know if I am on some kind of road, and can stumble on, or in a swamp' (*Village Voice*, 19 March 1958, p. 8 and 15).

Fin de partie (French title)

First publication   Les Editions de Minuit, Paris, February
    1957. Since this was before the first production of the play,
    Beckett incorporated changes made subsequently into the
    first English edition.

First performance   3 April 1957, Royal Court Theatre,
    London

Endgame

First publication in English   Grove Press, New York, 1958.

First English production   28 January 1958, Cherry Lane
    Theater, New York, directed by Alan Schneider

RECEPTION

The first production of *Fin de partie* caused almost as much difficulty as its composition, since no Paris theatre could be persuaded to risk putting it on. Eventually Roger Blin, the play's French director (to whom incidentally Beckett dedicated it), accepted the invitation of the Royal Court Theatre to bring it to London. Beckett described the experiment to Schneider as 'rather grim, like playing to mahogany, or rather teak'. The reviewers, with the exception of Harold Hobson and a French critic, were no more enthusiastic. Writing in the *Observer* (7 April 1957), Kenneth Tynan reacted forcibly: 'Last week's production, portentously stylized, piled on the agony until I thought my skull would split.' When the play reached Paris in April the French greeted it with respect but little warmth and the two most enthusiastic critics, Maurice Nadeau and A. J. Leventhal, both wrote from a reading of the already published text rather than as a result of seeing the actual staging. The latter realized that '*Fin de partie* cannot hope for the same success that attended *Waiting for Godot* ... an audience, faced with uttermost pain on the stage, is likely to wilt at the experience, though it may well be a catharsis for such who have hitherto refused in their euphoria to look beyond their optimistic noses' (*Dublin Magazine*, April 1957).

During the months following the creation of the play Beckett worked on an English translation under the title *Endgame*, and this, first produced by Alan Schneider in New York in January 1958, received considerable attention from the critics and was later remembered as 'a significant off-Broadway success' by John Unterecker (*New Leader*, 18 May 1959). The play's producer was, however, wry about Beckett's critics. They begin, he said, by saluting Play A as 'awful'. When Play B comes along, that too is awful, not nearly as good as A. Play C is then dismissed as being awful, worse than B, which though good was not a patch on A, which in the interval has become a masterpiece.

Endgame returned to London in October 1958 in a successful production by George Devine and since then it has been staged on several occasions and has been the subject of much critical writing and speculation. It would certainly seem that, as Beckett acknowledged to Alan Schneider, it is a difficult play to get right, and it may be that this was the main reason for the initial hostility of reviewers. Nevertheless, a good production 'will elevate the work to its proper tragic stature without sacrificing its corrosive, brilliant black comic values' (Tom Bishop, *The Beckett Circle*, Spring 1980).

DÉCOR

The dilapidated décor underlines the play's sense of an ending. The dustbins, the picture with its face to the wall, the dust sheets, all indicate a last 'refuge', outside of which is 'death' as nature's demolition experts prepare to move in. One window looks out on a dead plain, the other on a becalmed sea. To landward, Mother Pegg's light is extinguished; to seaward, the beacon is sunk. The audience can see nothing of this, of course, and has, like Hamm, to rely on Clov's reports on what he espies through the small, high windows; this makes for a strikingly claustrophobic effect essential to the play's impact. Alan Schneider's New York production exploited the authentic interior provided by the brick wall at the back of the stage, and the windows (complete with wooden frames) were painted in. This design, Schneider wrote, 'produced sound of great effectiveness and could be lit well and simply' (*Twentieth Century Interpretations*, ed. Chevigny, p. 19). It is amusing to note that just before the first performance of this production someone turned off the central heating, which caused the radiators and pipes to click loudly as they cooled off. The critics assumed that this was intentional and praised the originality of the idea with the result that Schneider had to ensure that it happened again on subsequent nights.

DRAMATIS PERSONAE

As previously mentioned, the play proved hard for Beckett to get right. The various stages the work went through can be traced in the holograph and three successive typescript drafts. The first typescript (T1) represents to all intents and purposes a fair copy of the manuscript, and the second (T2) does not differ substantially from the published text: the great majority of the changes, therefore, occur between these two drafts, both typed by Beckett himself. A study of them reveals that Beckett added relatively little to his original conception but struck out a great deal. The early drafts are undoubtedly richer in that they are packed with incident and variety. But they are also more diffuse: the dramatic line is much clearer in the final version, and the point pushed home more forcibly. The characters are more rounded at the outset, but also less consistent: Clov, for example, is a more expansive, a less dry and clipped figure, in T1, and Hamm's dread of solitude more obvious and his cruelty more crudely expressed. In pruning his work Beckett undoubtedly improved it, although sometimes he compressed things so drastically that the surviving statement is somewhat obscure.

In the drafts, the characters are simply designated as A, B, P and M. In the dialogue, however, A is addressed as Guillaume, B as James, P as Pépé (by A) and Walther (by M), and M as Mémé. It is clear that P and M are A's parents, and there is a suggestion (which survives in the final version) that B is his son; but the holograph notes preceding T1 speak only of a 'père adoptif' and 'fils adoptif'. Beckett clearly intended all along that the precise nature of the relationship between Hamm and Clov should remain vague and ambiguous.

In the published text, Hamm, articulate, erudite, ironical, is set off against Clov, whose linguistic and mental range is narrower. Nagg, coarse and earthy, is contrasted with Nell, who has feelings, and memories that she cherishes. The atmosphere between these four is electric and can erupt into angry rage at the slightest provocation. They are not made sweeter tempered by their handicaps. Hamm cannot stand and Clov cannot sit, and Nagg and Nell, being legless, are kept upright by their dustbins. So they all react peevishly to each other. Even their names show this: Hamm is the 'hammer' that drives in these particular nails (Fr. *clou*, Ger. *Nagel* and Eng. 'nail'). There is, naturally, little love lost between them. Hamm and Clov detest each other, and yet they need each other – Hamm needs Clov to wait on him, and Clov needs Hamm to open the larder; sometimes they come close to giving voice to an *élan* of affection, but their pride and reticence stop them. Usually they address each other harshly and without sentiment, as Nagg and Hamm do too. There is little tenderness in this decaying universe. The characterization, therefore, like the dialogue and the general construction, is all fully consistent with the static, inconsequential, claustrophobic and potentially explosive nature of the play.

STRUCTURE

The drafts corroborate Beckett's assertion that the play began as a two-acter. The second act was distinctly shorter than the first; at the head of the latter on T1 Beckett has scribbled '75 minutes' and at the head of the second act '35 minutes'. In reducing the two acts to one, he did not radically restructure the play, but simply ran the first into the second without a break; the original second act began with the words 'Our revels now are ended' (p. 39). His reason for making the change was probably that the division into two acts had little *raison d'être*. The second act opened a few moments later with Nell's dustbin gone, but otherwise the play continued very much as before. Beckett had clearly hoped that there would be a significant difference of tone between the two acts: a holograph note preceding T1 reads 'Act I. Hilare. Act 2 Mortellement triste'. But it did not come out that way.

The eventual form chosen is simple enough. Beckett himself has insisted on 'the extreme simplicity of dramatic situation and issue' in the play. In a 'bare interior' bathed in a 'grey light' four people live out their time: Hamm, his parents Nagg and Nell, and his servant Clov. The only event of some note is Nell's death about two-thirds of the way through. Otherwise such action as there is constitutes time-filling. All the characters, with the exception of Nell who is beyond caring, are waiting for something: Hamm for his sedative, Nagg for his pap and for a change of sand, and Clov for Hamm to die. It might be a day like any other: at the beginning, Clov gets Hamm up by removing the dust sheet covering him. But we never see him replace it. He may leave at the end, or his final appearance may be just a routine fancy-dress show – we never know. There are, however, indications that this day is unusual. As it progresses, there is a distinct feeling of 'running down'. Nell dies; even the resilient Nagg falls silent; provisions of various kinds, especially the precious sedative, are exhausted; and Hamm says, 'It's the end, Clov, we've come to the end. I don't need you any more' (p. 50). There is in fact a marked 'sense of an ending' in the play: the word 'end' occurs at least nine times in the text and is, of course, picked up in the title. John Spurling comments that the function of many elements in the play is

to lack definition when placed one on top of the other, while

remaining, each in itself, as clear as glass... This complex
web of references, recurrences, reflections might easily turn
into a mere tangle. It is given coherence by the play's dominant and almost absurdly simple theme, which is stated in
the opening sentence of Clov's prologue: 'Finished, it's finished, nearly finished, it must be nearly finished.'

(Fletcher and Spurling, *Beckett*, pp. 74–5)

Hamm, however, has one permanent resource, and that is his
'story'. It provides the play's leitmotif which helps to give it cohesion. Whereas in a two-act work Beckett, whose plays show
no dramatic development of the traditional kind, can rely on a
quite elaborate system of asymmetrical counterpoint, in a one-
acter he does not have this resource and so must rely more
heavily on leitmotif and the recurrence of themes. In this play
there are words and phrases that keep cropping up, but the
principal leitmotif is Hamm's story. This is first mentioned on
p. 34 and peters out temporarily on p. 37, only to crop up again
on p. 39. Dropped on p. 41, it recurs on p. 45, and then for the
last time in Hamm's closing tirade (p. 52). It thus weaves in and
out of the play like a phrase in a sonata.

Another thread is provided by the metaphors relating to play
of various kinds, and especially that enacted on the stage itself,
for Hamm, like a ham actor, plays to an imaginary audience.
He delivers his 'story' in a theatrical manner, pausing every so
often to comment on his own performance; likewise Nagg, in
his tailor joke. Clov points his telescope at the audience and
remarks ironically on their delirious enjoyment of the fun.
Nagg and Nell whisper to each other 'What was that he said?'
(p. 20) like spectators who have not understood. The chasm between stage and audience is reconstructed on the stage itself
because Hamm cannot bear to become too involved in his own
drama. We are in a world where all is illusion and all is play: we
are in the theatre, but, as we pointed out earlier, a theatre that
Shakespeare would have understood – *theatrum mundi*, or all the
world a stage.

For the stage, in Beckett, has a particular reality. It is not a
facsimile of a middle-class living room, as in 'drawing-room
comedy', but a place in its own right. There is no let-up: 'Let's

stop playing!' pleads Clov; 'Never!' replies Hamm (p. 49). The stage is an emblem of the notion of imprisonment that pervades the play; there is 'nowhere else' (p. 14).

If the metaphor is playing itself, the game is chess. 'There is no return game', writes Beckett in *Murphy* (p. 85), 'between a man and his stars.' The fates are playing with Hamm a game of chess which he is losing, a game now in its last moves. 'Old endgame lost of old,' says Hamm in his last speech, 'play and lose and have done with losing.' Stoically, he concludes: 'Since that's the way we're playing it . . . let's play it that way.' He has run the gamut, shot his bolt; there are too few pieces left on the board. Strategy is dead, tactics no longer feasible. Having blundered in the game, he is losing the endgame. He tries to resist despair, but he is afraid. 'His assurance', Beckett said at a rehearsal in London, 'is always put on.' Edgy nervousness causes him frequently to burst into a rage. His parents only disturb and irritate him all the more. Clov sadistically reminds him of Mother Pegg and his lack of human charity towards her; but most of all, Hamm plagues himself with unacknowledged remorse. 'A bit of a monster,' was Beckett's comment, 'the remains of a monster.' His 'novel' is autobiographical, and he can't let the subject drop. A man came to him, starving, and he tried to fob the man off with reasoning: 'Use your head, can't you, use your head, you're on earth, there's no cure for that!' (p. 37). He was right enough, no doubt, but this comment, uttered by a well-fed, pessimistic intellectual, returns to haunt his last days. He cannot be still: he acted in bad faith, and he knows it. Clov, probably the starving man's son, lives with him, a permanent, nagging reminder of the day when he bandied words with human misery. Thus Hamm may strike different spectators in different ways. Some may be reminded of Rouault's remarkable painting *The Old King*. He is indeed like a decrepit king, surrounded by a diminished court (see *Twentieth Century Interpretations*, ed. Chevigny, p. 61). Others may view Hamm as the last survivor of the great holocaust, the radiation from which is rotting his bones. Others, again, may simply take him as an ordinary enough person, with the usual arrogance, cruelty, repressed tenderness, and frailty cohabiting in uneasy harmony in his heart; a man who longs to bring the whole pointless farce to an end, but fears what lies beyond.

LANGUAGE AND DRAMATIC EXPRESSION

Throughout the play the dialogue reflects the often pointless to-and-fro of everyday conversation. This effect is achieved by two principal devices. The first is the way matters tend to be lost sight of and then picked up again in a desultory fashion later (cf. 'And the rat?' on p. 45). The second is the habit of annulment; for example, Nell says 'no' when Nagg offers her a piece (of biscuit), only to ask at once what it is he is offering her a bit of; and she refuses to scratch him, only to ask 'where?' (pp. 19, 20). Similarly, Clov says 'Then we'll die', and then cancels this statement a few lines further on (p. 14). These two devices imitate the inconsequential nature of usual conversation, as overheard in buses and public places.

Apart from its everyday aspect, Beckett's dialogue is characterized by the high incidence of question asking that goes on. Hamm is a particularly assiduous questioner, plaguing Clov like a precocious child its harassed mother. It is interesting to note that in the first forty exchanges of the play, Hamm asks Clov twenty-seven questions. He uses Clov's replies very much as he does his sedative; they are as it were verbal pain-killers. 'All life long the same questions, the same answers,' Clov is moved to complain, but for Hamm 'Ah the old questions, the old answers, there's nothing like them!' (pp. 13, 29). They fill his life and give him something to say. So that when Clov asks 'What is there to keep me here?' Hamm can truthfully reply, 'The dialogue . . . Ask me where I've got to' (p. 39).

There are other features that mark the dialogue as typically Beckettian. One of these is the twisted cliché, that is, a common expression which one of the characters alters, to amuse himself if no one else. Examples are 'If age but knew!' (p. 16 – the usual French expression is 'if youth but knew, if age but could'), and 'We lose . . . our ideals!' (p. 16). There is better humour, however, than this rather feeble sort: Hamm's false modesty about his creative powers, for example (p. 40). Most of the jokes, though, are meant to misfire – Nagg's tailor story, for instance, and Clov's wry comment on the audience's stony silence (p. 25).

For this is a rather introverted world: the humour is private, as are the allusions. These are sometimes literary. Shakespeare, for instance, is twisted by Hamm, who may not be unaware of his own Richardesque aspect, in 'My kingdom for a nightman!' and Descartes's *cogito* is frivolously invoked (pp. 41–2). And what else should Hamm quote, as he goes down at the end, but Baudelaire's sublime sonnet 'Recueillement'? For the dialogue is by no means uniformly coarse. It can rise, when necessary, to great beauty, as in Nell's nostalgic musings on the fact 'that we once went out rowing on Lake Como. One April afternoon' (p. 21).

The dialogue thus ranges from the elegiac in Nell's sequence to the explosively violent in some of the bickering between Hamm and Clov. The writing is, contrary to appearances, economical. Words like 'once' and 'yesterday' (cf. pp. 14, 18) have a profound resonance in dialogue that is frequently trivial in expression: the triviality sets off the lyrical utterances all the more forcefully.

NOTES ON THE TEXT

p. 11

(*Bare interior.*) Beckett never had any hesitation as to the setting of his play. On the other hand, the drafts do show a general tightening up of the expression here; the concision and economy of the present opening were not achieved at once. At the same time, Clov's 'business', for example with the steps, is stretched out as the play develops.

(*Hamm, Clov.*) These names, and those of Nagg and Nell, do not occur before T2, and even then are not used in the draft itself, but only scribbled by hand in the top left-hand corner of the first sheet. For a possible meaning of the names see the introduction to this play, *Dramatis personae*.

(*Very red face.*) This is now dropped in productions Beckett is associated with. He had learnt from a newspaper report that imprisonment tends to make people red in the face. Hamm and

Clov are therefore given red faces (and Nagg and Nell white faces to distinguish them from Hamm and Clov). But he is no longer interested in this idea, finding it too 'manichean', and also liable to introduce a note of clownery, which he thinks should be played down. Here and throughout the play, therefore, all references to facial colouring should be ignored.

(*Stiff, staggering walk.*) In the holograph notes preceding T1 Beckett has scribbled 'James doit boiter' (i.e. must limp). In the original production, Jean Martin moved as if his knee joints were frozen; his torso inclined forwards as if his spine were locked in that position. As the drafts progressed, therefore, Beckett inflicted a severer disability on Clov than a mere limp: cf. 'I am so bowed I only see my feet' (p. 51). Most of his creatures are disabled to a greater or lesser extent: firstly, because Beckett is a Cartesian for whom the mind-body split is total and simply the more obvious in handicapped people; secondly, because mutilation is for him a symbol of mankind's serious metaphysical handicap in the game of chance we are all forced to play (and lose) with our fates.

p. 12

(*a large blood-stained handkerchief over his face.*) This is also cut. Here and in a few other places Beckett hints at internal haemorrhage, but now wishes to play this down, at least as far as its visible manifestations are concerned.

(*a whistle hanging from his neck.*) Hamm summoned Clov originally by means of a small drum and drumstick. This is dropped, in T2, in favour of a whistle. In T1, too, Hamm's dressing gown, rug and headgear (a nightcap) are all red.

Finished, it's finished. Cf. John 19: 30, 'When Jesus therefore had received the vinegar, he said, It is finished: and he bowed his head, and gave up the ghost.' An apt allusion to start a play that is all about ending!

Grain upon grain, one by one, and one day, suddenly, there's a heap, a little heap, the impossible heap. This refers to one of the

97

paradoxes of the pre-Socratic philosopher Zeno (*fl. ca.* 460 BC), 'who used the example of a heap of millet to show the discontinuity between movements in space and time on the one hand and reality on the other, the essence of reality being infinity' (Hayman, *Samuel Beckett*, p. 37). Zeno argued that if you halve a pile of millet, then divide one of the resulting two piles in half and add it to the other, then divide the smaller pile in half again and add one half to the larger pile, and so on, you can never complete the operation (that is, remove the smaller, diminishing heap completely) because you are operating in space-time; only in infinity would the operation be completed. Beckett sees life as forcing us to attempt, Sisyphus-like, the completion of the 'impossible heap'. In one of his poems we read: 'my peace is there in the receding mist / when I may cease from treading these long shifting thresholds' (*Poems in English*, p. 49). That peace, of course, is by definition unattainable – which is why his characters can never die but must go on telling their stories, and resisting engulfment by the 'silence of which the universe is made' (*Molloy*, p. 122), until the end of time.

Old stancher! Note how these two words recur at the very end of the play, giving it a rounded completeness that is characteristic of Beckett's dramatic method. He is fond of beginning and ending works on the same note: cf. *Molloy*, Part II. His aesthetic model is that of the serpent swallowing its tail, a very ancient magical symbol.

My . . . dog? In T1 this reads 'Ma femme?', all hint of whom has of course disappeared from the published text. There is a suggestion in T1 that Clov could be Hamm's son, born when he was young, but it is soon dismissed by Hamm as unlikely. In T1, just as Clov wonders whether he will leave Hamm, Hamm asks himself whether he won't drive Clov away.

Yes, there it is, it's time it ended and yet I hesitate to – to end. T1 is more explicit that Hamm feels the time has come to put an end to things. Beckett's characters (cf. Molloy, Estragon and Vladimir) frequently contemplate suicide, but (perhaps because of the 'shifting thresholds') never seem to manage it. In any case even the pessimist Schopenhauer argues that suicide is a snare and a delusion, and Beckett clearly agrees with him.

p. 13

You pollute the air! Note the sudden and violent change of tone, typical of the brooding menace of the situation. Actors find the constant rise and fall in pitch difficult to handle: the problem is to prevent the eruptions sounding merely shrill. This, together with the difficulty of remembering one's cues in dialogue as evenly similar as this, makes *Endgame* an exhausting play to perform. But, as so often with Beckett, when the tones are pitched exactly right, all the pauses carefully respected, and the actions kept crisp, simple and exact, the impact on the audience is a very powerful and moving one.

Both Hamm's and Clov's opening statements show the drift of their relationship and concerns. Both begin with an arresting statement, try a philosophical statement, personalize it, and come quickly down to domestic chores and inanities.

I don't complain. A conventional reply, again typical of the conversational tone of the whole play. But, as so often, Hamm is not content with this routine answer, and pesters Clov for more details.

Have you not had enough? Yes! (Pause.) Of what? An example of annulment. See the introduction to this play, *Language and dramatic expression.*

Of this . . . this . . . thing. As in everyday conversation, Hamm gropes for the right word, and fails to find it.

p. 14

Have you bled? In this desultory conversation matters are taken up, and dropped as rapidly again, for no very good reason, as in everyday life.

(Clov goes to back wall.) Like a child sent into the corner for a misdemeanour.

p. 15

I don't know the combination of the larder. Without Hamm, therefore, he would starve.

Go and get two bicycle-wheels. Perhaps these are to enable Hamm to move his armchair about without Clov's assistance. Bicycles, in any case, are common in Beckett's world: they seem to symbolize the body, because like it they are subject to mechanical failure.

When you inspected my paupers. This is the first of several indications that Hamm was formerly (like Pozzo in *Godot*) a man of substance and property, in a time when such things existed, and had Clov visit his paupers. Note that like Pozzo, again, Hamm smokes a pipe (p. 35).

Outside of here it's death. Beckett, as always, refuses to circumscribe the import of his play by offering an explanation (such as earthquake or nuclear bombardment) for this state of affairs.

We're getting on. That's just what they are not doing! In *Godot*, likewise, Estragon and Vladimir alternate between this kind of optimism and the gloomy realization that nothing is happening or can happen.

Me pap! Because Nagg is toothless, Hamm's offer of a hard biscuit a little later is an act of typical sadism.

Accursed progenitor! Hamm's language is characteristically formal even when he is hurling insults.

The old folks at home! 'is a sardonic quotation from the sentimental nineteenth-century popular song of the same title by S. C. Foster' (Jeremy Treglown, *Times Educational Supplement*, 2 June 1978).

No decency left! At this point in T1 Hamm strikes Nagg with his drumstick.

p. 16

I'm back again, with the biscuit. The frequency with which the characters, and Clov in particular, describe their actions, may disconcert. This is, however, typical of everyday conversation once again. It is also characteristically Beckettian in that every drop of word-play is wrung from a given situation.

Spratt's medium. A type of dog biscuit.

p. 17

And what do you see on your wall? Mene, mene? This does not appear in the manuscript. T1 has 'Les lettres de Ninive'. This recurs in T2, where it is struck out and replaced by the present words, in ink. The reference is to Dan. 5: 26: 'MENE; God hath numbered thy kingdom, and finished it.' The ominous warning written on Belshazzar's wall is clearly seen by Hamm, who knows his Bible, as disturbingly relevant to his own situation.

p. 18

Why this farce, day after day? At a rehearsal, Beckett has been quoted as saying to Nagg and Nell: 'Murmur. No smile at all, completely impassive.'

p. 19

When we crashed on our tandem and lost our shanks. In T1 the passage is more explicit in that we are told that the accident occurred 'au lendemain de notre nuit de noces. Broyées jusqu'à l'aine. Heureusement que ce n'est pas arrivé la veille.' These ribald comments on the accident have of course disappeared from the published text.

It was in the Ardennes. On the road to Sedan. The former is both a range of mountains and a Northern French *département*, of which Sedan is a *sous-préfecture*.

There's something dripping in my head. Hamm can feel a throbbing in his head, which he later (p. 20) attributes to a 'little vein'. See note to p. 12, 'a large blood-stained handkerchief'.

Endgame

p. 20

Are you crying again? Even the spontaneous and irrational expression of human suffering – tears – is put under the rational yoke of symmetry: 'They cry three times in the play, to each his tear' (Beckett quoted in Anon., *Materialien*, p. 54).

p. 21

It was on Lake Como. A lake in Northern Italy, chosen here for the euphony of its name, which adds to the elegiac quality of Nell's evocation.

p. 22

And you are not bloody well capable of making me a pair of trousers in three months! At this point Nagg's public-house joke veers off into a full-scale onslaught on the Creator, and ceases to be a funny, if rather crude, story; cf. the 'Let us pray to God' passage, pp. 37–8. Beckett's own fondness for the joke is shown by the fact that he used it in 1945 also, as an epigraph to an essay in French on the painters Bram and Geer van Velde.

You could see down to the bottom. Nell has not been listening to Nagg's joke, but has continued musing about the day on Lake Como when she had known happiness.

My kingdom for a nightman! . . . Clear away this muck! Chuck it in the sea! Note the particularly harsh cruelty of Hamm's language. See *Richard III*, V, iv, 7.

Desert! This is the imperative form of the verb 'to desert'. Clov understands this and soon afterwards connects the word with the noun 'desert', since for him to desert Hamm would be to go into the desert outside.

p. 23

Beyond is the . . . other hell. At a rehearsal in London Beckett spoke of Hamm's 'anxiety': 'There should be nothing out there, there *must* be nothing out there . . . He wants Clov to see what he's going out into, but if there is something out there alive, it is not as he supposed, and that would be terrible.'

p. 27

To think perhaps it won't all have been for nothing! Hamm is horrified at the possibility that their existence may not, after all, have been entirely pointless.

Catch him, for the love of God! As when the boy is spotted later, Hamm is terrified that there will remain some living organism to survive him.

Unless he's laying doggo. The ensuing exchange is typical of Beckettian bawdy verbal play.

p. 30

Flora! Pomona! . . . Ceres! These Roman goddesses were responsible, respectively, for flowers, fruit and crops.

Is my dog ready? In T1, this dog reminds Hamm of 'Zoulou'. This is the name of a dog in *Molloy* which belongs to Moran's neighbours. Such echo from work to work is characteristic of Beckett.

He's a kind of Pomeranian. Cf. 'A little dog followed him, a pomeranian I think' (*Molloy*, p. 12). For the Berlin production Beckett changed the breed to 'poodle' in homage to the philosopher Schopenhauer, who owned one.

Your dogs are here. An ironic comment on the fact that Clov is a sort of dog too.

(The dog falls on its side.) Both dog and Clov have leg ailments. Beckett emphasized their similarity even more by making the Berlin Clov look at Hamm like a poodle, squatting beside the armchair. When asked whether Clov with his physical disability can kneel down at all, Beckett refers to Hamsun's captain: 'He cannot sit either, although he is very mobile otherwise' (*Materialien*, p. 74).

p. 31

Is Mother Pegg's light on? She is called Cochard in T2, her name is left blank in T1. Between the dog passage and this one, there is a long development in T1, running to about seven pages, in which Hamm asks Nagg whether the two old people could crawl if they had to; in which, too, we learn that Hamm picked up Clov when the latter was about 7 years old. Then Hamm orders Clov to read to him from the Bible (Gen. 8: 21–2, and 11: 14–19). The first fragment, the Flood, is not to Hamm's taste, although it was he who requested it, so Clov jumps a few pages to the next passage, which gives Hamm the idea he too would like to 'beget'. Clov calls to 'Mélanie', and then returns summarily disguised as a woman, alternately speaking in his own voice and a falsetto. Hamm seems to be convinced there really is a woman there, and talks to 'her' as if she were his wife, mentioned early on in T1. Hamm, as always, soon tires of his wish to 'beget', and taunts Clov to stand in for him. Clov, too, hesitates, and flees offstage. An explosion is heard, Clov returns to say that nothing has in fact occurred between him and 'Mélanie', and then Hamm asks about Mother [Pegg's] light.

p. 32

That means that bloody awful day, long ago, before this bloody awful day. T1 is more explicit on the point that Clov has learnt all he knows from Hamm.

I once knew a madman who thought the end of the world had come. From here to 'I prefer the middle' (p. 34) inclusive makes up an insertion appended to the end of T2 and intended for incorporation at this point. It is thus one of the few passages that were added late in the play's development. This story of the madman is obviously important to Hamm: his vision has come to resemble the painter's, and unfortunately for him it is reality and not illusion. That is why Hamm corrects the tense of 'is' to 'was not' – the insane hallucinations of the past have become present painful realities.

All he had seen was ashes. Clov slowly turns round towards Hamm showing a growing interest in what he tells him about the world in ashes (Beckett's stage directions in Berlin). Clov,

who describes nature as a desert and who enjoys watching the
wall in the kitchen, seems to identify with the madman. Note
his eager questioning of Hamm for details.

p. 33

An idea, have an idea. A bright idea! The following exchanges
are similar to several in *Godot*, especially the argument about
hanging near the beginning. Logic-chopping is, in fact, a
favourite pastime with Beckett's heroes.

p. 34

(*They listen to it ringing to the end.*) The Berlin production shows
a symmetry of two heads framing the alarm clock – Clov closing
his eyes as if asleep.

Vaguely. It wouldn't do for Hamm to show enthusiasm for
something; he cultivates an air of refined boredom to cover his
growing anxiety.

p. 35

Got him that time! Hamm is delighted to see, by Clov's slamming of the door, that he has scored a point in the continuous
battle of wits raging between these two. In T1 this episode
occurs in Act II, and is immediately followed by a section in
which Pépé is forced (like the victim in Beckett's novel *How It
Is*) to recount his life story, which is smutty but quite witty. He
also agrees with Hamm that he is glad Mémé (Nell) is dead; this
incongruous note disappears, of course, from the published
version.

Why did you engender me? 'may be an allusion to the last speech
of Marlowe's Faustus ("Curs'd be the parents that engender'd
me!")' (Jeremy Treglown, *Times Educational Supplement*, 2
June 1978).

Something dripping in my head. This meditation recurs from
pp. 19–20.

Enough of that, it's story time, where was I? Note the literary register of Hamm's narrative passages, in marked contrast to his normal vernacular.

It was an extra-ordinarily bitter day, I remember, zero by the thermometer. Hamm refers here and subsequently to instruments used in meteorology.

p. 36
but already the sun was sinking down into the . . . down among the dead. In the *Iliad* Hades, the realm of the dead, is situated in the remote West, hence where the sun sets. Hamm is pleased to be able to show off his familiarity with the classics; note the self-congratulatory 'Nicely put, that'.

p. 37
I'll soon have finished with this story. This tirade is one of the high points of the play. In dramatic terms, its function is to reveal how Hamm is trying to stifle his remorse by an elegant narration, in which he attempts to show himself (note that he has insisted on having an audience in the person of his father) in a less compromising light. But it is also another instance of Beckett's meditation on the role of the creator of fiction, a question pursued relentlessly in the novels. The last few words are not only Hamm's, but the anguished query of every narrator in Beckett's *oeuvre*: fiction for them is always an alibi of some sort, and a matter of life and death. The Unnamable, for instance, and the Voice in the radio play *Cascando*, are forced to narrate 'stories' in order to attain the 'true silence'; if they could tell the 'right story', they could cease, and rest. But this is never vouchsafed to them, any more than peace of mind is attainable by Hamm. Meanwhile, it is hard not to be impressed by the artistry with which they carry out their self-imposed creative task: Hamm's story has us spellbound. It uses all the tricks of the trade: suspense, characterization, dialogue and variation of pace and tone.

p. 38
I was asleep, as happy as a king, and you woke me up to have me

listen to you. Nagg means just now, of course, and not when Hamm was a baby. T1 makes this clearer.

Yes, I hope I'll live till then, to hear you calling me like when you were a tiny boy. Hamm does so, of course, in the closing minutes of the play.

p. 39
Our revels now are ended. See *The Tempest*, IV, i, 148. The quotation underlines the hint that Hamm is a kind of 'toppled Prospero'.

p. 40
Ah you mean my chronicle? Hamm is being pedantic, of course, but he is also trying to keep Clov with him by spinning out their dialogue.

Keep going, can't you, keep going! Cf. Pozzo, in *Godot*, getting Estragon to beg him to regain his seat (Act I).

He's offered a job as gardener. Hamm is still 'getting on with his story', since this is the first mention of the man's being offered a job as gardener.

p. 41
Oh tiny. T1 has 'six ans, sept ans' struck out. This was precisely the age at which Hamm took Clov in. Beckett evidently dropped this as making the identification of Clov as the child too certain.

I'm afraid it will. It never truly ends, in fact.

(HAMM *raises his toque.*) In respect for the dead. Cf. p. 32.

p. 42
Then he's living. A play on Descartes's dictum 'Cogito, ergo sum' – 'I think, therefore I am'.

Am I very white? Hamm, being blind, is naturally not very sure about colours (he thinks the dog is white, for instance – see p. 30).

p. 44

HAMM: (*head bowed, absently*). Hamm is no longer listening to Clov, but is plunged in his own thoughts. It is evident that the situation is rapidly deteriorating: a good production will put this across palpably.

Me to play. As at the beginning of the play, Hamm sees his situation as that of a chess player called upon to make a move.

All those I might have helped. Note the nagging sense of guilt. Hamm is returning to his self-justificatory 'story'.

Lick your neighbour as yourself! A bitter twist on Christ's commandment (Matt. 19: 19).

All that, all that! Cf. 'Be again, be again. All that old misery. Once wasn't enough for you' – Krapp's words, recorded on his 'last tape', in acid reaction to 'that stupid bastard I took myself for thirty years ago' heard on an old tape (*Krapp's Last Tape*, pp. 62–3).

The end is in the beginning and yet you go on. The source of this is probably that used also by T. S. Eliot in *Four Quartets*, namely the pre-Socratic philosophers, especially Heraclitus. It is in any case a very old image (cf. Rev. 22: 13) for that which is eternal, continuous, infinite and permanent, as opposed to the fleeting impermanence of individual existence. Beckett is, throughout his *oeuvre*, fascinated by circularity, by returns to points of departure, and this is why he finds the pithy saws of Heraclitus so congenial; 'and yet you go on' is Hamm's ironical rider to what is, after all, a mystical idea, a paradox not accessible to pure reason.

p. 45

and drag myself forward with my fingers. This is what Molloy in fact does, at the end of his chronicle, which forms the first part of *Molloy*.

There I'll be ... alone against the silence. Like the Unnamable and so many other Beckettian characters.

I'll have called my father and I'll have called my ... (he hesitates) *... my son.* This is the nearest Hamm comes to recognizing Clov as his son; it is also prophecy of what occurs at the end of the play.

Breath held and then... Perhaps a reference to suicide by apnoea, or suspension of breathing, which 'has often been tried, notably by the condemned to death. In vain. It is a physiological impossibility... Mr Endon had insisted that if he did it at all, it would be by apnoea, and not otherwise. He said his voice would not hear of any other method' (*Murphy*, p. 185).

Then babble, babble, words, like the solitary child who turns himself into children, two, three. It is no coincidence that Beckett came relatively late to drama, when he had almost exhausted the possibilities of monologue in fiction.

Moment upon moment, pattering down, like the millet grains of ... that old Greek. Most critics, particularly Ross Chambers, have assumed this is Zeno (see note to p. 12 on the 'impossible heap'). But Chambers writes 'In "Beckett's Brinkmanship" [a previous article], I took Hamm's "old Greek" to be in fact Zeno. Mr Beckett assures me that I am wrong, although, like Hamm, he cannot recall the name of the "right" philosopher. He comments on the compulsion this reveals not to divulge more about the play than is included in it; I would add that it shows a desire to protect the *allusiveness* of the text, as being more important than the elucidation of its actual allusions' (*Twentieth Century Interpretations*, ed. Chevigny, pp. 76–7 n.).

p. 46

Is it not time for my pain-killer? Pain-killing drugs occur quite frequently in Beckett's *oeuvre*; cf. 'The End' and 'The Calmative' in *No's Knife*. Hamm, whose only hope of oblivion and rest lies in his sedative, is panic-stricken at Clov's news. He must now face his end unaided by chemical stupefiers.

(CLOV *starts to move about the room* ... CLOV *goes, humming, towards window right*.) This is the first time Clov has not moved from *a* to *b*, the first time he has shown any independence – humming without having been instructed to. He also asks Hamm several questions, and even comments on himself. Clov's changed attitude becomes even more marked on p. 48 where he strikes Hamm with the dog.

p. 47

I was never there. Cf. the story of the 'little girl, very strange and unhappy in her ways ... The trouble with her was she had never really been born!' (*All That Fall*, pp. 35–6).

p. 48

When old Mother Pegg asked you for oil for her lamp and you told her to get out to hell. In the subsequent exchange, T1 makes Hamm more adamant in his excuses.

(*He loses balance, clutches on to the ladder*.) This kind of clownish pratfall is characteristic of much in *Godot*; there is more of it in T1, but it has largely disappeared in the final version.

p. 49

There's your dog for you! Beckett suggested that 'dog' should be spoken softly (soft as the object), whereas the other words should 'hit' like sharp blows. See *Materialien*, p. 76.

Of darkness! Hamm is harking back to Clov's accusation about Mother Pegg, p. 48, and still trying to justify himself in his own eyes.

I'm warming up for my last soliloquy. Note the theatrical metaphor. 'Behind the knockabout turn of Hamm and Clov', comments Katharine Worth, 'it is easy to hear Sean O'Casey's sad, sardonic and farcical double acts' (*IDE*, p. 242).

p. 50

It's the end, Clov, we've come to the end. Although Clov's change process is already well under way, for Hamm this is the beginning of the end of the play: endgame of *Endgame*, in fact! From now on the rundown, which has been gradual so far, speeds up. (Hamm's statement is much less final in the manuscript and thus less impressive.)

p. 51

When I fall I'll weep for happiness. Clov's tirade is charged with the sombre poetry so characteristic of this play. For him, too, the end is in sight: he envisages opening the door and walking out to his death in the surrounding wastes like Oates on Scott's last expedition, but for less heroic reasons. Right from the opening of the play, to his next to last words ('This is what we call making an exit'), we can discern a continuous strengthening of his will to leave.

(*Enter* CLOV, *dressed for the road*). T2 has Clov watch Hamm, but not dressed for a journey as here. 'Clov's difficulty in leaving the room through [the kitchen door] is of the same order as the fearsome effort called for in [Maeterlinck's] *Pelléas and Mélisande* to open the castle door and let the day begin' (Worth, *IDE*, p. 246).

p. 52

Wipe . . . And put on again. Beckett said: 'Here Hamm is playing a double role: first he gives the orders, then he obeys them' (*Materialien*, p. 84).

A little poetry. The first stanza of Baudelaire's sonnet, which Hamm half translates, reads:

> Sois sage, Ô ma Douleur, et tiens-toi plus tranquille.
> Tu réclamais le Soir; il descend; le voici:
> Une atmosphère obscure enveloppe la ville,
> Aux uns portant la paix, aux autres le souci.

'Now cry in darkness' is of course Hamm's sardonic mistranslation of the last two melancholy lines of this quatrain.

Beckett's quotations are not there for their own sake, but because they are (like this one) fully appropriate to the mood.

(*Pause. Narrative tone.*) Introducing the last recall of Hamm's story. Although he never finishes it, he seems satisfied that he has got as far with it as is necessary to his purpose.

No? Good. In the Berlin production Beckett adds here another 'No!' and another 'Clov' to enhance the symmetrical rhythm. When asked to whom the second 'No!' was addressed, he replied: 'Hamm utters his No against Nothingness' (*Materialien*, p. 75).

p. 53
(*He covers his face with handkerchief.*) When asked whether Hamm covers his face in order to die, Beckett replied: 'No, only the better to be able to be silent' (*Materialien*, p. 87). When asked whether the handkerchief represented the curtain, he retorted testily: 'Yes' (*Materialien*, p. 56).

ACT WITHOUT WORDS I

Written in French in 1956 with music by John Beckett, the author's cousin.

First publication   Les Editions de Minuit, Paris, 1957, as *Acte sans paroles*, in the same volume as *Fin de partie*
First publication in English   Grove Press, New York, 1958, in the same volume as *Endgame*.
First performance   3 April 1957, Royal Court Theatre, London, as an afterpiece with *Fin de partie*

RECEPTION
The reaction of the critics has been as slender as the mimes themselves, largely, it seems, because this first one in particular is usually performed as an afterpiece with a difficult play which deflects the critics' exegetical powers. When comment is made it tends to exaggeration, as when Roy Walker (*Listener*, 9 May 1957) claimed to have seen it 'precisely imagined by Bosch in a detail of the *Temptation of Saint Anthony*'.

STRUCTURE
The text is largely self-explanatory. Beckett, who attempts to resolve the formal problems involved in a one-player situation in a wordless type of drama, makes specific use of the proscenium stage and the area of hidden wing space, and in this first mime there is conscious, almost pantomime use of the flies. After discussing the mimes with Beckett, Charles Marowitz wrote in *Encore* (March 1962): 'His interest is not so much in mime but in the stratum of movement which underlies the written word,' and in productions with which he is associated Beckett attempts to bring out the 'stylized movement' in accordance with which all his plays are structured.

   This piece is a variant on the Greek myth of Tantalus, who was punished for his sin 'by being set, thirsty and hungry, in a pool of water which always receded when he tried to drink from it, and under fruit trees whose branches the wind tossed aside when he tried to pick the fruit' (*Oxford Companion to Classical Literature*, p. 414).

In this mime, as in *Act Without Words II*, the player is prodded into action by an external stimulus (the whistle) – cf. the bell that awakens Winnie in *Happy Days* – which represents both the author and the malevolent kind of divinity that haunts Beckett's universe. The character is clearly intended to be exemplary of suffering humanity.

NOTES ON THE TEXT

p. 43
The man is flung backwards on stage from right wing. The entry on to the stage is seen by Barnard as illustrating 'Beckett's favourite view of birth as being a forcible ejection of the child who wishes to remain in the womb' (*Samuel Beckett*, p. 109).

p. 44
A big cube descends from flies, lands. This business with the cubes parallels experiments with monkeys in which bananas are placed beyond the animals' reach and various tools are provided to allow them to reach them. In these experiments, carried out to study the psychology of learning procedures, successful use of the tools usually involves the animals in a more complex task on the following occasion.

ACT WITHOUT WORDS II

According to Beckett this was written in French at about the same time as *Act Without Words I*, that is in 1956.

First publication   *New Departures*, I (Summer 1959)
First performance   25 January 1960, Institute of Contemporary Arts, London, directed by Michael Horovitz

RECEPTION

Like the first mime, this has attracted little attention and when there have been comments they have been exaggerated. Irving Wardle, writing in the *Observer*, 15 July 1962, of Charles Marowitz's production at In-Stage in London, praised it for its 'strong surface humour and real sense of tragedy', but little more has been said.

STRUCTURE

Like *Act Without Words I*, this text is largely self-explanatory and is for Beckett a kind of five-finger exercise of exploration of the formal problems involved in a two-player situation in a wordless type of drama. Hugh Kenner notes the parallels between it and *How It Is* and the metaphor, central to both, of life as an endless track where people are as objects to other people. He also points out the differences, however, and comments that '*Act Without Words II*, being a mime, is utterly explicit as to the empirical facts, though tacit as to their possible meaning' (*A Reader's Guide*, p. 143).

Once more the cycle of action is stimulated in its various stages by an external agent, the goad, and we are left to imagine what the protagonists make of it and to decide what it represents for us.

NOTES ON THE TEXT

p. 49

A is slow, awkward ... absent. B brisk, rapid, precise. Beckett
here follows Jung's psychological typology: A is introverted, B
extroverted. Barnard sees A and B as the inner and outer selves
of one man and the whole mime as symbolizing 'the emptiness
of a life which consists of an alternation between the two split
portions of a man' (*Samuel Beckett*, p. 131).

A, wearing shirt ... prays. Cf. Winnie's prayer in *Happy Days*.

broods, takes a large partly-eaten carrot from coat pocket. Cf. *Waiting for Godot*, p. 20.

p. 51

A crawls out of sack. The mime could continue indefinitely,
with only the position of the sacks in relation to each other
being changed. For this hint of infinity cf. *Play*; for the exploration of all possible variations on the positioning of the players, cf. *Come and Go*. As Hugh Kenner says, 'One supposes
that the proprietors of the goad keep an infinity of wheels' (*A
Reader's Guide*, p. 143).

ROUGH FOR THEATRE   I

Written in French but based on an English manuscript entitled 'The Gloaming', dated December 1956.

First publication in English   Grove Press, New York, 1976, in
    Ends and Odds
First performance   May 1979, Schiller Theater, Hamburg, by
    Ralph Schermuly and Ulrich Kuhlmann, directed by
    Walter D. Asmus, with *Rough for Theatre II*

The play has a Yeatsian flavour. The only textual matter calling for comment is the rather apposite allusion to *As You Like It*, II, vii, 174–5 on p. 73.
    James Knowlson, one of the few critics to have written at any length on this work, noting its similarity to *Endgame*, comments:

> The relationship between A, a blindman, seated on a folding-stool and scraping a fiddle, and B, a one-legged cripple, confined to a wheelchair and pushing himself along by means of a pole, seems to represent a point prior to a state of interdependence such as that in which Hamm and Clov are found. In this case, the mutual needs rapidly become clear and the advantages of a symbiotic relationship seem obvious, in theory at least: B would offer A company and access to food – corned beef and potatoes – and would act as his eyes; A would push B about in his wheelchair and tuck his rug around his feet (or his foot since he only has one!). But when put into practice, however tentatively, the theory conspicuously fails to lead to any satisfactory state of companionship. For there is in A and B the same juxtaposition of contradictory impulses and the same striking ambivalence of behaviour that was present in the relationship of Estragon and Vladimir and of Hamm and Clov. Irritability and the desire to help follow one another in rapid and apparently random

succesion ... In fact, although the theatre fragment was written after the French *Fin de partie* [*Endgame*], it is much closer to this play in time than its dating in *Ends and Odds* as 'circa 1960' might suggest. It is now clear that it was first written ... between *Fin de partie* and the English translation, *Endgame*. The similarity with *Endgame* may be one reason why Beckett did not attempt to develop the play further and why he only published it at a much later date among the 'odds'.

(*Frescoes*, pp. 228–9)

KRAPP'S LAST TAPE

Written in English early in 1958 for the Northern Irish actor Patrick Magee, who had pleased Beckett with his Third Programme readings of extracts from *Molloy, Malone Dies* and *From an Abandoned Work*. Michael Robinson points out the great similarities between *From an Abandoned Work* and *Krapp's Last Tape*, and says: 'It is almost certain that Beckett abandoned the novel in favour of the play, retaining its best features' (*The Long Sonata of the Dead*, p. 212). We might, then, assume that it was Magee's readings themselves that led Beckett to use this material for a dramatic monologue. Professor Knowlson tells us that the manuscript first draft is dated 20 February 1958 and is entitled 'Magee Monologue' (*SBaE*, p. 80).

First publication   *Evergreen Review* (New York), Summer 1958
First performance   28 October 1958, Royal Court Theatre, London, in a double bill with *Endgame*. Krapp was played by Magee and Donald McWhinnie directed. These two also collaborated in a television production, first shown in *Thirty Minute Theatre* on BBC2 on 29 November 1972.

RECEPTION

The work was early recognized as a minor dramatic masterpiece. Writing in the December 1958 issue of *Twentieth Century*, Roy Walker felt that 'the soliloquy has found, for the first and probably the last time, a form which combines the immobile mask and the mobile face, mime and speech, monologue and dialogue, and offers all their various resources to one performer'. Performed in New York in January 1960, it was enthusiastically reviewed by Robert Brustein as Beckett's 'best dramatic poem about the old age of the world', flawless and economical, haunting and harrowing (*New Republic*, 22 February 1960). Played in Paris in March 1960, it was seen as 'a kind of lyrical poem of solitude' (Robert Kanters, *L'Express*, 31

March 1960) and there was general critical acclaim. The definitive performance, however, has perhaps been that of Martin Held, in a production directed by Beckett himself for the Berlin Schiller-Theater Werkstatt, which has been universally acknowledged as outstanding.

DÉCOR

The strong contrast between light and dark – very bright in the playing area, and the rest dark – is central to the play, although in the Berlin production Krapp's drinking hole was lit, as was his way to it in the television production. This contrast is most striking, pinpointing the use of only a very small part of the stage for most of the action, and it is also of dramatic importance. It justifies Krapp's turning round anxiously once or twice, as if, Beckett told Martin Held, 'Old Nick' were there: 'Death is standing behind him,' he explained, 'and unconsciously he's looking for it [because] it's the end ... he's through with his work, with love and with religion.' But there are also metaphysical reasons for the light/dark dichotomy that may not be obvious on first viewing to most spectators. They are explained by Professor Knowlson, who sees this as being a further expression of Beckett's concern with man's basic dualism, the Cartesian separation of mind and body. He quotes one of Beckett's own notes from the manuscript notebook that he wrote and used for his own production of the play in Berlin in 1969:

> [Krapp] turns from [the] fact of anti-mind alien to mind to thought of anti-mind constituent of mind. He is thus ethically correct (signaculum sinus) through intellectual transgression, the duty of reason being not to join but to separate (deliverance of imprisoned light). For this sin he is punished as shown by the aeons.

Professor Knowlson comments:

> The consequence of this view of the incompatibility of sense and spirit and of Krapp's attempts to reconcile them intellectually is seen embodied in the play in frequent images of light and dark, of eyes opening and closing, of light, fire and clear

water on the one hand, and of darkness, mist, and heat on the other.

He also points out, though, that

> there is . . . throughout the play a consistent attempt made to mingle the light and the dark, expressing Krapp's desire to reconcile and promote a kind of union between sense and spirit. Both setting and costume are dominated by a mixture of the colours black and white.
>
> (*Light and Darkness*, pp. 21–2)

Professor Knowlson interprets his movement from the light to the dark and back again as giving Krapp a sense of well-being because

> in this way he came to believe that he could separate clearly the light from the dark, as he separated 'the grain from the husks', and still identify his essential self with the light.

Knowlson has studied the different ways in which Beckett has envisaged the decor in productions that he has directed:

> The set has remained extremely simple throughout with a plain table and chair on a bare stage. In Schiller and subsequent productions directed by Beckett, the table was bare at the beginning of the play, until Krapp went backstage (audience left) into a visible, lit cubby-hole or closet to fetch in turn the ledger, the metal tins – which by then had replaced the cardboard boxes of the printed text as containers for the reels of tape – and, finally, the tape recorder. This closet is not mentioned in the English or French printed texts and made its first appearance, in Schiller, in 1969. The cubby-hole was lit from the inside by a white light in Schiller and in later Beckett productions. This rather weak light, invisible at the opening of the play, remained on after Krapp's triple journey into the cubby-hole; it was finally extinguished along with the rest of the lighting at the end. In Schiller, the entrance to the cubby-hole was masked by an opaque, black curtain which was drawn until Krapp opened it. It then remained half open until the end. In San Quentin, Beckett emphasized the sound made by the heavy metal rings and rod

when the curtain was drawn. In Orsay, Beckett introduced for the first time the dark shadow of Krapp drinking on a side wall of the cubby-hole.

(*KTWB*, p. 32)

DRAMATIS PERSONAE

Although only one person is on stage, Beckett manages to have two characters, in effect, by means of the recorded voice of the younger Krapp. In most productions this voice is prerecorded and then played over the public address system by a technician while the actor mimes the operation of the tape recorder. However, if great care is taken over timing and control of the machine, it is possible actually to have Krapp play his prerecorded tape before the audience himself, the sound then being amplified more appropriately from the tape recorder. This is more effective since it clearly locates the recorded sound in the machine to which he cocks his ear. The play, then, is only in a technical sense a monologue, in that the same actor plays both roles; but it comes over as a dialogue, conducted between an old man and the middle-aged hopeful he was in former and happier times. Indeed there is even a shadowy presence of a third Krapp, in his late twenties, who is referred to when 39-year-old Krapp mentions 'these old P[ost].-M[ortem].s' which he usually indulges in, as indeed does the old Krapp also, 'before embarking on a new ... retrospect' (p. 58).

Krapp's purple nose is due to his drinking, of course. His shabby garb not only reveals his present poverty and neglect, it also shows him as a clown (the white face and boots especially, and the slipping on the banana skin) and thus links him to other Beckett clown figures, such as Vladimir or Clov; cf. 'Played the clown, all alone, hour after hour, motionless ... spell-bound, groaning' (*Malone Dies*, p. 195). It is interesting to note, however, that in the Berlin production the external clownish indications – purple nose, trousers too short, boots too big and the four capacious pockets – were cut out. This made it all the more necessary for Martin Held to emphasize the clown in his performance. Krapp's poor sight is something that Beckett himself is familiar with, since he suffered from cataracts for several years and is thus making a kind of wry joke at his own expense.

STRUCTURE

This looks complicated when the play is read in an armchair, but is perfectly straightforward in performance. Old Krapp opens in his own voice; the middle-aged Krapp then speaks on tape; Krapp senior stops him, croaks out a fragment of a hymn, resumes his listening, interrupts it again to consult the dictionary, listens further, switches off when the younger man announces the imminent end of the tape and winds back to the account of the 'farewell to love'. Then Krapp the elder records his own comments, sings his hymn again, remembers the love story, throws away his current recording (his 'last tape' of the title), returns for the third time to the love affair, and this time allows the old tape to be concluded and 'run on in silence'. The structure is thus one of counterpoint, with more time given to the younger man's tape and less to Krapp's last tape.

Many critics congratulate Beckett on his imaginative dramatic use of the tape recorder and several point out that this device enables him to return to something explored in his first book, *Proust*, the problem of the ever-changing identity of the self. Thus Kenner is led to describe *Krapp* as 'a last bitter parody of those vases celebrated in *Proust*, where the lost past is sealed away' (*Samuel Beckett*, p. 185), and Michael Robinson points out that Beckett has brilliantly overcome the problem of incorporating material from the past into the play and has 'fashioned a vehicle which manages to combine, not only the background which drama normally requires, but also the Proustian past of an individual in time' (*The Long Sonata of the Dead*, p. 284).

LANGUAGE

Although Irish names and references creep in, there does not seem to be anything specifically Irish about Krapp's language. He is not as self-conscious about his use of language as Maddy Rooney, but he does show a writer's enjoyment of words and sensitivity to them. Beckett uses this latter characteristic as a means of distinguishing between the Krapp that we see and the one that we hear on tape. The language of Krapp the younger is more learned and even precious compared with Krapp senior's;

note the latter's irritation at the former's pompous, pedantic style and his stopping the tape whenever the younger Krapp begins to declaim. He fails to understand the word 'viduity' used by his former self (p. 59), although Katharine Worth suggests that even young Krapp may have used a dictionary for this, wishing to make a good impression on tape. Certainly even at 69 Krapp can still revel childlike in the joys of a word like 'spool' with its sensuous plosive and its elongated vowel (p. 56). But the language of the play operates on another important level, as Alec Reid has pointed out:

> As we listen, we become aware of something else, of three distinct sound patterns. Gradually we distinguish an even-paced measure for narrative speech, a slower, long-drawn-out lyrical tempo, and a brisker, harsh, sardonic tone, and we notice the periods of silence marking the change from one rhythm to the next. From the interplay of these rhythms we gradually realize that Krapp-at-39 is torn by two radically opposed elements in his character, and that the conflict still racks the old man sitting at the table in front of us. The sound patterns do not depend on any 'interpretation' imposed by the actor or the director. They are inevitable; deliberately constructed by Beckett through the words he has chosen, the way he has arranged them, and the pauses which he has put down to separate them.
>
> (*All I Can Manage*, pp. 21–2)

NOTES ON THE TEXT

p. 55

(*A late evening in the future.*) Beckett was forestalling the reviewer's quibble that, as the magnetic tape recorder is a relatively recent invention, it was not possible in 1958 for an old man to listen to tapes recorded in his youth.

(*a wearish old man.*) Feeble, withered, shrunk.

(KRAPP *remains a moment motionless, heaves a great sigh.*) Note the extended mime of this opening section. In performance, especially for television, it has usually been modified; in the German production with Martin Held, for instance, there was only one drawer at the side of the table and the envelope and keys were omitted. Indeed, in productions directed by Beckett much of the stage 'business' is cut out.

p. 57

Mother at rest at last. . . . The black ball . . . This is both a précis of the tape we are about to listen to with Krapp, and a haunting image in itself. Professor Knowlson makes this comment on the full version of this scene (pp. 59–60):

> Here images of darkness are not only associated with death, but also juxtaposed with images of whiteness . . . In giving the black ball to the white dog, 'I might have kept it. But I gave it to the dog', apparent opposites are integrated one with the other. For if, as Samuel Beckett himself has pointed out in his production notebook, this gesture is one of sacrificing sense to spirit, the form here too is that of a mingling.
>
> (*Light and Darkness*, p. 24)

Slight improvement in bowel condition. The juxtaposition of this with the preceding and following items is bound to have a comic effect on stage. Constipation is an appropriate affliction for a man of this name, although it should be noticed that the abandoned play *Eleuthéria* involves a Monsieur Victor Krap.

Memorable equinox? This may have a sexual meaning for Krapp senior; cf. Watt's 'biannual equinoctial nocturnal emission in vacuo' (*Watt*, p. 232). But for Krapp junior it is a religious or aesthetic notion – see note to p. 60 below. Professor Knowlson considers that the phrase is included 'because it evokes a perfect balance of light and darkness, since "equinox" means "the time at which the sun crosses the equator and day and night are equal" (OED)'.

Farewell to – (*he turns page*) *– love.* It is easy to visualize the comic effect of short-sighted Krapp poring over the large ledger and finally dropping flatly the word 'love'. Professor Knowlson points out that 'Farewell to Love' is the title of a poem by John Donne.

(*hand cupping ear towards machine.*) In Berlin Beckett suppressed this gesture and made Held emphasize Krapp's overall listening posture.

sound as a bell, apart from my old weakness. Does he mean bananas, or the 'demon drink'? Or does he consider his bowels his weakness? Professor Knowlson thinks the latter, i.e. that he is referring to a more or less permanent state of constipation.

crest of the wave – or thereabouts. A characteristically comic qualification. Note the cliché, followed by hesitation, then bathos.

Celebrated the awful occasion. His birth. Krapp is not alone among Beckett's characters in this feeling. Cf. Mr Tyler in *All That Fall*: 'I was merely cursing ... the wet Saturday afternoon of my conception' (p. 15).

Cut 'em out! He is still talking about bananas, which cause constipation.

The new light above my table ... With all this darkness round me. See comments on *Décor* above.

p. 58

Connaught, I fancy. A province in the west of Ireland. 'In the San Quentin production, 1977, this was changed to "Kerry, I fancy" only because of the difficulty experienced by the American actor, Rick Cluchey, in pronouncing the name' (*KTWB*, p. 26).

Bianca in Kedar Street. There is no such street in Dublin or London, nor does it seem to be an anagram of Drake Street. Perhaps it is an anagram of 'Darke', in contrast to the girl's name which means 'white' in Italian: cf. a heroine in *More*

Pricks Than Kicks called 'the Alba' (also lit. 'the white one' in Italian), to whom the poem of *ca.* 1935 entitled 'Alba' is addressed (see *Poems in English*, p. 23); indeed, in an early draft of the play, Bianca was called Alba. There is clearly some play here on the light-and-darkness motif: in Hebrew 'kedar' means 'black'.

(*Brief laugh in which* KRAPP *joins.*) Note how the two Krapps laugh together over the youthful foolishness of their self on the earliest tape. The Berlin production shows a deliberate symmetry in Krapp's intermittent laughs; first he laughs once, then twice, then four times but alone. This mechanical sequence stands in shrill contrast to a liberating laugh, it is a laugh into the void. His laugh is also self-derisory because nothing essential has changed over the thirty years since the recording.

A girl in a shabby green coat. Cf. the 'Smeraldina', another of the heroines in *More Pricks Than Kicks*, and 'the green one' in *Eh Joe* (see p. 205 below). This girl is, clearly, *not* the Bianca mentioned earlier. Some complex self-disguising by the author seems to be going on here: Beckett's mother, like Krapp's, died after a 'long viduity'; in her case it lasted from 1933, the year Beckett's father died when Beckett himself was (like Krapp) in his late twenties, until 1950. Harvey tells us that Beckett gave the 'green girl' the name Smeraldina ('little emerald') because she was Irish, had greenish eyes and often wore green (see *Samuel Beckett*, pp. 122–3). If, as one suspects, there is a carefully refracted amount of autobiography in the play, this would help account for its poignancy and pathos.

p. 59

Now the day is over. From the hymn by Sabine Baring-Gould (1834–1924), who also wrote 'Onward, Christian soldiers'. Beckett's devout Protestant upbringing accounts for his precise recollections of this form of popular verse. Notice that it is also another instance of 'darkness'. Beckett now feels that the allusion is too self-conscious and omits it from productions he is associated with (*KTWB*, p. 26).

perhaps a glint of the old eye to come. The eye of the future Krapp whom we see before us on the stage.

the house on the canal. The Dublin Grand Canal crops up in several of Beckett's works, such as 'First Love' and *Malone Dies*.

where mother lay a-dying. An example of the pompous speech of the earlier Krapp that irritates the old Krapp, it seems to play on 'a-flying' in the Herrick poem also alluded to in *Happy Days*, p. 45 (q.v.). If so, the allusion is apt, since Herrick's fourth line is 'Tomorrow will be dying'.

vidua-bird! There are a number of species in the genus *Vidua*; the male's breeding plumage is a sombre black. Professor Knowlson comments:

> The definition is not (as far as I have been able to establish at least) a standard dictionary definition. It contains additional information which adds considerably to the resonance of the definition. 'Viduity' is extended to include men, women, animals and birds. 'Black plumage of male' offers yet another sombre death image. *Encyclopedia Britannica* gives under 'weaver-bird': 'sub-family of the widow-birds (*viduinae*); have long tail feathers reaching in *Vidua paradisea*, a bird the size of a sparrow, a foot in length'. This plumage is confined to males. Newton's *Dictionary of Birds* quotes Edwards's remark in 1745 that he was informed that 'the Portuguese call this bird the widow from its colour and long train' and adds that an extraordinary growth of tail feathers is to be found in males at the breeding season.
>
> (*KTWB*, pp. 26–7)

p. 60

the blind went down. A traditional signal that a death has occurred. Cf. Wilfred Owen's line in 'Anthem for Doomed Youth': 'And each slow dusk a drawing-down of blinds.'

In the end I held it out to him and he took it in his mouth. Origin, childhood and the *past* are all made present in the death of the mother; but the immediate animal life with its vital urge contains *future*. Two time dimensions are composed into one *moment* with the black ball as an emblem for the *hic et nunc*. The sudden incursion of death into a harmless game with a dog highlights death as being inherent in life.

I shall feel it, in my hand, until my dying day. The subdued yet intense emotion of this remark shows that Krapp's longing for his mother to be 'gone' (p. 59) was not callousness. Krapp is, in fact, unusual among Beckett's heroes for the tenderness revealed in this passage and in the later description of love in a boat.

The vision at last. This 'memorable equinox' appears to have been the occasion of a religious or aesthetic illumination of some kind, very similar to one that Beckett himself is reported to have experienced at the same age (see Bair, pp. 350–1). But, as Kenner points out,

> Krapp-69 cannot be bothered to rehear the account of this vision, pregnant though it was with promise of great works now (at 69) not achieved and not achievable. We hear the account in snatches, notably the fragment, 'clear to me at last that the dark I have always struggled to keep under is in reality my most – '. A man struggling to keep the dark under, that is how Krapp-39 saw himself: a man who should rather draw on it, as on a capital asset. It seemed a revelation.
>
> (*A Reader's Guide*, p. 132)

Professor Knowlson comments that for the 39-year-old Krapp this was

> clearly a key memory. He believed that this vision had revealed a way of reconciling light and dark and of transforming his life and work in the light of this revelation. But the old Krapp cannot bear to listen to this account of the vision and reacts with impatience and anger.
>
> (*KTWB*, p. 28)

The only passage that interests old Krapp, however, is 'my face in her breasts' and he winds back eagerly to hear the beginning of the story.

p. 61

after a few moments she did. Cf. the emphasis on 'moments' at the time of his mother's death (p. 60).

Let me in. The French version '*M'ont laissé entrer*', 'they [her eyes] let me in', makes the meaning clear, i.e. they let him into her inner being.

We drifted in among the flags. Rushes. Cf. *Happy Days*, p. 39.

p. 62

The eyes she had! Even cynical old Krapp is betrayed into an elegiac utterance here. He has always been moved by women's eyes, though. Cf. p. 58 (Bianca's eyes) and p. 60 (the nurse who had eyes like chrysolite; see *Othello*, V, 2, 145).

everything on this old muckball. Our planet.

The sour cud and the iron stool. Indigestion and constipation respectively. Cf. *Malone Dies*: 'What matters is to eat and excrete. Dish and pot, dish and pot, these are the poles' (*Three Novels*, p. 185).

Seventeen copies sold. Not a brilliant total for the 'opus magnum' which, one assumes, was engendered by the vision on the night of the memorable equinox.

One pound six and something, eight I have little doubt. ' "The standard lowest solicitor's fee before the war"; Beckett as reported by Ruby Cohn' (*KTWB*, p. 28). Expressed to the nearest penny in today's decimal currency, £1 6s 8d is £1.33.

Sat shivering in the park, drowned in dreams and burning to be gone. Note this death wish. Cf. 'last effort' (p. 63). Does this mean suicide or an effort to mingle successfully the conflicting sense and spirit?

Scalded the eyes out of me reading Effie *again*. Theodor Fontane's great German novel *Effi Briest* (1895). See note on *All That Fall*, p. 29. It is characteristic of both Krapp and his creator that this delicate evocation should be undercut by the coarse reflections upon Fanny's visits immediately afterwards.

but I suppose better than a kick in the crutch. There is a pun on 'crutch' as crutch and crotch. The Berlin version of the text brings out the sexual connotation by alluding to Krapp's masturbatory inclinations. Indeed, in productions that he directs, Beckett now makes this explicit by changing the text to 'better than the thumb and forefinger' (*KTWB*, p. 29).

p. 63

lie propped up in the dark – Professor Arthur K. Oberg finds confirmed, in this sentence, many critics' suggestions that in *Krapp* Beckett is attempting to dramatize the Proustian vision. He sees Krapp likened to Proust the asthmatic, lying propped up in bed in his cork-lined room (*Modern Drama*, vol. ix no. 3, pp. 333–8).

Be again on Croghan on a Sunday morning. One of Beckett's early English poems, 'Serena II', commemorates a walk in the hills near Dublin with a Kerry Blue Terrier bitch.

(winds [tape] forward to the passage he wants.) This could happen only if Krapp had previously rewound the tape, but most often he removes both spools and thus leaves the tape at the end of the passage. Whatever the directions, it is certainly at this point that having Krapp work his own machine would incur the risk of making a pause too long for the maintenance of dramatic tension.

gooseberries, she said. I said again I thought it was hopeless. This is repeated verbatim, not only to extract extra pathos from it, but also because Beckett's dramatic technique relies heavily on repetition and *da capo*. Cf. the plays in two acts like *Godot* and *Happy Days*, and cf. *Play*, which can be 'repeated exactly'. Note that this time Krapp hears it through the end, only moving his lips as if attempting to say something.

Recent critics have laid stress on the tenderness to be found in *Krapp*, but the importance of love in the play is perhaps best shown by an early critic, Richard N. Coe: 'There is, however, another theme in Krapp, emerging to the surface again after years of underground existence, and that is the theme of love. It may seem paradoxical to suggest, in view of the almost legendary sordidness and impotence with which Beckett invests his lovers (most typically, Macmann and Moll in *Malone Dies*), that love is in fact one of the most persistent ideals in Beckett's writings. But there is an analogy with Beckett's people in their search for God. Just as the majority of his characters revile the God that they can conceive, as a malevolent and impotent impostor, yet by their very imprecations hint at the existence of an Absolute beyond conception, so do they also revile the love they know, and by so doing, hint at the same time at the existence of a love which they have never known and cannot know – the love which is 'music, *music*, MUSIC'. If Beckett's people turn away from love, it is in an agony of disappointed idealism. Love seems to promise a *Nirvana à deux*, an annihilation of time, and has failed to fulfil its promise . . . Krapp, if he fails to find the 'end' that all Beckett's people are searching for, none the less finds a strange quietus – not a happiness, but a sort of stilling of movement, a slowing down of time, a hesitation on the brink of oblivion' (*Beckett*, pp. 104–5).

Describing the evolution of the play through successive drafts, S. E. Gontarski concludes that 'the play, as Beckett shaped it, became a study of recurrent failure more universal than personal sexual inadequacy', a portrait of 'a beaten man who now curses his younger selves at least in part for the decision to abandon love', and that 'the final masterful pathocomic balance was achieved [only] through careful revision' (*KTWB*, pp. 19, 22).

Not with the fire in me now. The 39-year-old Krapp rejected happiness for the 'fire in him', which is, one assumes, the creative energy and insight engendered by his experience at the time of the 'memorable equinox'. The old Krapp shows only too clearly the dismal consequences of that ascetic act of renunciation – the fire is now not even a glow in the embers. On the other hand we are well aware that had Krapp opted for common happiness it would in any case by now long since have turned to ashes. The paradox is that the decision confronting him was in fact a non-choice: as a writer he was not in a position to prefer ordinary happiness, which for Beckettian man is neither of this world nor the next; that is why Krapp, like the tape, runs on finally into silence. The play has 'fuse[d] most successfully a moving human situation with philosophical issues that lead one directly into judgements on the nature of existence' (Knowlson, *Frescoes*, p. 91). This is summed up, in Beckett's own production, in the striking image, in a set otherwise plunged into darkness, of Krapp's face at the end picked out by the reflection of a small beam of light playing off the rotating spool as it runs on in silence.

ROUGH FOR THEATRE   II

Written in French in the late 1950s, probably 1958, between *Krapp's Last Tape* and *Embers*.

First publication in English   Grove Press, New York, 1976, in
    Ends and Odds
First performance   May 1979, Schiller Theater, Hamburg,
    with *Rough for Theatre I* (same actors and director)

The play reads like a revue sketch, but Beckett says he did not have this in mind. Noting similarities not only with *Krapp* and *Eleuthéria*, but also with *Rough for Radio II* (to which might be added *Catastrophe*) for the manner in which 'the pain of the subject is treated with indifference or even mockery', Professor Knowlson continues:

> It has a lively, varied, even at times sparkling dialogue from two sharply drawn characters. A variety of incidents focuses on the same central issue of suffering and pain. It has a relatively wide intellectual and emotional range and blends tragicomic elements together smoothly. In the end it remains, however, a fragment, twice as long as *Footfalls* but clearly lacking its sense of completeness. On the other hand, it is difficult to envisage it being extended successfully.

In any case, he goes on,

> Beckett's work in the theatre after *Play* has differed fairly drastically from that found in [the *Rough for Theatre*] fragments. He has focused more recently on simple, stark, fraught situations, on an extreme concentration and economy, and on a musical style of patterning of motifs. Reduction in the number of characters, reduction of the human body to a part rather than the whole, and reduction in other elements involved has not meant a similar reduction in density or in emotional power. In the miniatures of the seventies

indeed, this density and power derives partly from the juxta-position or confrontation of different time states, and partly again from establishing an unusual relationship between the material of the play and the audience watching. A comparison of the dramatic 'Odds' [*Roughs for Theatre I* and *II*] with the 'Ends' (*Not I*, *That Time* and *Footfalls*) emphasizes therefore the essentially innovatory quality of Beckett's recent writing for the theatre.

(*Frescoes*, pp. 232–4)

EMBERS

Written in English and completed at the beginning of 1959. Beckett was urged by the BBC to write more for radio after the success of *All That Fall* but other preoccupations made it impossible for him to do so immediately.

First publication   *Evergreen Review* (New York), November–
     December 1959
     It appeared very soon after this in a double volume
     (London, Faber and Faber) with *Krapp's Last Tape*.
First broadcast   24 June 1959, BBC Third Programme

RECEPTION

Embers was awarded the 1959 RAI Prize for a literary or dramatic work, with or without music. The BBC production was by Donald McWhinnie and Jack MacGowran played the leading role. In spite of this the play attracted little critical attention and that was mixed. The playwright John Whiting praised 'a dramatic prose which has the precision of fine poetry' and the musical 'exactness' of the play's notation (*London Magazine*, May 1960), but Karl Miller condemned 'technical weaknesses, boring repetitiveness, obscurity' and the whole 'pathetic and presumptuous' drift of Beckett's work and its lack of the 'means of control which art is supposed to need' (*Encounter*, September 1959). Likewise Frank Kermode dismissed the play, in *Encounter*, July 1960. Hugh Kenner attributes the relative failure of *Embers* to the BBC production, which is the only one he knows of and which, he says, made Henry's voice of 'so stylized a decrepitude that it was difficult in the extreme to make out the words, the all-important words'. But he adds, 'And yet the script is fascinating' (*A Reader's Guide*, p. 163). Clas Zilliacus agrees with this, adding: 'The text of *Embers* is a carefully wrought shorthand version of a larger statement which exists in an aural dimension only' (*B&B*, p. 94).

Embers

DÉCOR

See under *All That Fall*, p. 77 above. The sound effects are even more consciously artificial (see the direction concerning amplification, p. 95); whereas in *All That Fall* the sounds were ostensibly intended to be audible to all the characters within earshot, in *Embers* they are, it is strongly suggested, audible only to Henry, within his head, and even controlled by him. (Cf. the slamming of the door, p. 96.) In the BBC production this notion was emphasized by the use throughout of an insistent hum to represent the sound of the sea. This continually wells and dies away, becoming much louder in the pauses but never excessive. It is interesting to note how often Henry refers to sounds, especially during his story – 'no sound in the house of any kind, only the sound of the fire . . . and no sound of any kind, only the fire . . . Outside all still, not a sound, dog's chain maybe . . . not a sound, bitter cold . . . Dead silence then, not a sound, only the fire . . . Shifting, lapsing, furtive like, dreadful sound . . . white world, great trouble, not a sound, only the embers, sound of dying' – etc. (pp. 94–5). And his final words (p. 104) are 'Not a sound'. In the stereo version recorded by the University of London Audio Visual Centre in 1975, the producer, Katharine Worth, sought to indicate the movement of mind by locating passages in different 'zones' of sound. (In that recording, Patrick Magee played Henry, Elvi Hale Ada, and the director was David Clark.) 'In *Embers*', Professor Worth comments, 'the focus is always on the mysterious relationship between the willed and unwilled sounds, between those that stay in place and those that get out of hand, like Addie's uncontrollable paroxysms or the sucking sound of the sea' (*IDE*, p. 253).

DRAMATIS PERSONAE

As suggested above, the whole play seems to be performed in the mind of Henry, a man in late middle age: 'Henry above all needs to be perceived, if only by a mute presence of his own evoking' (Zilliacus, *B&B*, p. 77). His wife, Ada, his daughter, Addie, and his daughter's music and riding masters are all assigned separate voices and in the BBC production are performed by separate actors; whereas Henry's dead father is

137

'impersonated' by Henry himself. Given a sufficiently versatile performer, the sequential nature of the utterances, and the fact that the voices are, as it were, summoned from the past, there is no intrinsic reason why all the parts should not be taken by a single actor, although it must be emphasized that the author does not envisage this possibility. 'Bolton' and 'Holloway', the men who appear in Henry's 'story', are probably fairly complex fictionalizations of Henry's father and his father's doctor, respectively. Certainly the associations are close.

STRUCTURE

The play falls roughly into three sections. On pp. 93–6 Henry's first monologue introduces the themes and characters that will loom large throughout the work. From p. 97 to p. 103 we have a section of dialogue. The play ends (pp. 103–4) with Henry's monologue continuing the story about Bolton and Holloway, interrupted on p. 96, line 9.

LANGUAGE

Again, as in *All That Fall*, the speech is often Anglo-Irish in idiom; cf. 'Will I play my piece now please?' (p. 98). For the play's title, cf. p. 95, line 16. Martin Esslin tells us, however, that 'Ebb' was first suggested as a title but by April 1959 *Embers* had been chosen definitively (*Encounter*, September 1975, p. 42).

In the BBC production the language was slightly modified; 'trying to toast his arse' was cut (p. 95), as was the expletive 'Christ!' on p. 99. 'It was not enough to drag her into the world' (p. 103) became 'to bring her into the world' and 'Why are you always coming down here?' (p. 100) was repeated. Ada's colloquial use of 'don't, 'didn't', 'What's', etc., was expanded in the BBC production to 'do not', etc. This gave her voice a formal tone which seemed in keeping with the differentiation made between her and Henry in the type of voice they used. Henry's voice was old and cracked with a fairly bitter tone throughout: in contrast Ada's voice was extremely remote and almost ghostly in its soft, lilting, toneless expression.

NOTES ON THE TEXT

p. 93

(*Sea scarcely audible.*) Several of the plays begin inaudibly; cf. *Happy Days, Play, Not I.*

[First nine lines.] The sound effects underscore and illustrate the words, e.g. 'Slither of shingle as he sits'. Note the clear indication of where sea sounds overlap words and where they are distinct. Henry talks to overcome the sound of the sea and its unpleasant memories.

That sound you hear is the sea. 'You' refers to Henry's father. The 'dialogue' with his father continues overleaf.

we are sitting on the strand. Note the archaic ring of this word; but it is in current use in Ireland.

pp. 93–4

You would never live this side of the bay . . . I think the last time I went in was with you. John Fletcher offers the following explanation of this passage in terms of the sado-masochistic syndrome:

> The sea represents the mother whose person is denied firmly to the son. After the death of the father (whose body was never found, a symbol of the repression by the son of the paternal image), the son finds the courage to defy his interdicts by crossing the bay and thereby indulging his own incest fantasy. But the son's temerity is a relative thing, for he still depends on the father: before he disappeared, the father 'glared' at his offspring, calling him a 'washout', and thus denied all valid connection between his wife and their son.
>
> (*Samuel Beckett Now*, ed. Friedman, pp. 162–3)

p. 94

I'm like you in that, can't stay away from it. 'It' is the sea. It is also the 'cursed thing' that he once went to Switzerland to get away from, a few lines further on.

I usen't to need anyone, just to myself, stories. Like Hamm, and like the narrators in the novels, Henry survives by fictionalizing the pain in his existence. The story about Bolton is resumed, no doubt for the hundredth time, in the middle of p. 94. The hesitations (e.g. 'shutters ... no, hangings') show that Henry is 'composing', making it up as he goes along. The staccato rhythms of the story are very like those in *Not I*, although, of course, the latter is far less coherent.

p. 95
Vega in the Lyre. Vega is the chief star of the northern constellation, Lyra.

hands behind his back holding up the tails of his old macfarlane. This garment is not mentioned in the SOED but the French dictionary *Le Petit Robert* states that it used to be a man's sleeveless cloak, with a cape around the shoulders.

A drip! A drip! Cf. *Endgame*, p. 19: 'There's something dripping in my head.' In the BBC production 'the dripping sound has the inexorable insistence of a metronome, with an echo effect added' (Zilliacus, *B&B*, p. 91).

Try again. To tell his story about Bolton and Holloway.

p. 96
urgent need, bring the bag. The doctor's bag, of course.

chilled to the medulla. A typical Beckett joke, like the following 'washout', characteristic of his way of twisting clichés.

Washout. Wish to Christ she had. Vulg.: 'I wish to Christ my mother had washed me out [e.g. with a douche] before I was conceived.' Cf. *All That Fall*, where Mr Tyler curses 'the wet Saturday afternoon of my conception' (p. 15). Note the close association in Henry's mind between his longing never to have

been born and his recollection of his and his wife's efforts to
have Addie (p. 101); this association is revealed by the immediate mention of Ada, line 19, after his talk of the mother.

that's what hell will be like, small chat to the babbling of Lethe.
Lethe is a river of Hades, the underworld, from which souls
drank before reincarnation. Its waters induced oblivion of their
former life.

Price of blueband now! A common brand name of margarine.
Note the bathos in the contrast between images of hell and this
humdrum comment about groceries.

p. 97

*You shouldn't be sitting on the cold stones, they're bad for your
growths.* The 'growths' are haemorrhoids (piles), which are
popularly said to be caused by sitting on cold surfaces like
stones.

Raise yourself up till I slip my shawl under you. In the BBC production no sound accompanies these words, implying that the
scene is imaginary. Note Beckett's explicit direction '*No sound
as she sits*', a few lines further on. On the other hand Henry
makes sounds as he gets up (e.g., p. 99).

I hope you put on your jaegers. These are long johns.

The ones I used to fancy all did. 'Fancy' here in the sense of 'bet-
ting on'. A rather feeble joke; no wonder Henry fails to laugh.

p. 98

Listen to it! The sea again.

The Pampas! The inland grassland plains of South America.

It was rough, the spray came flying over us. References to rough
and calm sea, as pinpointing memories and reflecting states of
mind, are frequent in Beckett's plays. Cf. Krapp's vision and
affair (pp. 60–1), Nagg and Nell in *Endgame* (p. 21), Estragon

and Vladimir and the Rhône (*Waiting for Godot*, p. 53), and later on in this text (pp. 99–100).

Santa Cecilia! Addie's incompetent playing no doubt pains the ears of the patron saint of music.

Fa! Italian for 'F'. 'Qua!' a few lines on, is Italian for 'here'. Note the humour of this section, with its comic exaggerations.

p. 100

(*Sea suddenly rough.*) This direction refers back to p. 98 and introduces an evocation of the consummation of Henry and Ada's love affair. This memory is further evoked on p. 101.

It's silly to say it keeps you from hearing it. Henry claims that his incurable habit of talking to himself prevents him hearing the sound of the sea. Beckett maintains throughout an ambiguity as to whether Henry is 'really' by the seashore, or has something 'wrong with [his] brain', which causes him to hear the 'sucking' (p. 101) sound of the sea all the time, wherever he is. See also p. 101, 'Listen to it!' onwards.

you ought to see Holloway. A hint that Henry's Bolton story is not entirely fictional, since Holloway has something of a 'real' existence.

Stone! (Clash.) Stone! 'It seems to me that Beckett, with this sound complex, has overstrained the expressive powers of his medium' (Zilliacus, *B&B*, p. 93). It is a confusing sound and, Zilliacus says, 'gives the listener an irritating notion of hidden significance'.

p. 101

What age is she now? Addie.

p. 102

Keep it going, Ada, every syllable is a second gained. This could be the motto of all the Beckett heroes, especially the narrators in the novels.

Left soon afterwards, passed you on the road. The 'you' here referred to is Henry's father, who is addressed from this point on.

'*I have a panhysterectomy at nine.*' This is put more simply and
more crudely in *All That Fall*, p. 14, as 'the whole . . . er . . .
bags of tricks'.

white, black, white, black. Cf. note on light and dark in *Krapp's
Last Tape*, pp. 120–1 above.

Bolton: 'Please!' . . . *'Please!'* . . . *'Please, Holloway!'* We
never learn exactly what Bolton wants from Holloway. Some
critics have assumed that he wants a pain-killing injection,
which would be not untypical of a Beckett character; but Holloway offers him a 'shot', which he refuses. It seems more likely
that his 'great trouble' is acute mental distress and loneliness
and that Holloway either fails to understand this or, more
likely, cannot take upon himself responsibility for the anguish
of yet another being, apart from himself, condemned to existence. 'Bolton's object, it seems to me, is euthanasia. He begs
for it both verbally . . . and . . . by showing Holloway the acute
anguish in his eyes' (Zilliacus, *B&B*, p. 86).

and the glim shaking in your old fist. Barnard writes:

> Why does Beckett suddenly use the second-person 'your' in a
> story where before and after this he uses 'his'? Surely it is an
> intentional slip indicating that Henry has for the moment for-
> gotten to maintain the fiction of Bolton and thus reveals that
> he is really telling himself a story about himself, a fictional
> situation symbolizing his own real isolation.
>
> (*Samuel Beckett*, p. 117)

Note too how the mention of 'glim' (i.e. candle) reminds Henry
of Portia's words in *The Merchant of Venice* (V, i, 90–1), which
is why he changes his usual phrase 'white world' to 'naughty
world' three lines further on.

great trouble, no good . . . No good. Henry's story is still 'to be continued'. Commenting on the importance of this incident to the narrator, Professor Worth notes that

> he cannot get it out of his mind; perhaps has to disguise it in fictional form before he can tolerate the tale of the two old men by the dying embers and somehow do what he feels he has to do, relate it to the other story of his father, whose spirit haunts the entire piece.
>
> (*IDE*, pp. 250–1)

Little book. Henry's diary. ' "Plumber at nine" echoes "panhy-sterectomy at nine", and both plumber and doctor deal with the "waste",' writes Kristin Morrison, noting how 'Beckett turns a simple ordinary word into a complex pun . . . When all is drained, when all is discarded, when all is lost, nothing remains. And this, in fact, is Henry's ideal state' (*Canters and Chronicles*, p. 93).

Not a sound. This last enigmatic use of the phrase *outside* the Bolton and Holloway story (and after the last pause during which the sea is heard) could be confirmation that the whole play – *including* the sound of the sea – may be a figment of Henry's imagination, and that in reality his world is soundless, like that of a stone-deaf person.

THE OLD TUNE

Adapted from Robert Pinget's French text about 1960.

First publication   Les Editions de Minuit, Paris, late 1960, in
    a bilingual edition with Pinget's original
First broadcast   23 August 1960, BBC Third Programme,
    with Jack MacGowran as Cream and Patrick Magee as
    Gorman, produced by Barbara Bray
First British stage performance   October 1964, Traverse
    Theatre, Edinburgh, with Leonard Maguire as Gorman
    and Declan Mulholland as Cream, directed by Michael
    Geliot

Beckett has skilfully transposed into pure Dublin the colloquial
French of his friend Robert Pinget (b. 1920). The play, which
the BBC called 'a conversation piece for radio', was commissioned by its producer, Barbara Bray. Since this is not an
original Beckett text it calls for little comment here, apart from
the names. Toupin in Pinget here becomes Gorman, a common
Irish name that Beckett also uses in *Watt* (the fishwoman is a
Mrs Gorman), and Pommard (the name of a famous red Bur-
gundy) becomes Cream (evidently an allusion to 'cream'
sherry). The title in French, *La Manivelle*, means the crank of a
hand organ, but Beckett, as is his practice, uses as title a phrase
from the text (p. 177, line 2).

    The translation has been praised by Richard N. Coe as being
'more effective from every point of view – poetically, dramatically, atmospherically – than the original' (in Morris Beja *et al.*,
eds., *Samuel Beckett: Humanistic Perspectives*, p. 37), and Clas
Zilliacus notes that Pinget's neutral French idiom is 'trans-
figured into something strongly reminiscent of the great Irish
tradition, and of Synge in particular', Beckett's version being
'more persuasively figurative', with 'highly filigreed rhetoric'
(*Moderna Språk*, vol. 68 (1974), p. 7). Turning to Bray's direction of the play, Zilliacus writes:

The overall impression given by the production is that of a delicate balance between the poetic realism of the dialogue and stylization in the handling of sound: the footsteps of passers-by were rendered in a metronome-like beat, and the din of traffic sounded the way it would sound to two men from another epoch, rather than to listeners overhearing the two. This, of course, reinforces the subjective point of view. On the other hand, Barbara Bray's silences which separate Gorman's 'When you think . . .' and the resurgences of the old tune are very much shorter than the ten seconds indicated by the author.

(p. 9)

The BBC's treatment of this work seems therefore to have been influenced by their earlier handling of *All That Fall* and *Embers*.

The music chosen by Beckett for 'the old tune' played by Gorman was 'The Bluebells of Scotland'. Deirdre Bair considers that 'he used this play as an illustration of how important the proper use of music could be to a playwright' (*Samuel Beckett: A Biography*, p. 552).

There were few reviews, and those few not always enthusiastic. Frederick Laws declared himself 'most woundily bored by these old bores' (*Listener*, 1 September 1960).

HAPPY DAYS

Written in English, 1960–1.

First publication   Grove Press, New York, 1961
First performance   17 September 1961, Cherry Lane Theatre,
   New York
First British production   1 November 1962, Royal Court
   Theatre, London, with Brenda Bruce as Winnie, directed
   by George Devine

RECEPTION

The play attracted attention from the critics at its first performance in New York but there was little real enthusiasm. Upon a
'substructure of gloom, defeat and impotence Mr Beckett has
constructed a portrait of an incurable optimist', wrote *The
Times*'s New York correspondent, but denied the play much
theatrical quality (25 September). *Village Voice*, usually well
disposed to Beckett, found the play 'thinner in texture, slighter
in consequence than all its forerunners' (21 September).

In London in November 1962 the play was better received.
For *The Times*, 'The text is an elaborate structure of internal
harmonies with recurring clichés twisted into bitter truths, and
key phrases chiming ironically through the development as in a
passacaglia.' Bernard Levin thought 'this terminus in the
drama' would 'haunt those who see it' and Kenneth Tynan
urged his readers to see it although 'it is a dramatic metaphor
extended beyond its capacities.'

By the time the play reached Paris the critics were unreserved
('*inoubliable*', '*sublime*', '*admirable*') but these comments were
perhaps prompted more by the actress than by the play: Madeleine Renaud played Winnie.

DÉCOR

This is simpler than Beckett originally intended. His

147

manuscript notes, dated 8 October 1960, give details of his first conception of the play. They are thus summarized by James Knowlson:

> In this early version, there are two ledges on the mound in the centre of which Winnie is imprisoned. The man is first referred to as sitting in striped pyjamas on the lower one of these ledges, with his back to the audience. Later, in the same notes, he is said to be sleeping *behind* the mound and is referred to for the first time as going into his *hole*. The man is first addressed as Tom, later is called Edward, then finally is named as Willie, whereas the woman's name is changed from Mildred (preserved in her story in the printed text) to Winnie. On another page there is a list of the numerous objects which Winnie keeps in her bag and to which she is strongly attached, together with the observation 'Cut out alarm clock. Invisible bell.'
>
> (*SBaE*, p. 85)

S. E. Gontarski comments:

> The early drafts of *Happy Days* tend to be more 'realistic' than the printed version. The major structural and thematic alterations in the manuscripts demonstrate not an evolution toward fuller explanation of character and situation, but the opposite, a development away from what Beckett has called, 'the grotesque fallacy of a realistic art – "that miserable statement of line and surface", and the penny-a-line vulgarity of a literature of notations' (*Proust*, p. 57). The composition of *Happy Days* is almost a process of decomposition, a direction consistent with Beckett's professed aesthetic: 'The artistic tendency is not expansive, but a contraction' (*Proust*, p. 47). As such, the development of *Happy Days* is virtually a microcosm of Beckett's overall artistic development: the pattern from *Godot* to *Breath*, from *Murphy* to *The Lost Ones* is toward absence, whiteness, silence.
>
> (*Beckett's 'Happy Days'*, p. 33)

Coe (p. 105) and Robinson (p. 289) both see Winnie's mound as Zeno's impossible heap of finite time (see also *Endgame*, p. 12). It could also be regarded as an objectivization of Winnie's past, similar to Krapp's tape. Robinson also notes a parallel with Dante, which is probably intended by the playwright: 'Like the Violent against God, Nature and Art, [Winnie] is confined to a burning desert under a rain of perpetual fire, visible at first from waist to head like the Heretics in their burning tombs, and then from forehead to neck like the Traitors Dante saw in the Lake of Cocytus' (p. 290).

DRAMATIS PERSONAE

Once again we have a couple (cf. Estragon–Vladimir, Hamm–Clov) and even, like Maddy and Dan Rooney, a married couple, for even if the legal tie does not exist they have certainly cohabited for a long time. A. Alvarez sees the play as 'a sour view of a cosy marriage', which is what it certainly is on one level. Winnie and Willie are bored with each other, even sexually bored (see particularly the revelatory remark on p. 42). But the couple also serves a philosophical purpose, which Edith Kern draws attention to: Winnie is sure of her existence only in so far as Willie acknowledges it. This is part of the Berkeleyan idealism that Beckett feels so much sympathy for (see Introduction, p. 37) and that also underpins *Film* (q.v.). Willie, in other words, serves to assure Winnie that she exists.

In reply to a question from Billie Whitelaw at rehearsal, Beckett said of Winnie:

> I don't think she knows herself what kind of a woman she is. She's a mess. An organized mess. Her strength is through unawareness. She has a kind of profound frivolity, she's scatterbrained, she babbles . . . One of the clues of the play is interruption. Something begins, something else begins. She begins but she doesn't carry through with it. She's constantly being interrupted or interrupting herself. She's an interrupted being. She's a bit mad. Manic is not wrong, but too big. The first act establishes a kind of quality – the interruption, the strangeness, the gracefulness – she's not stoic, she's unaware. A child woman with a short span of concentration – sure one minute, unsure the next.
>
> (*The Beckett Circle*, Summer 1979)

Winnie is meant to look 'blousy' but she has other

connotations apart from those of a middle-class matron: 'Winnie, buried in sand to her waist, succeeds at times in making the earth around her appear as a coquettish skirt and at others appears like an earth goddess whose womb and bosom are meant to enfold and nourish all' (Edith Kern). According to Alan Schneider, the first director of *Happy Days*, Beckett originally envisaged Winnie's as a male part but decided against it since trouser pockets are not as capacious as a shopping bag. 'This alone', Mrs Kern remarks, 'should prevent us from considering the chattering woman and her silent newspaper-reading companion as symbolic of marital "togetherness", as some reviewers have done' (*Yale French Studies*, Spring–Summer 1962, pp. 51, 53). The play indicts what Beckett calls, in *Proust*, people's 'smug will to live', which Winnie's optimism certainly epitomizes. There is striking contrast between her vitality and the desert place around her.

Note the piercing bell that arouses Winnie; it performs the same function as the goad prodding the characters into action in *Act Without Words II*.

STRUCTURE

The two-act structure of the play has been questioned by many critics, among them Alvarez, who considers that the play 'labours a single point at inordinate length' and serves merely to provide an 'effortless' technical solution to an 'absurdly difficult' theatrical problem (pp. 110–11). Doherty, on the other hand, suggests there is a third act implicit in the structure – silence – where the mouth is buried but the mind still made to think (p. 117). Structural difficulties in production, notably the length and stasis of the first act, explain to some extent perhaps its mixed reception by theatre audiences. However, the change that occurs between the acts has considerable dramatic impact and is essential to the play as a whole. Certainly any production needs to be particularly aware of the dramatic implications of the pauses, the pattern of movement, sound, fragmented and completed sentences and of what Kenner calls the actress's 'hundred chances to show what a voice can do' (p. 147).

LANGUAGE AND DRAMATIC EXPRESSION

The Irish-American critic Vivian Mercier considers that Winnie may have been modelled on the author's aunt Cissie, a cripple for a number of years: 'She remains', he writes, 'the stoical epitome of an Irish Protestant gentlewoman, a loyal member of the [Anglican] Church of Ireland like Maddy Rooney, but less prone to complain than the fat heroine of *All That Fall*.' He sees her language as 'Common Anglo-Irish' and cites in support of his claim expressions like 'what ails you?' and 'put a bit of jizz into it' which, he says, 'survive only in Ireland'. On the other hand, there is at least one example of an Anglo-French bilingual joke: 'Them? Or it?', a play on the French plural *les cheveux* for 'hair' (p. 19). Alvarez considers Winnie's language merely 'suburban prattle', which, given its richness in quotation and literary allusion, hardly does it justice. Neither does he take into account the considerable rhythmic and poetic effects of Winnie's utterances, the flow of which is so carefully controlled by pauses, movements, repetitions and variations.

The larger point about language in this play is that it is represented, as everywhere in the Beckett canon, as failing, breaking down: cf. 'Words fail, there are times when even they fail . . . What is one to do then, until they come again?' (p. 20). Winnie's speech is punctuated by broken quotations. Like all other Beckett heroes, she is terrified of silence and like them she has recourse to story-telling (the tale of Mildred and the mouse) in an attempt to keep the silence at bay.

The importance of the minutiae of movements in this essentially static play cannot be overestimated, and the reader needs to visualize each action as it is related and avoid the habit, bred of reading plays with less vital stage directions, of concentrating solely on what is said. Notice how movements alternate rather than overlap with spoken lines, particularly in the earlier part of the play: indeed examples of simultaneous speech and action are extremely rare throughout the whole play whilst speech frequently arrests gesture. Given Winnie's intention, this is understandable enough: to fill the day with words and actions at the same time is clearly wasteful when both are at such a premium.

The play clearly progresses towards being more verbal and

less movement orientated: it begins with much stage business and inaudible prayers and moves through the initial stages of manipulation of props alternating with speech to a greater emphasis on pauses, tone of voice and facial expression. By Act II, of course, Winnie's movements are restricted to eyes right, left or front, and Willie is not seen until his dramatic entrance at the end. The tension at this point owes much to this progressive reduction of emphasis on movement, and to the fact that for the first time in the play we actually see a character move across the stage!

NOTES ON THE TEXT

[Title.] This common English expression (e.g. for a cheery toast when drinks are served) is often used sardonically and establishes an initial ambiguity since Winnie, on the whole, means it literally but the spectator views it ironically.

It may well allude – as Winnie would – to a religious poem, Vaughan's 'The Retreat':

> Happy those early days! when I
> Shin'd in my Angel-infancy
> Before I understood this place . . .

It's obviously a translation, too, of Verlaine's 'Ah! les beaux jours' in 'Colloque sentimental', from which the play's French title comes.

> (Jeremy Treglown, *Times Educational Supplement*,
> 2 June 1978)

p. 9

(*Expanse . . .*) *Happy Days* belongs to the group of Beckett plays that occur in an indefinite and endless landscape; cf. *Godot*, *Embers* or *Cascando*, in contrast to the group which take place in closed cells, e.g., *Krapp*, *Endgame* or *Eh Joe*.

(*scorched grass.*) This is due to the considerable heat accompanying the blazing light, which causes Willie to get singed (p. 14), Winnie to perspire (p. 28) and presumably the parasol to burst into flames (p. 28). If we are to believe Winnie, the heat is increasing (pp. 27–9) but so is her ability to withstand it (p. 28), although in a more philosophical frame of mind she decides 'it is no hotter today than yesterday' (p. 29). It is ironical that Winnie also sees this heat, which would seem to be a form of torture, as a blessing: it stops the grass from growing.

(*low mound*.) The reason why Winnie is set in a mound rather than in level earth may be purely dramatic functionalism. It has also been seen as suggestive of a skirt of Mother Earth, a breast, a boil, a burial mound. It certainly excludes the idea that she is sinking into a swamp.

(*Blazing light*.) Renée Riese Hubert writes: 'This perpetual sunlight possesses some of the infernal qualities which characterize the spotlight in *Play*, a spotlight which arouses the characters from complete darkness and provokes reluctant confessions' (*Modern Drama*, vol. ix no. 3, p. 339). Winnie comments that it is 'holy light' and 'hellish light' (p. 11). It would seem to make little difference to Beckett if this were heaven or hell.

(*pompier*.) A French term meaning conventional, emphatic, trite.

(*trompe-l'oeil*.) Imitation – literally eye-deceiving.

(*exact centre*.) The mound is placed centrally on the stage and Winnie placed centrally in the mound: her position thus ensures 'maximum of simplicity and symmetry'. It recalls Hamm's insistence on being placed in the exact centre of the stage (centre of the world) in *Endgame*, p. 24.

(*capacious black bag*.) Ulf Schramm sees it as a symbol of the limited possibilities of helping her through the day (p. 43). Its dark depths (p. 25) store potential experience (Schramm, *Fiktion und Reflexion*, p. 192). This limitation forces her to economize her activities and she warns herself, 'Do not overdo the bag, Winnie' (p. 25). In the second act when she cannot rummage in her bag, it is replaced and compensated for by fantasies (stories, memories, etc.) For the origin of the bag see p. 38, 'the one you gave me . . . to go to market.'

(*collapsible collapsed parasol*.) Beckett's humour extends even to the stage directions which only the actor and reader can appreciate.

(*Long pause*.) The play begins in stasis (cf. *Krapp*) and it is important to conjure up the initial scene: blazing light against the darkness of the auditorium, one character (Willie is at first invisible) in an unforeseen situation, asleep, a bag and a parasol. Her sleeping posture could well obscure the fact that she is embedded and she might appear as some grotesque malformed giant who fills the stage but is relatively pea-brained. In this respect Winnie's aspect would be a reversal of the common theatrical convention of masks, where the head is enlarged and caricatured but the body remains unchanged.

(*A bell*.) Who rings this bell? We can ask but not answer the question. It could suggest a malevolent god that denies Winnie rest and free will; or the assistant stage manager whose job it is to ensure that actors are ready for their cues and entrances.

Doherty notes that 'she mentions the bell for sleep, but we never hear it' (*Samuel Beckett*, p. 116); clearly it is not only the arbitrary divider of the day and the night (a night without darkness if we are to believe that Winnie is being permitted to sleep at the beginning of each act), for it is quick to insist on her continuing her happy day on occasions when she seems to falter (see pp. 37, 40), like the goad in *Act Without Words II*. Winnie sees this as a blessing: 'Someone is looking at me still. Caring for me still. That is what I find so wonderful' (p. 37). The factor controlling the bell can clearly see Winnie's every move, like the factor controlling the various things that appear before the man in *Act Without Words I*, or the manipulator of the spotlight in *Play*.

(*piercingly*.) Beckett's originally intended alarm clock would not have been adequate. In the Berlin 1971 production a loud shrill fire alarm bell was used. The ten seconds during which this piercing bell rings are – and are intended to be – intensely irritating.

(*gazes front. Long pause.*) Initial confrontation with the audience but no acknowledgement of the fact.

Another heavenly day. The oppositional implication of night is, of course, ironic or meaningless since the sun never stops burning and therefore loses its traditional function as a soundless watch. Time references are always subjective: Winnie decides what time it is – 'The day is now well advanced' (p. 42), 'Not long now, Winnie' (p. 46), and the adverb 'now' consequently sounds somewhat hollow.

(*inaudible prayer.*) Beckett's orchestration of sound mentioned above is evident throughout the plays, and the beginning of *Happy Days* affords a first-rate example of the manipulation of different sounds and volume. The sequence in the first few minutes is this:

Silence. Piercing bell 10 seconds. Silence. Bell 5 seconds. Silence. Phrase spoken at normal stage volume. Silence. Inaudible prayer 10 seconds. Silence. Phrase spoken low. Silence. Inaudible addendum 5 seconds. Phrase spoken low. Silence. Phrase spoken at normal stage volume. Silence. Phrase spoken at normal stage volume. Silence. Stage action. Spit. Loud 'Hoo-oo!' Silence. Louder 'Hoo-oo!' Silence. Phrase spoken at normal stage volume.

p. 10

World without end Amen. Doherty (*Samuel Beckett*, p. 116) notes that 'World without end Amen', the ending of the *Gloria*, is both the indication of this unending but downward descending purgatory and the central irony of the 'Happy Days': 'Glory be to the Father, and to the Son, and to the Holy Ghost. As it was in the beginning, is now, and ever shall be, World without end Amen.'

(*toothpaste*.) This is running out, like a lot of other requisites: medicine to aid lack of spirits (p. 13); memory of classical quotations (*passim*); and love. But note that everything is *running out*, nothing that Winnie needs has *run* out, unlike *Endgame* where, for example, the sugar-plums (p. 38) and the pain-killer (p. 46) have run out.

(*Tender smile . . . smile off*.) The latter is not only a convenient directive shorthand: when Beckett says 'off' he means just that, as opposed to a smile fading. He uses the technique frequently in this and other plays, to change suddenly facial expression. Its purpose can vary: it can be comic, intentionally foreground 'stageyness', it can reveal preoccupation or, as in this case, it can suggest the fleeting and precarious nature of tenderness. A good Winnie uses 'puckish facial expressions to set to rest any gloomy intent' (*The Beckett Circle*, Spring 1983).

running out . . . can't be helped . . . just one of those old things. All this section can be applied to Willie just as well as to the tube of toothpaste.

[Repetition and alteration.] We can note early on the frequent use of repetition and variation: 'can't be helped – just one of those old things – another of those old things – just can't be cured – cannot be cured' (p. 10), or 'no worse – no better, no worse – no change – no pain' (p. 10, repeated pp. 12–13). The most frequently repeated phrase, 'the old style', becomes something of a musical leitmotif throughout the play. See below, notes to p. 13.

p. 11
woe woe is me. From *Hamlet*, III, i.

p. 12
(*fixed lost gaze, brokenly*) – *prayers perhaps not for naught* – (*pause, do*.) – *first thing* – (*pause, do*.) – *last thing* – (. . . *wipes eyes*.) The first hint, and fairly early in the play, that perhaps even Winnie herself is not fooled by her own sparkle and optimism. These moments of possible/probable insight into her

own situation seem to be more felt than explicit, and owe much to the pauses where we can only speculate whether or not she is thinking, and if so, of what. Cf. p. 30: 'That is what I find so wonderful, the way things ... (*voice breaks, head down*) ... things ... so wonderful. (*Long pause, head down. Finally turns...*)'. Cf. also 'voice breaks' or 'falters' on pp. 20, 23, 27, 33, and her reference to 'gnawing doubt' on p. 22.

(*handle of surprising length.*) Both a joke prop and a dramatic convenience, in that it will reach far enough to strike Willie. Beckett does not insist that the light should come from directly above, so a parasol with so long a handle might prove rather ineffectual against a diagonal light; it is up to the actress to ensure that it does not appear so.

Damp. Winnie is very conscious of her physical state. Notice her careful inspection of her teeth.

p. 13
the old style! See also various references on pp. 16, 18, 19 (twice), 20, 25, 26, 32, 33, 37, 40.

Oh fleeting joys – oh something lasting woe. See Milton, *Paradise Lost*, 10: 741–2.

(*Willie's bald head, trickling blood.*) Willie's macabre and comic entrance some minutes into the play finally assures the audience that he does exist: up to that moment he has been frequently referred to but never seen. It is unclear whether his bleeding head has been caused by the breaking bottle or by Winnie's striking him with the beak of the parasol. What is noticeable is that he is not alarmed by this treatment (he even returns the parasol to her when she drops it) and does not complain. His procedure for dealing with the trickling blood seems well established and is reminiscent of Hamm's 'old stancher' in *Endgame* (p. 12).

p. 14

Ensign crimson... Pale flag. See *Romeo and Juliet*, V, iii, 94–6:

> Thou art not conquered. Beauty's ensign yet
> Is crimson in thy lips and in thy cheeks,
> And death's pale flag is not advanced there.

(WILLIE *reads*.) Willie's first snippet of news, the death of Dr Hunter, does have some value for Winnie and, of course, is in itself a typical Beckettian pratfall. Snippets from the Occupations Vacant column serve at least a double function: firstly, nostalgia for the youth and vitality Willie no longer has, interrupting Winnie's reminiscences of her first kiss; secondly, they are as useless (or useful) as reading material as Winnie's daily reading of her toothbrush handle.

(*arrests gesture as* WILLIE *reads*.) Even with Willie's appearance speech and gesture do not coincide. It is ironical that Winnie should indulge in memories of her (alleged) lover as soon as Willie appears.

Borough Green. A small town in Kent.

horse-beech. A pun on horse chestnut.

p. 15

Very bushy moustache, very tawny. Willie's moustache, not revealed until the end of the play, is also very bushy and very long but it is white.

The tangles of bast... The shadows deepening among the rafters. This reminiscence seems momentarily genuinely lyrical, like Krapp's sad lyricism of 'Be again in the dingle on a Christmas Eve' (*Krapp's Last Tape*, p. 63). The deepening shadows are in ironic contrast to the blazing light of Winnie's present situation and the memory is lost once she opens her eyes. It is interesting to note that she has her eyes closed for several seconds without the bell insisting that she open them.

(WINNIE *lays down glass and brush.*) Cf. Clov's routine with the glass (*Endgame*, p. 25).

p. 16

Hog's setae. The audience, kept in suspense by characteristically Beckettian delaying tactics, has expected 'bristle'. Note that Winnie understands the learned (Latin) word '*setae*' but is unclear about the definition of the plain Anglo-Saxon 'hog'.

not a day goes by ... hardly a day. A typical gesture of withdrawal which sometimes denotes a significant shift in meaning. Cf. when Winnie shifts from 'can't complain' to 'mustn't complain' (p. 11).

(*She looks for spectacles.*) 'Beckett's production notebook for the Old Vic revival (1975) indicates that he intends Winnie to appear ambivalent about sex; he states that she "*feels* for glasses and mag. glass without taking eyes from card", thus suggesting her fascination despite her stated disgust' (Morrison, *Canters and Chronicles*, p. 48n.).

(*Impatience of* WILLIE'*s fingers.*) Note the comedy of Willie's fingers itching to regain possession of the card. Beckett is scrupulous about the stage directions concerning the visibility of Willie's hands: in handing back the parasol (p. 12) his hand is 'invisible' so as not to reveal his presence and thus add to the comedy of the parasol reappearing. In placing the handkerchief on his bleeding head it would seem unnecessary to specify 'His hand appears...' Strangest of all is Beckett's insistence on 'hands invisible' when Willie is opening his newspaper (p. 14 and p. 36), fanning his face (p. 15) and presumably when turning the pages (p. 36). But it all adds to the general mystery of his activities behind the mound. The manner in which he and things appear and disappear behind the mound is almost mindful of a glove puppet show.

p. 17

creature in the background. Applicable also to Willie.

What is *the alternative? (Pause.) What* is *the al* – (WILLIE *blows*

nose loud and long.) This dramatic device never fails to be effective in Beckett's plays. It is usually employed when his figures
come close to an awareness of their central situation. Cf.
Krapp's Last Tape: when Krapp is faced with images of
approaching death his song is upset by a fit of coughing.

p. 19
The sweet old style. Cf. Dante's *dolce stil nuovo*, to which Winnie
is making conscious learned allusion.

It. Comic, of course, because of its abruptness after the long
pause and because of Winnie's excited response to this contact.
Willie has only read from the newspaper up to now. Since
Willie is bald 'It' may well be appropriate.

p. 21
Fear no more the heat o' the sun. From *Cymbeline*, IV, ii, 258.

p. 22
There will always be the bag. . . Even when you are gone, Willie.
She cynically weighs off a man against an object.

p. 23
when two are gathered together. A characteristic allusion to the
Anglican liturgy and Holy Communion.

emmet. An ant; cf. 'pismires' in *All That Fall*, p. 23. The emmet
is an image of life and therefore something negative for Winnie,
just as the flea upsets Hamm in *Endgame*. Cf. p. 27 where
Winnie says: 'What a blessing nothing grows, imagine if all this
stuff were to start growing.'

The Latin for ant is *formica*, hence 'formication' below with its
comic intention. Normally it means the sensation of ants crawl-
ing over the skin. Cf. Harvey (*Samuel Beckett*, p. 193) on 'formi-
cante' in Beckett's poem 'être là sans mâchoires sans dents'.

p. 24
(*laughs*.) These orchestrated laughs are perhaps one of Winnie's
and Willie's rare moments of 'togetherness', although Winnie

raises in her next speech the possibility that they were 'perhaps diverted by two quite different things?'

p. 25

amid severest woe. From Gray's 'Ode on a Distant Prospect of Eton College', a poem perhaps better known for having given the phrase 'where ignorance is bliss,/'Tis folly to be wise' to the language.

paradise enow. From Fitzgerald's *The Rubáiyát of Omar Khayyám*, v. 11.

To sing too soon is a great mistake, I find. Is she thinking of the proverb 'If you sing before breakfast, you'll cry before night'?

p. 26

Brownie. From Browning, an automatic pistol invented by J. M. Browning of Utah. 'Ever uppermost' refers to another Browning, the poet Robert, whose *Paracelsus* reads (at 11, 3, 372), 'I say confusedly what comes uppermost'.

I'll leave you out. A possible double meaning of leaving the revolver outside the bag and of leaving out suicide as a method of resolving her situation.

p. 27

when I was young and . . . foolish. W. B. Yeats, 'Down by the Salley Gardens', lines 4 and 8.

p. 28

Reason says, Put it down. The Cartesian mind-body dualism is likely to have inspired this scenic tension.

(*The parasol goes on fire*.) Due to spontaneous combustion, no doubt, caused by the intense heat of the place. This presents a difficult technical problem in production but if it is accomplished successfully it is the most dramatic and magical moment of the play. The only people not surprised by the event are Willie who doesn't notice it and Winnie who, we assume, has seen it happen before. It is ironical that it occurs immediately after Winnie's statement about one of her two lamps burning brighter. The event is both a curse and a blessing: the parasol can no longer be used for protection against the blazing light; on the other hand Winnie was tired of holding it up anyway.

p. 29

With the sun blazing so much fiercer down. This stands in sharp contrast to what she says at the bottom of the page: 'It is no hotter today than yesterday...' Her first statement could be seen as hallucinatory in the same way as 'The earth is very tight today' (p. 23).

p. 30

something has seemed to occur, and nothing has occurred. This, together with the immediately preceding thoughts of Winnie, is a restatement of the Zeno paradox of the eternal present in which nothing can change: the arrow cannot reach its destination; it cannot even leave the bow.

it will be in the bag again tomorrow. And so it will, if the performance is one of a run. Similarly stage hands will have replenished the flat tube of toothpaste, the almost empty bottle of red medicine, restored the charred parasol and so on. By his awareness of playmaking Beckett supports the very illusion/reality his play and its characters create. Kenner comments:

> It is a curious effect, the hidden functionaries of the theatre who check the contents of bags and arrange combustible umbrellas being transformed, by a few words, into presiding powers, workers of mysterious miracles since resources are replenished, merciless since no headway is made, not even headway toward some abyss.
>
> <p align="right">(<i>A Reader's Guide</i>, p. 149)</p>

(*Waltz Duet 'I love you so' from The Merry Widow.*) This serves the same nostalgic function in Winnie's life as 'Death and the Maiden' does in Mrs Rooney's, or the 'Ghost' Trio in the play of the same title.

162

The musical-box song may seem extremely sentimental when read. But in its dramatic context it is, first, rather grotesquely comic, as Willie sings it hoarsely without the words. Then, at the end, when sung by Winnie, it manages to sound moving . . . capturing something of the yearning which transcends the banality of its words.

(Knowlson, *Frescoes*, p. 106)

p. 31

Winnie, sing your song. Harvey claims that Winnie's reference to her song 'recurs during the difficult moments when other resources fail [and that it both] betrays a need and holds out a hope' (*Samuel Beckett*, p. 169).

the bird of dawning. The cock. See *Hamlet*, I, i, where after the ghost's disappearance Marcellus uses the expression.

Mr Shower. This couple serves to some extent to forestall audience reaction. Cf. 'I've been better entertained', *Waiting for Godot* (p. 38). The names are once again appropriate to the function: 'Shower' and 'Cooker' recall the German words *schauen* and *kucken*, both meaning 'to look'.

p. 32

keep yourself nice. This is ironical and pathetic at the same time, contrasting sharply with Willie's disgusting habit of eating the pickings of his nose a few lines further on. Michael Robinson compares Winnie's mania for 'keep[ing] herself nice' with the action of a prisoner buttoning his flies carefully as he leaves the condemned cell for the last time.

pp. 35–6

Castrated male swine . . . Reared for slaughter. An oblique reference to Willie's own situation.

p. 37

[Act II.] Note the brevity of this act: it is less than half the length of Act I. It has sometimes been suggested that the second act of *Happy Days* is an irrelevance. Professor Knowlson disagrees: 'The existence of two acts renders a whole series of dramatic contrasts possible as well as numerous subtle modulations of mood', and permits a 'much fuller, more ambiguous' picture of the Willie–Winnie relationship being given. (*Frescoes*, pp. 107–8).

(*Her head, which she can no longer turn, nor bow, nor raise, faces front motionless throughout act.*) The first instance of total physical immobility in Beckett's drama. Nagg and Nell in *Endgame*, although restricted to dustbins, could at least turn and attempt to kiss, but now the head is held. The same technique is used in the later plays *Play* and *Not I*.

Willie. (*Pause. Louder.*) *Willie.* We can only assume that Willie is still behind the mound: even the reader is not told of his whereabouts until he appears 'dressed to kill' (p. 45).

(*Bell rings loudly.*) Doherty writes:

> This act is very short and the bell is more insistent that the eyes do not close. In the beginning of the first act Winnie was allowed to close her eyes and pray, but immediately she does close her eyes in the second act the bell shrills her into opening them immediately and will keep on insisting on 'eyes open'. So no prayer.
>
> (*Samuel Beckett*, p. 117)

Hail, holy light. From Milton, *Paradise Lost*, 3: 1. See also p. 11 where Winnie first says 'holy light' but then corrects herself to 'hellish light'.

p. 38
beechen green. From Keats, 'Ode to a Nightingale', line 9.

p. 39
no damask. Cf. 'feed on her damask cheek', *Twelfth Night*, II, iv.

the lake . . . the reeds. Cf. *Krapp's Last Tape*, p. 61.

p. 42

Aristotle. The phrase *omne animal post coitum triste est* is usually attributed to Galen.

p. 43

What are those exquisite lines?

> Her memories of quotations are even more fragmentary than in Act I; yet she prides herself on remembering parts of the classics, and specifically summons 'those unforgettable . . . exquisite . . . immortal' lines, as opposed to the merely 'wonderful lines' of Act I. She actually quotes from such sentimental versifiers as Charles Wolfe [as here], rather than from the great poets of the English language.
>
> (Cohn, *Samuel Beckett*, pp. 255–6)

S.E. Gontarski elaborates:

> The pattern of literary allusions and echoes in *Happy Days* is complex. The themes of the failure of love, the misery of the human condition, the transitoriness of all things, the disjunction between the real and ideal, the misery of awareness, have been carefully reinforced in Winnie's literary allusions and reverberate throughout the play like a constant drumbeat. The word 'mercy' itself becomes a refrain, like 'happy'. And in Beckett's selection of quotations and obliquer references virtually every historical epoch is represented: pre-Christian Greek philosophies, the blind religiosity and Christian Idealism of the Middle Ages, Renaissance Humanism, eighteenth-century Rationalism, and nineteenth-century Romanticism. The philosophies, literature, and religion of Western man comprise the fragmented mythology against which Winnie fails and suffers, and like a jeweller's foil, mythology highlights the suffering.
>
> (*Beckett's 'Happy Days'*, p. 73)

I call to the eye of the mind. A quotation from Yeats's play *At the Hawk's Well*.

p. 44

Bibby. A child's nanny; cf. 'Text for Nothing III' in *No's Knife*,
p. 82. The story of Mildred and the mouse is a true one.
Dorothy Coote (see note to *All That Fall*, p. 37) recalled that
one day when her sister Mildred was visiting the Becketts
a mouse ran up her leg; moreover, Miss Coote's nickname
was Dolly, so here again Beckett is drawing on childhood
memories.

Too late. For what? Is defloration by a mouse really meant?
Doherty comments: 'If this mouse-experience has been
Winnie's, then the power of the story is that of obsession; if not,
then it is a substitute or metaphor for some terror which she
cannot articulate or put into words' (*Samuel Beckett*, pp. 117–18).

p. 45

The pink fizz. A drink based on champagne and grenadine.

The flute glasses. Tall, narrow champagne glasses frequently
seen in France.

Life a mockery. Notice Winnie's use of stock phrases from
romantic novelettes.

Where are the flowers? Cf. 'And this same flower that smiles
today' in Robert Herrick's poem 'To the Virgins, to Make
Much of Time', which is also referred to in *Krapp's Last Tape*,
p. 59. Here is the stanza in full:

> Gather ye Rose-buds while ye may,
>   Old Time is still a flying:
> And this same flower that smiles to day,
>   To morrow will be dying.

p. 46

Reynolds' News. This was a popular Sunday newspaper.

(Shocked.) What ails you, Willie, I never saw such an expression!
Much of the dramatic tension of the final scene comes from

Winnie's being *shocked* out of her complacency for the first time. Up to this point even the most surprising events have been seen as commonplace and have yielded little response: Winnie's being embedded in the mound, Willie's bleeding head, the flaming parasol. Winnie's later fear and vehemence are all the more forceful because we cannot ascertain the exact cause of them and momentarily she seems to be faced with a situation she has not met before.

jizz. Irishism for 'life'. Beckett uses the same expression in 'Text for Nothing III': 'a week in spring, that puts the jizz in you' (*No's Knife*, p. 81).

p. 47
(*He slithers back to foot of mound.*) Kristin Morrison comments:

> Winnie's fear of the mouse running up her thigh and Willie's lack of 'jizz' constitute mutual sexual disability which results in that barren mound in which Winnie lives, rigid and extinguished, a state even more fatal than the death, the revolver Willie cannot reach.
>
> (*Canters and Chronicles*, p. 51)

(*musical-box tune.*) The *Merry Widow* waltz again.

> This most static of plays is also, paradoxically, almost a dance play; through the rhythm, music, the words of a song we arrive, in Yeatsian mode, at a revelation of a profound deep of the mind.
>
> (Worth, *IDE*, p. 258)

p. 48
(*They look at each other. Long pause.*) Death governs this moment of a petrified gaze and a third act could surely be only a quasi-death with the mind alone still at work after speech has gone. As mentioned in the *Introduction*, p. 39 above, Beckett safeguarded, in his 1979 London production, the carefully structured ambiguities of the text, which Professor Knowlson refers to as 'Willie's closing attempts to reach Winnie, either to kiss her or to kill her or himself' (*Frescoes*, p. 108).

WORDS AND MUSIC

Written in English and completed towards the end of 1961. Martin Esslin describes it as 'finally reali[zing] Beckett's long-cherished intention of collaboration on an original work with John Beckett' (but see under *Décor*, below).

First publication   *Evergreen Review* (New York), November–December 1962

First broadcast   13 November 1962, BBC Third Programme, with Felix Felton as Croak, Patrick Magee as Words, directed by Michael Bakewell.

RECEPTION

Once again there was relatively little attention from the critics but *The Times*'s reviewer was characteristically respectful. In the *Observer*, however, Paul Ferris called it a 'hoarse and unsatisfactory assault on ideas that makes as little concession as possible to formal playwriting' (18 November 1962).

DÉCOR

The sonic décor is very similar to that of *Embers* (see p. 137 above), except that there is a musical score by the author's cousin, John Beckett. 'Music' is, however, more than a score. It has the qualities of a character rather than an accompaniment. Twelve musicians were employed for the BBC recording, strings, brass, percussion and electric organ (see Zilliacus, *B&B*, p. 115). Beckett was not fully satisfied with his cousin's score, so for a later recording, produced by Katharine Worth and directed by David Clark at the University of London Audio Visual Centre in 1975, in which Patrick Magee again played Words, Humphrey Searle composed the music.

DRAMATIS PERSONAE

For the first time Beckett uses abstractions ('Words', 'Music') as characters in his drama. 'Music' personified is capable of being humble: it is capable too of expressing love and age, and capable of rebuking and making suggestions to 'Words'. This, of course, confronts the reader with considerable difficulty that can be satisfactorily overcome only by listening to a performance.

Croak is not without analogies to Krapp; in the manuscript drafts he was first called Old Man's Whisper, then Whisper, then Senile Croak, and finally Croak. His names for his minions are Joe and Bob. 'Words' is noticeably unoriginal in his thoughts, fitting whatever happens to be the chosen theme (e.g., sloth, love) into the same sequence of sentences, although on the subject of the face (p. 131ff.) it is 'Words' who is insistent and cruel to Croak whereas 'Music' would prefer warm and loving associations. At this point 'Words' escapes from the control of his lord, Croak, and wounds him with memories he would rather not hear.

Martin Esslin, who was Assistant Head of Radio Drama when this play was produced, has an interesting comment to make on it:

Beckett's preoccupation with the process of human consciousness as an incessant verbal flow ... here found its logical culmination, and one which only radio could provide. For, after all, human consciousness – the self's awareness of its own existence – does not *only* consist of a constant stream of language. It has a non-verbal component as well, the parallel and no less unbroken stream of wordless consciousness of being made up of body-sensations, inner tensions, the awareness of body temperature, aches, pains, the throbbings of the flow of one's own blood: all are the multiple facets of non-verbal consciousness summed up in the overall concept of emotion. This stream of non-verbal life-awareness, of life-force or *Will*, is the subject matter of *music* which portrays and represents the ebb and flow of the emotions. To give an adequate representation of the Beckettian exploration of the self's experience of itself, music therefore had to be added to the verbal stream of consciousness ...

In this radio play the listener, Croak, commands one of his

servants to regale him with a verbal, the other with a musical (i.e. emotional) stream of consciousness.

(Encounter, September 1975, p. 43)

STRUCTURE

This is very straightforward. At the command of their master, the two servants perform in turn upon themes he gives them. All is not well between them, however. Croak eventually leaves, perhaps in despair provoked by the melancholy of 'Words's' words, and peace is at last restored between the two servants.

LANGUAGE

'Words's' language is deliberately 'literary' and even includes original poetry (by Beckett). Note the garbled quotation from Yeats's 'Lake Isle of Innisfree', 3 lines from the foot of p. 128. In the BBC production the 'orotund' performance of his lines by 'Words' suggests a Shakespearean rhythm of speech, perhaps akin to the Fool performing at Lear's bidding.

NOTES ON THE TEXT

[Title.] This was merely provisional when the script arrived at the BBC, but it stuck. It 'points forward, in its generic simplicity, to other neutral Beckett titles like *Play* and *Film*' (Zilliacus, *B&B*, p. 100).

p. 127

Theme . . . sloth. Professor Knowlson tells us that in the manuscript the word 'hope' occurs here.

Sloth is of all the passions . . . this is the mode in which the mind is most affected and indeed – 'Passion' and 'mode' are terms from speculative rationalist philosophy. The whole of 'Words's' declamation is a parody of philosophical writing. He is clearly 'tuning up' in his own manner, since he uses the same material on the next page.

(*Tuning dies away. Shuffling louder. Silence.*) In sound production the effect of the orchestral tuning and 'Words's' ineptitude, plus its repetition and Croak's shuffling entrance, are very humorous. Such features as this can easily be overlooked in a reading of the play, particularly where 'Music' plays an equal role to 'Words', or suggests how he might perform a given sentiment.

p. 128

By passion we are to understand a movement of the mind. In the BBC production this became a 'movement of the soul'.

and they are legion sloth is the LOVE is the most urgent. 'Words' momentarily forgets the theme of tonight's performance.

p. 129

all the cursed deadly. Sc. 'sins'.

> The numerous manuscript references to sins that flesh is heir to [are compressed] into one rather opaque phrase, 'all the cursed deadly'. The text as it stands has done away with most of the content of this moral debate; what is left is the chiselled rhetoric used to convey it.
>
> (Zilliacus, *B&B*, pp. 107–8)

MUSIC: *Long la.* This was considerably expanded in performance. 'In *Words and Music*, Music acts the pathfinding, encouraging Ariel to Words's truculent Caliban' (Zilliacus, *B&B*, p. 113).

p. 130

CROAK: *Groans.* Here, as elsewhere where Croak groans, the sound is not a simple groan but a vulgar, earthy rattle in the back of the throat, full of phlegm, disgust and despair.

p. 131

Age is when to a man. After numerous false starts, 'Words' at last recites the poem without mishap.

The face . . . The face. Cf. *Krapp's Last Tape*, p. 60 – Krapp's
memory of the nurse.

p. 132

Lily! Evidently Croak (like Krapp and like Joe in *Eh Joe*) has
some accusing figures in his past who are liable to return to
haunt him.

Mira in the Whale.

> Among the stars are several which, though no way dis-
> tinguishable from others by any apparent change of place,
> nor by any difference of appearance in telescopes, yet
> undergo a more or less regular periodical increase and dimin-
> ution of lustre, involving in one or two cases a complete
> extinction and revival. These are called periodical stars. The
> longest known and one of the most remarkable is the star
> 'Omicron' in the constellation Cetus (sometimes called Mira
> Ceti), which was first noticed as variable by Fabricius in
> 1596.
>
> (Sir John F. W. Herschel, *Outlines of Astronomy*, p. 597)

p. 133

Then down a little way. This time 'Words's' verse emerges
smoothly from his prose; but he still takes a little while to recite
the poem without hitch.

p. 134

My Lord! (*Sound of club let fall.*) '[This] indicate[s] that the
memory of fleeting fulfilment, "one glimpse of the well-head",
has silenced Croak in total despair' (Martin Esslin, *Encounter*,
p. 43). Clas Zilliacus (who sees more erotic significance than
most critics do in the text generally) offers a rather different interpretation: 'Croak leaves the scene because his artists are
moving beyond the prescribed confines of their art into more
dangerous territory. The fare they are offering is, in fact, getting rather too rich' (*B&B*, p. 111).

ROUGH FOR RADIO   I

Written originally in French late in 1961.

First publication in English   *Stereo Headphones*, 7 (Spring 1976), pp. 3–7; collected in *Ends and Odds* (New York, Grove Press, 1976).

At the time of writing there are no plans for radio production. Beckett's attitude is that the play has been overtaken by *Cascando*, which it formally resembles rather closely. The text calls for no other comment than that a Turkoman (p. 109) comes from Turkestan, and that 'breech' (p. 111) reflects 'a typically Beckettian anomaly signifying unwillingness to be born; cf. the player flung backwards on stage in *Act Without Words I*' (Zilliacus, *B&B*, p. 121).

CASCANDO

Written in French in 1962 at the suggestion of the Romanian-French composer Marcel Mihalovici, whose music for *Cascando* is his opus 86.

First publication in English   *Evergreen Review* (New York), May–June 1963

First broadcast   13 October 1963, ORTF, France Culture, directed by Roger Blin, who also played Opener; Voice was played by Jean Martin

First broadcast in English   6 October 1964, BBC Third Programme. The BBC broadcast (described by the announcer as 'a meditation for radio by Samuel Beckett') followed a text intermediate between that printed in the *Evergreen Review* and that published by Faber and Faber in 1964; see Zilliacus, *B&B*, p. 123. In the BBC production, directed by Donald McWhinnie, Patrick Magee played Voice and Denys Hawthorne Opener.

RECEPTION

Although it has been little mentioned since, *Cascando* did attract some attention at the time of its first broadcast. P. N. Furbank, writing in the *Listener* (15 October 1964), conceded that it would make little sense to anyone who had not followed the previous stages of Beckett's development, but asked: 'Isn't that rather unusual at the moment, to find an author whose development matters?' He continued: 'This work of genius is about the impossibility of *not* writing, of not telling oneself stories.' John Holmstrom was also quite enthusiastic: 'The flavour, the whole quality that makes his despair bearable and even lively, lies in the words, that inimitable partnership of misery, music-hall and the English prose tradition' (*New Statesman*, 16 October 1964).

Cascando

DÉCOR

Beckett has finally, in this radio play, removed all specificity from the sonic décor. The play could take place anywhere – or nowhere. Moreover, the notion of sonic control by the protagonist is carried one stage further than in *Embers*.

DRAMATIS PERSONAE

Whereas Croak was a kind of shabby impresario, Opener's voices are in his head and he gives the impression of a creator having difficulties in creating. This is much more evident in the BBC production than from a reading of the text. Opener is a kind of technician, opening channels and closing them off, and thus seems to represent the artist attempting to control his medium and its material (cf. 'it's in his head', top of p. 140). Katharine Worth comments:

> Much of the interest in *Cascando* is centred on the vain attempts the Opener makes to keep remote from the story it is his function to open; he ends by being drawn in but never ceases to be perplexed by the power he has to open.
>
> (*IDE*, pp. 252–3)

As in *Words and Music*, 'Music' becomes a character in his own right, capable of acceleration and softness, of pausing and expressing despair. In production, Zilliacus shows, wind instruments are the 'main providers of melodic content' (*B&B*, p. 132). As a complement to this, Voice is orchestrated and, in the performance of its 'low, panting' and staccato quality, puts a greater emphasis on this factor than on the linear development of the inconsequential story. In contrast to those of *Words and Music*, who remain unreconciled, the characters here seem to have some degree of unity; they 'link arms' in a doomed attempt to pin down Woburn, the subject of Voice's story, who is curiously like O in *Film* or Macmann in *Malone Dies*. His name, Clas Zilliacus suggests, conveys the idea of a 'woe-burnt' existence (*B&B*, p. 129).

STRUCTURE

The three 'characters' either alternate or work together; the form of the play is patent from even a rapid glance at the text, and it is in any case explained by Opener.

LANGUAGE

The panted 'story' of Voice is set out very like the statement of the speaker in *Not I*, or the accusing words in *Eh Joe*.

NOTES ON THE TEXT

[Title.]

> Perhaps to avoid confusion [with a poem of 1936, 'Cascando'], Beckett's first title was *Calando*, a musical term meaning 'diminishing in tone' (equivalent to *diminuendo* or *decrescendo*). It was changed when it was pointed out by RTF officials that 'calendeau' was slang for '[Camembert] cheese' in French.
>
> (Federman and Fletcher, Samuel Beckett, p. 70)

Cascando itself is a musical term meaning 'falling tone' and is thus appropriate for a play about 'dying away'.

p. 137

It is the month of May. Such allusions to a lost world are ironical. Cf. Winnie's humorous allusions to the 'old style' in *Happy Days*. See also p. 141, where the word 'reawakening' is added; 'May, as Malone mused [*Three Novels*, p. 234], is named after Maia, goddess of increase' (Zilliacus, *B&B*, p. 124).

I open. Inevitably this has caused speculation amongst critics as to what is opened – Opener operating a tape recorder, opening his ears, opening the doors of a lunatic asylum, tuning into a radio. All such interpretations are misleading, seeking a concrete explanation, whereas to Opener himself such details are 'an image, like any other' (p. 143). Such interpretation also does disservice to the work as orchestration and meditation. It is, however, worth remembering the use of 'open' in technical jargon as 'opening a channel'.

story ... if you could finish it. Cf. the closing words of the

Unnamable, another Beckettian hero who is chasing hopelessly the 'last' words of an impossible-to-end fiction:

> I'll go on, you must say words, as long as there are any, until they find me, until they say me, strange pain, strange sin, you must go on, perhaps it's done already, perhaps they have said me already, perhaps they have carried me to the threshold of my story, before the door that opens on my story, that would surprise me, if it opens, it will be I, it will be the silence, where I am, I don't know, I'll never know, in the silence you don't know, you must go on, I can't go on, I'll go on.
>
> (*Three Novels*, p. 418)

Cf. Clas Zilliacus's comment: 'instead of focusing on a story, [*Cascando*] focuses on the storytelling condition' (*B&B*, p. 143).

And I close. In the BBC production Voice's words were not cut off when interrupted by Opener but the actor dropped his voice. Unfortunately this undermined the notion of abrupt opening and closing, controlled by Opener. In the lack of any specific directions as to pace, Voice was generally slow in this production.

p. 138
boreen. Anglo-Irish word meaning a lane or narrow road.

(*Silence*.) The sequence here is as before (Voice solo, Music solo, Voice and Music together) but without explicit instructions from Opener – he can control without verbalizing.

pp. 139–40
It's my life . . . I open and close. The central dilemma of Opener and the artist – there are voices and sounds in his head that others cannot hear and the artist can only release them, not seek to express or interpret them.

p. 140
Full strength. I.e. full volume.

p. 141

no tiller ... no thwarts ... no oars. Woburn, like the hero of the short story 'The End' (1946), drifts out to sea to certain death in an open boat. This is a powerful dramatic image: it occurs in a number of places, for example, at the end of Ingmar Bergman's film *Shame*.

p. 143

As though they had linked their arms. 'They' are Voice and Music.

p. 144

Woburn ... he clings on ... come on ... come on – For some reason the BBC production stops the music after 'he clings on' which makes 'come on ... come on' seem to refer to the music. This was surely not Beckett's intention: in the text music and voice continue together to the end. Voice's plea should surely not be aimed at Music, but at Woburn and the *inability to end*. As Kristin Morrison puts it, 'Like the snake that swallows itself, this radio drama tries to use its own sound to bring about a final silence' (*Canters and Chronicles*, p. 119).

ROUGH FOR RADIO   II

Written first in French in the early 1960s, perhaps c. 1962.
Ruby Cohn thinks it may even predate *Rough for Radio I* (*Just
Play*, p. 283 n. 10).

First publication in English   Grove Press, New York, 1976, in
    Ends and Odds
First broadcast in English   13 April 1976, BBC Radio 3, as
    'Rough for Radio', as part of the events to celebrate Beck-
    ett's 70th birthday. Stenographer was played by Billie
    Whitelaw, Fox by Patrick Magee, Animator by Harold
    Pinter and Dick by Michael Deacon. The play was pro-
    duced and directed by Martin Esslin.

RECEPTION

Writing in the *Listener* (22 April 1976) Alex Hamilton called the
play a 'trouvaille', but did not much appreciate its 'Arctic
draughts homing ... from every speaker'.

DÉCOR, ETC.

The technical aspects of this play are neither particularly
remarkable nor innovatory, though the inclusion of a mute
character in the cast list of a work for radio is unusual to say the
least. (In the BBC production Dick substantiated his presence
by a grunt as he wielded the bull-whip or 'pizzle'.) The interest
of the play resides in its involvement with traditional consider-
ations of radio drama such as indication of character through
voice and tone. In the BBC production the voice of Animator is
educated and authoritative to the point of arrogance, but is subject to lapses into a romantic tone. The Stenographer sounds
absurdly pert and well organized and only occasionally loses the
cool composure of an efficient personal secretary. Patrick
Magee's Fox is a voice one associates with *the* persona of
Beckett's radio drama, a remote voice that is wavering and

inconsequential, otherworldly in its relationship to the voices that surround it and command it to speak.

A further interesting aspect of this piece is that instead of presenting the listener with something that he must ponder, the play itself is someone pondering on a testimony and its meaning. As we have pointed out elsewhere in this book, audience reflects play. The Animator is a critic/investigator/interpreter who orders and admonishes his secretary while clearly fancying her. His investigation of Fox is painful rather than painstaking as he pains him physically for no purpose. If there is more than a suggestion of the critic/academic making the life of the author unpleasant, and perhaps there is, we are also given a reply in the satiric portrait of the Animator who is verbose, given to cliché, adept at literary allusion, proud of what he considers a poetic turn of phrase ('so sibilant'), and of a philosophic turn of mind. He refers to spectres from the days of book reviewing, and is clearly a person who assumes that the theories he puts forward with false modesty are authoritative although they convey nothing. Most damning of all, however, is his willingness to insert a new sentence in Fox's testimony so that it fits into his theory and he can be done with the business that he is responsible for in the first place (hence 'Animator') but is clearly not very interested in exploring diligently.

NOTES ON TEXT

p. 115
The plugs. Earplugs. In the BBC production they popped loudly when extracted from Fox's ears.

p. 116
per buccam. By way of mouth.

Mauthner. Fritz Mauthner (1849–1923) was perhaps the first philosopher to investigate systematically ordinary language and the philosophical problems raised by it; his major work, *Contributions Towards a Critique of Language*, dates from 1902.

crabbed youth. The usual phrase is 'crabbed age' and comes from Shakespeare's *Passionate Pilgrim*, xii.

p. 118

There all sigh, I was, I was. Beckett is struck by the fact that souls in Dante's *Purgatorio* habitually look back on their past life ('*Io fui*' being something of a refrain) instead of looking forward joyfully to Paradise as one might expect. Cf. Beatrice, Dante's great love and the poet's guide in Paradise, who is mentioned on p. 122.

p. 119

Sterne. Laurence Sterne (1713–1768), author of the comic novel *Tristram Shandy*, was the grandson of Richard Sterne, Archbishop of York.

p. 120

in milk. Able to give suck to a baby.

p. 121

Peter out in the stones. See note to *Waiting for Godot*, p. 44. 'Tied' immediately afterwards also recalls *Godot*, of course.

p. 122

micaceous schists. See COED; 'micaceous' is the adjective of 'mica'.

fodient. Digging, burrowing.

or some other part. A bawdy innuendo.

PLAY

Written in English late 1962–3.

First publication   *Theater Heute* (Hanover), July 1963, in the
    German translation, by Erika and Elmar Tophoven, *Spiel*
First publication in English   Faber and Faber, London, 1964,
    in a volume with two radio plays, *Words and Music* and
    Cascando
First performance   14 June 1963, Ulmer Theater, Ulm-
    Donau, [*Spiel*], directed by Deryk Mendel
First British production   7 April 1964, Old Vic Theatre,
    London, National Theatre Company, with Rosemary
    Harris (w1), Billie Whitelaw (w2) and Robert Stephens,
    directed by George Devine

RECEPTION

As the first Beckett play to be given its British première at the
National Theatre, *Play* received plenty of attention from the
critics and a little more warmth than did the Ulm world première. *The Times*'s correspondent commented on the latter as a
'depressing no-man's land of the after-life' (24 June 1963),
although Barbara Bray, writing in the *Observer* (16 June), noted
'Beckett's inventiveness, formal mastery and poetic power'. By
the following year the enthusiasm increased. Harold Hobson
appreciated the *da capo* repetition: 'All in the story that had
seemed vague becomes sharp and clear. The incidents stand
out: only the emotions – the sadness, the compassion, and the
pain – are still beyond computation' (*Sunday Times*, 12 April
1964). Laurence Kitchin suggested that the play communi-
cated like 'tightly compressed chamber music' on a subliminal
level (the *Listener*, 30 April). But the usual criticism was still to
be read: The *Times Educational Supplement* saw the play as only
an 'amusing technical exercise' (15 May), and Bamber
Gascoigne saw it as a further stage in 'the gradual desiccation
and boxing-in' for which Beckett's theatre is notorious. The

Daily Express even headlined its notice as 'The Three Faces of Beckett's Contempt'.

DÉCOR

This is reduced to three identical urns, a head protruding from each, and a moving light. Given the simplicity and detailed directions of the text, it is surprising how frequently these seem to be taken as indications of what is desired rather than being obeyed to the letter. For example, the production photographed on the cover of the first Faber edition has bulky urns; Beckett specifies at length that they are not to be bulky and even supplies a number of technical alternatives (p. 159); moreover, these urns are neither 'identical' nor 'touching' as specified (p. 147); they are fully lit, whereas Beckett specifies 'just discernible' and 'spotlight projected on faces alone' (p. 147), and the faces are not noticeably 'so lost to age and aspect as to seem almost part of the urns' (p. 147). Far more satisfactory is the photograph of the National Theatre production (see Fletcher and Spurling, *Beckett*, plate 7), where the faces are encrusted with the same decay as the urns, a production addition approved by Beckett but never specifically incorporated into the text. This is not simply a matter of attention to detail: it is argued below that *Play* is a matter of situation rather than meaning and communication, and the situation *is* as presented in the text. Alteration of this situation does not therefore only give rise to further misinterpretation but changes the very substance of the play. And the substance of *Play* is a stage area in almost complete darkness, with speech from the fixed heads provoked by a light 'at close quarters and from below' (p. 158), a light of varying intensity, voice volume being in ratio to the strength of the light. Beckett indicates that this spotlight is 'expressive of a unique inquisitor', and that even when all three faces are lit simultaneously the light 'should be as a single spot branching into three' (p. 158). This 'merciless interrogator', the spotlight, has a Yeatsian ancestor in *Purgatory*, known to be one of Beckett's favourite plays:

> Like the light at the window of Yeats's ghostly house it is a palpable force in the action, stirring the trapped characters

into an obsessive replay of their past drama, a 'dreaming back', in the Yeatsian phrase it is so natural to use of Beckett's characters also.

(Worth, *IDE*, pp. 253–4)

DRAMATIS PERSONAE

Faceless faces in many ways, the characters have no names but are reduced to digits: W1, W2, M, where M = Man and W = Woman. It is often assumed that M and W1 are husband and wife and W2 M's mistress, although this is not expressly stated in the text. However it is quite clear that Beckett had adapted for his own purposes a literary cliché – the eternal triangle – and is doing to the Feydeau farce in this play what he does with circus and music-hall routines in *Waiting for Godot*. There is enough evidence in the narrative sequences to establish their former (past tense) characters, though this is in sharp and ironic contrast to the situation which now faces them and us (present tense). All three are typecast as fairly wealthy, upper middle class. W1 'has means' and thinks of 'a little jaunt to celebrate, to the Riviera or to our darling Grand Canary' (p. 150). She has time to sit 'stricken in the morning room' (p. 149), and hires a private detective when she thinks M is being unfaithful to her. W2, too, sits in the drawing room, sewing or doing her nails, and employs a servant, Erskine. Both ladies love green tea and show a coyness about sexual matters, but W1, in particular, becomes uncouth when talking about the other woman: 'I began to smell her off him again' and 'Calves like a flunkey' (pp. 150–1). W2's breeding is perhaps a little more thoroughly aristocratic and her spite more refined and consciously superior: 'I understood why he preferred me' (p. 148) or 'Who he, I said filing away, and what it?' (p. 150). M, for his part, has convenient 'professional commitments' (p. 150) and is capable of great deceit ('God what vermin women. Thanks to you, angel, I said' – (p. 151), swearing he truly loves both women. He has an inflated impression of his own prowess and is a coward, weakly confessing and then unable to cope with the consequences. But in the situation that confronts them and us, these previously separate identities have been eroded so that they now occupy identical urns, speak in similar tones, each

'lost to age and aspect'. Perhaps minor traces of character differentiation remain: WI seems more concerned and hysterical
concerning her position; W2 assumes she will escape hers by a
breakdown, and M fantasizes and analyses the situation. But
these are all mere words, compelled by the light: their situation
betrays this possibility and they are the mere ciphers of the cast
list, without movement, expression, tone, props, costume or
background. There is nothing but the weight of their situation
and the experience of the present.

STRUCTURE

The narrative outline that the three separate testimonies indicate is as follows: WI suspected M of being unfaithful to her; WI
had 'a scene' with W2; WI became ill and threatened suicide; M
confessed and asked forgiveness; WI returned to W2 to gloat
over her victory, but unknown to her the affair continued; WI
again became suspicious; M agreed to go away with W2 but 'finally it was all too much'. At this point the testimony becomes
obscure: M, it seems, 'disappeared'. And at this juncture the
narrative changes from the past to the present, and among
much anguished reflection on the characters' present situation a
few further narrative details of the affair become apparent: WI
thinks M has gone away with W2; W2 thinks M has deserted her
for WI. M imagines that WI and W2 are now friends in their
sorrow, exchanging happy memories of him! The audience can
see that none of these beliefs can be sustained: each of the trio is
isolated with endlessly repeated questions and imaginings that
can never be answered or brought to fruition as they remain in
the present, in the present tense, in the situation as it is.

Martin Esslin tells us that when Beckett heard a playback of
an experimental radio adaptation of *Play*, he was driven to
explain how he saw the work in order to defend his dislike of
what had been done. Esslin's recollection of his explanation was
this:

> The text fell into three parts: *Chorus* (all characters speaking
> simultaneously); *Narration* (in which the characters talk
> about the events which led to the catastrophe); and *Medi-*
> *tation* (in which they reflect on their state of being endlessly

suspended in limbo). These three parts are repeated, and the play ends, as it began, with the Chorus. But, Beckett explained, there must be a clear progression by which each subsection is both faster and softer than the preceding one. If the speed of the first Chorus is 1 and its volume 1, then the speed of the first Narration must be 1 plus 5 per cent and its volume 1 minus 5 per cent. The speed of the following segment, the first Meditation, must then be (1 plus 5 per cent) plus 5 per cent, and its volume (1 minus 5 per cent) minus 5 per cent. The implication is quite clearly that any quantity plus or minus still has to be a finite quantity; however soft, however fast, the same text will go on *ad infinitum*, even faster and even softer without quite ceasing altogether.

(*Encounter*, September 1975, p. 44)

LANGUAGE AND DRAMATIC EXPRESSION

The moving spot provokes speech, and as response is immediate, there is a semblance of dialogue. It is rapidly apparent, however, that there is no attempt to communicate, no semblance of intentional verbal contact between the three characters, but rather three separate monologues controlled by the moving spotlight. The three characters relate in their monologues firstly a series of events in which they seem to have once been interdependent (in dialogue, as it were), and secondly their concern with their present situation. Unaware of one another throughout, each suffers his own thoughts (in monologue); but perhaps 'suffering' only in so far as the play writes in 'suffering' – that is to say that, although the light interrupts them by moving on mid-narrative, mid-sentence, and even mid-word, forcing them to backtrack in an attempt to make coherent statements, the backtracks too are written in, and the light is simply switching on and off a tape loop that includes repetition. In this respect it controls the 'play' button of the tape recorder, and this may well be another ambiguity of the title *Play*. The spotlight provokes language as an inquisitor, but this does not mean that it is demanding answers or even communication. Beckett changed an earlier stage direction from 'At every solicitation a pause of about one second before utterance is achieved except where a longer delay is indicated', which would suggest question, into 'The response to light is immediate' (p. 147), which suggests automation. This 'light-inquisitor' does not follow any set pattern of questioning, nor insist on coherence or continuity of the point under discussion, and in the repeat section no new information comes to light, but the light continues to move as before. The variations and deviations permitted by Beckett (p. 160) even include a changed order of speeches 'as far as this is compatible with unchanged continuity for actors', which again suggests that the light provokes speech without seeking to acquire meaning or information from it. And this situation *is* the play.

It is important to remember throughout any reading of *Play* that it is a further essential of the production that 'faces [are] impassive throughout' (p. 147); 'voices toneless except where an expression is indicated' (only four places in the whole text: italicized 'I', pp. 147 and 157; 'Vehement', p. 16 of the first edition only; and 'Hopefully', p. 156); and that pace of delivery is 'rapid tempo throughout' (p. 147). Also that when the spotlight is faint on all three faces, the voices are 'largely unintelligible' (p. 147), and that a permitted variation in the repeat section is 'breathless quality in voices from beginning of Repeat I and increasing to end of play' (p. 160). These restrictions on dramatic delivery add to the mechanically compulsive situation of speaking at the expense of communicating the cliché-ridden details of the affair. Beckett's emphasis on the aural fabric of the play is also indicated by his careful orchestration of the *chorus*, which is divided into something approaching musical bars in the additional notes (p. 159), and by the brief variations and highlights to the continuous verbalization of volume and silence; by W2's wild laugh (p. 147 'faint', p. 157 twice, both times cut short), and by M's hiccups (pp. 148, 151 and 154).

NOTES ON TECHNICAL ASPECTS OF THE
1976 ROYAL COURT PRODUCTION
Royal Court Theatre, London, 19 May (preview) to 19 June 1976, with *That Time* and *Footfalls*

W1	Anna Massey
W2	Penelope Wilton

Play

M   Ronald Pickup
Light operated by Duncan M. Scott
Directed by Donald McWhinnie

The fact that the programme has the unusual credit 'Light operated by' emphasizes the degree to which this play depends on a technical device. In this particular production the manipulation of the light was superb, and though it would be unfair to say the light 'makes' the play (it would not do justice to the split-second timing required of the actors), it would be true to say that the lasting image in this play is the sudden appearance and disappearance of the heads caught in the light, rather than the words they say. The light does not even sweep from one to another and so gives no warning to head or audience of approach, and the result resembles the ducks on a fairground rifle range, which pop up and disappear before you have time to take proper aim. And it is partly for this reason that the exact repetition of the play is so effective. The text of the play on its first rendering sports a great deal of comedy, especially in the first half, but these voices do not obey the cardinal rule of pausing for laughter, with the result that lines are 'lost'. But towards the end of the play jokes are scarce (the exceptions being 'Lipton's' and 'Par . . . don'), and when the whole play is repeated the inconsequential details of gossip that were savoured the moment before become stale and turn sour, the situation rapidly becomes clear to anyone who has not grasped it up to this point, and, as the 'jokes' run out, and with them the lines that were 'lost', so the audience is subjected to a greater amount of repetition, with a corresponding increase in their discomfort. It is by this point that the mood in the auditorium had changed from an inquisitive and relaxed atmosphere associated with comedy to a concentrated silence and tension associated with tragedy; and it is then that the basic themes of the endless voices, the lack of contact, pathetic details that seem to be the sum total of humanity, and a ruthless inquisitor and controller became paramount. Laughter decreased as realization increased that the jokes that hid the situation as it was were thin. Commenting on the same production, Professor Worth writes:

The production at the Royal Court in 1976 brought out with special vivacity [*Play*'s] droll comedy; the first time round was extraordinarily funny. Repeated, the selfsame lines and comic noises, like the hiccup, took on new seriousness, as they had to – it was a remarkable change of mood – but through it all, the sense of witty control remained: a great part of the pleasure was just this delicate balance between the impression of obsessed unawareness and humorous self-consciousness.

(*IDE*, p. 254)

NOTES ON THE TEXT

[Title.] This has many connotations and associations: (i) a play; (ii) an amusing pastime; (iii) free movement; (iv) play button of a tape recorder; (v) music; (vi) toying; (vii) difficulty of differentiating between reality and illusion (cf. p. 153, l. 17).

p. 147
(*Front centre, touching one another*.) This is now the only contact between M, W1 and W2. In *Endgame* Nagg's and Nell's dustbins are also just touching one another.

p. 148
I said to him, Give her up. The first of a great number of clichés in this testimony section. Cf. 'she burst in and flew at me', 'smelled the rat', 'made a clean breast of it', 'bygones bygones', and many others. The characters often repeat similar banalities – e.g. W2 in the following speech relates 'Give him up.' Variation and repetition of words and phrases assist the unity of the fragmented narrative and help the listener to make some sort of coherent story of the details.

(*hiccup*). Perhaps a music-hall hint to suggest that he drinks, although there is nothing else to reveal him as an alcoholic. Certainly it undercuts his metaphysical pretensions.

Though I had him dogged for months. This is perhaps a rather laboured joke since it is extended also by the detective's being called a 'bloodhound' and by W1's claim of smelling W2 off M: 'he stinks of bitch' (p. 148).

And there was no denying that he continued as . . . assiduous as ever. A coy reference to M's sexual capabilities.

p. 149

Fearing she was about to offer me violence. W2's aristocratic-legal words are in comic contrast to W1's slang.

I rang for Erskine. Cf. *Watt*, where there is an Irish manservant of the same name.

And of course with him no danger of the . . . spiritual thing. Cf. 'his horror of the merely Platonic thing' (p. 148).

p. 150

I could hear a mower. An old hand mower. An apt detail, mentioned by both W2 and M, and serving to link their testimony.

p. 151

The problem was how to convince her that no . . . revival of intimacy was involved. M's hesitation would suggest that he, too, is coy over sexual matters. The intimacy referred to is, of course, with W1.

On the way back by Ash and Snodland. Commuter-belt towns in Kent, fairly near to London.

All night I smelt them smouldering. This rather poetic image closes the narrative section. It has, of course, associations with cremation and urns, and is an ironic end to the 'animal scent' associations of M's sexuality.

p. 152

When first this change. Change to fainter light.

Or you will weary of me. W1 is addressing the light.

At the same time I prefer this to . . . the other thing. Like several of the comments, this one is applicable both to the narrated story and the present situation.

p. 153
You might get angry and blaze me clean out of my wits. W2 expects or hopes that the situation will unbalance her. Cf. 'a little unhinged already' (p. 156), and M's thought that continual light might cause him to rave (p. 156).

So it must be something I have to say. W1's desperate craving for peace and her desire to attain it by speaking the truth (p. 153), saying the right thing (p. 153), and penitence (p. 156), can never be realized in the present, and it parallels the likely failure of the audience in trying to find a true meaning in the situation. 'There is no sense in this . . . either, none whatsoever,' she comments (p. 154). As seen here, these concerns, certain failure, and the manner of phrasing suggests an early genesis of Beckett's later play *Not I*, where Mouth is unwillingly compelled to verbalize the same insoluble problems without pause.

p. 154
over a cup of that green tea they both so loved. Unfermented tea, roasted immediately after gathering, usually China tea. Cf. 'Personally I always preferred Lipton's' (p. 154); this is Ceylon tea.

Is anyone looking at me? Cf. M: 'Am I as much as . . . being seen?' (p. 157). A reminder of Bishop Berkeley's dictum *esse est percipi* which is central to *Film* (q.v.).

That poor creature – W2 is imagining how W1 refers to her.

p. 155
What do you do when you go out? Sift? Sift the testimonies, presumably. The notion that 'going out' is not an end or rest, but the beginning of a tiresome process of going over and over the same ground, is reinforced.

p. 156

Never woke together, on a May morning, the first to wake to wake the other two. Then in a little dinghy – These are M's fantasies of reconciliation between all three of them.

Penitence, yes. Cf. *The Unnamable, passim.*

they lolling on air-pillows in the stern . . . sheets. Stern sheets are seats for passengers in the stern of a rowing boat. Why the hesitation? Is it a joke about bed sheets, or linguistic hesitation caused by mental decay, such as Krapp experiences?

p. 157

(*Peal of wild low laughter from* W2.) 'This laughter is in shattering contrast to the swift, expressionist tempo of the past quarter of an hour' (Reid, *All I can Manage*, p. 43).

Mere eye. No mind. The light. Cf. *Film.*

p. 158

M: *We were not long together* – The play stops short of a third repeat quite deliberately: as in *Godot*, once would have been too little to establish the theme, three times would have laboured the point about the potential for infinity implicit in the dramatic situation. Unlike *Godot*, however, the play *is* repeated exactly; this underlines the dreary banality of the adulterous episode, because the jokes about it are less funny when heard a second time.

FILM

Written in English, April 1963, *Film* was commissioned for Evergreen Theater, New York.

First publication   Faber and Faber, London, 1967, with
    Eh Joe

It was filmed in New York in the summer of 1964 and first shown publicly in the summer of 1965 at the New York Film Festival. It provided Buster Keaton, the greatest comedian of the silent screen, with one of his last roles, for he died soon afterwards. The published text is merely a tentative working scenario for the use of a director and is not a dramatic work in its own right. The film itself runs for 24 minutes.

RECEPTION

The audience at the first showing booed *Film*, and the director, Alan Schneider, tells us that the American critics either 'clobbered or ignored it'. One critic called it 'vacuous and pretentious', and no one understood the message *esse est percipi*. Once shown in Europe at various film festivals, it attracted critical interest and won several prizes. British reviews followed the same pattern: 'personally I think *Film* is a load of old bosh' (*Sunday Times*, 21 November 1965), was Dilys Powell's comment. But echoing the awards of the film festivals, the British magazine *Film* (Winter 1965–6) wrote of a 'strange and haunting experience' provoked by 'a work more closely approximating to the definition of film as an art than we have seen for a long time'. Schneider tells us that after the first showing to the general public in New York in 1968, there were generally favourable reviews, and undoubtedly it has now established a better position in the *oeuvre* among Beckett devotees.

This has been helped by David Clark's remake of 1979, with Max Wall as O, produced by the British Film Institute Production Board. Filmed on location in semi-derelict London dockland, it expands the text by using soundtrack (but with no speech, only street noises, the sound of O's breathing, and the 'sssh!' in part I specified by Beckett on p. 163) and the controlled use of colour and texture to distinguish the viewpoints of E and O (but which failed to do so as unambiguously as the director hoped). There was also a musical accompaniment (flute), an arrangement of Schubert's song 'Der Doppelgänger'. Costumes were roughly of the 1920s, and Wall's talent for pratfalls (getting tangled in lengths of rope, tripping over his briefcase) was exploited to the full. Clark justified the remake in a note in *The Beckett Circle* (Fall 1978):

> Just as with any work, *Film* needs to be re-examined against the developments that have taken place in Samuel Beckett's theatrical style in the fifteen years since it was written. Not only that, but the text may, as published, mislead the casual scholar. There is evidence that the requirement of silence, except for one sibilant injunction, may be considered as a late emendation, more the result of the form 'taking over', rather than a structural necessity. Not only that, but there is the whole question of the use of colour. Nowhere does Samuel Beckett require that the film be made in black and white; what *is* certain is that the required images are not to be naturalistic. These considerations, then, form the basis for my new production. I am certain that the structural use of both sound and visual texture gives extra dimensions within which the comic unreality that is crucial to the feeling of the piece can be displayed. When, in May 1977, I discussed these ideas with him, Samuel Beckett gave me 'a free hand' to proceed.

Richard Cave felt that 'unlike Schneider's version, Clark's is aesthetically very beautiful to watch', but found the inclusion of a soundtrack 'oddly irritating [and] intrusive' (*Journal of Beckett Studies*, Spring 1982, pp. 135–7).

DÉCOR

This is as specified on p. 164 and is clearly an act of homage to the classics of the silent film. The original project was intended to last 30 minutes but the opening sequence (restored in Clark's version) was shortened and shots of street animation, cyclists and a cabman, and of an elderly couple peering at a newspaper were excluded because Beckett found them unsatisfactory on film.

Hugh Kenner explains the near soundlessness thus:

> It is established that this is a soundless world, uninvaded by acoustic space. This is established by the film's wittiest touch, the 'sssh!' which is the sole sound on the soundtrack, and posits that we are not in the silent world of the silent films which resulted from the mere unavailability of sound, but in a silent world where sound exists and one none the less hears nothing, not a footfall.
>
> (*A Reader's Guide*, p. 167)

THEME AND STRUCTURE

The protagonist's preoccupation with photographs recalls *Krapp's Last Tape*, where the 'snapshots' are aural. The second photograph (p. 173) resembles closely one taken of Beckett himself at the same age, praying at his mother's knee.

The entire work illustrates and exemplifies a tenet in philosophy (see *Notes on the text*, below); whether this is a recipe for a successful work of cinematic art is open to question. Beckett is frequently praised for his unerring exploitation of the particular facilities offered by the various media: in the case of *Film*, however, his conscious use of the medium is not wholly satisfactory and can be difficult to understand without reference to the notes. For example, the vital 45° camera angle is incomprehensible to the viewer, and, whereas in the script E determines this angle, in the film itself it seems to be O, moving unnaturally, slowly and awkwardly. Even with Keaton playing O, Beckett's direction 'O should invite laughter throughout by his way of moving' (p. 163) is rarely satisfied. The technical device of sometimes seeing through O's eyes, out of focus, is also not sufficiently prepared for and can be confusing. 'That look' (p. 169), an 'agony of perceivedness' (p. 165), is almost impossible to realize in concrete visual terms, and is liable to varied misinterpretation by an audience. Perhaps even the central point that 'It will not be clear until end of film that pursuing perceiver is not extraneous, but self' (p. 163) remains obscure to many viewers.

Beckett was partially aware of the difficulties and also of the possibility of overloading the film with intention and meaning (see his introductory comment on p. 163 and his note 8) and, in filming, the original project was greatly simplified. It is evident, however, that all the problems were not solved. Nor were they by David Clark. In either version, the film is not easy to watch, nor even cinematically very interesting once the first sequences are over and the camera is confined to limited movements within the room.

NOTES ON THE TEXT

p. 163

Esse est percipi. 'To be (exist) is to be perceived' (Lat.). This dictum forms the basis of the epistemology of Berkeley (see *Waiting for Godot*, notes to pp. 44 and 91, above). According to his theory the universe is maintained in existence only by virtue of God's continued perception of it.

p. 166

Side by side on floor a large cat and small dog. Schneider tells us that by the time filming reached this sequence Buster Keaton was in his element. Before that he made no effort to disguise his general bafflement and thought the script unclear and unfunny, although he was at the same time co-operative on the set (*Film* [complete scenario], p. 81).

COME AND GO

Written in English, early 1965, based on an earlier draft entitled 'Good Heavens' and inscribed 'for John Calder'.

First publication   Les Editions de Minuit, Paris, 1966, as *Va et Vient*

First publication in English   Calder and Boyars (the dedicatee's firm), London, 1967

First performance   14 January 1966, Schiller-Theater Werkstatt, Berlin, in the German translation, *Kommen und Gehen*, by Elmar Tophoven, directed by Deryk Mendel, in a triple bill with *Act Without Words II* and *All That Fall*

First production in English   28 February 1968, Peacock Theatre, Dublin, directed by Edward Golden

First British production   9 December 1968, Royal Festival Hall, London

RECEPTION

There is general critical approval for this slight piece; it is 'a beautiful, delicate, decorous work' according to Kenner (*A Reader's Guide*, p. 174), 'a fragile piece in a minor key' (Worth, in *Beckett*, p. 205), and a 'simple, yet moving little play' (Knowlson, *Frescoes*, p. 122), but real enthusiasm is lacking.

DÉCOR

This is extremely simple, stark and straightforward. See Beckett's very explicit production notes pp. 196–7. Professor Knowlson comments: 'Beckett concentrates as much upon the dress, voices and movements of the three women characters, and especially the distinctive manner in which they hold hands, as upon the spare vocabulary of the dialogue' (*SBaE*, p. 94). The fact that we cannot see what the women are sitting on gives them a slight air of unreality, as though they are suspended.

LANGUAGE

The three figures are 'apart from colour differentiation as alike as possible' (p. 196). This is reflected in their language, which follows a set pattern but avoids exact repetition, e.g. Flo: 'God grant not'; Ru: 'God forbid'; Vi: 'Please God not.' Even their 'Oh's' are differentiated (see p. 197). The three characters are similar and yet each has individuality that becomes a part of the formal, unified structure. One must not forget the importance of the long silences and of those words – the explanations of misfortune – that the audience does not hear. 'Words seem to represent something of an intrusion into the silence that constantly threatens to become the dominant reality' (Knowlson, *Frescoes*, p. 123).

NOTES ON THE TEXT

[Title.] Hugh Kenner sees 'an unstated epigraph by Eliot: "In the room the women come and go/Talking of Michelangelo"' (*A Reader's Guide*, p. 174). This title could suggest birth and death as well as the specific movements of the characters; it may also echo the words of Ps. 121: 8.

p. 191

A dramaticule. A Beckett neologism, chosen for its wry appropriateness, and meaning 'little play' or 'playlet'.

p. 193

Characters. Note the rather old-fashioned first names, Flo[ra]/[rence], Vi[olet] and Ru[by], which go well with the hats and long coats. Moreover, 'they resemble in appearance the three mothers in Fritz Lang's *M*, a film much loved by Beckett' (Knowlson, *Frescoes*, p. 122).

p. 194

When did we three last meet? No doubt an ironic allusion to Shakespeare's three witches in *Macbeth*. At the same time,

the banal situation of two women gossiping darkly about a

third not present has been transformed in *Come and Go* into a miniature dramatic piece of considerable formal beauty by means of a stylization of dress, movement, gesture and language that brings Beckett closer perhaps to the theatre of W. B. Yeats than at any other time in his plays, except for the ritualistic opening of *Endgame*.

(Knowlson, *Frescoes*, p. 123)

(*Appalled.*)

The appalled response of the one receiving the news indicates clearly enough that the gossip concerns the imminent death of the friend who has just left them, giving them the opportunity for this exchange of dark confidences. [The] earlier, and much longer, version of the play, entitled 'Good Heavens', had, much less successfully, made this more explicit, even spelling out the terminal date of the third friend's incurable ailment: 'Three months. At the outside ... Not a suspicion. She thinks it is heartburn.' The unspoken nature of the condemnation in the final version is more powerful precisely because it is less explicit. For while it leaves a mystery unresolved, it also tends to lead one beyond the particular illness of an individual woman to embrace the fate of all mankind.

(Knowlson, *Frescoes*, pp. 121–2)

p. 195

Dreaming of ... love.

The draft with the pornographic narrative ['Good Heavens'] also contains these sequences linking apparent good health to sexual activity. And there the details are presented quite explicitly. Each of the three women is terminally ill and does not know it; each one has a husband who is 'crazed with grief', or 'heartbroken', or 'weeping'; each has a lover, who apparently accounts for her radiant look; and in all three cases, both lover and illness are secrets kept from others or from the one affected. That Beckett decided to jettison this excessive symmetry along with the whole pornographic sequence was probably wise. In later versions the erotic stories, either read aloud or suggestively whispered, become simply 'dreaming of ... love', a much more neutral and romantic phrase, not competing in any way with the sense of mortality which permeates the play. Yet the hint of sexual interest remains.

By tempering the sexual explicitness and reducing the play altogether, Beckett has actually intensified the sense of loss which this 'dramaticule' conveys. In the early version, with its erotic novel used for imaginative escape (the three women deliberately focusing on 'the little death' to avoid 'the big death', eros rather than thanatos), the comic grotesque elements swamp the tragic ones. In the final version, the balance is very skilful indeed; and the balance point is precisely that element of erotic interest which began as a full-fledged narrative and has been boiled down to simple references to love and marriage. The three women are no longer leering old adulteresses; they have become cartoons. Beckett has reversed the artistic process by moving his characters from flesh (with all the luscious details of story) to sketch (where the story remains only as hint), that sure deft line with which some artists begin a picture and with which others choose to end.

(Morrison, *Canters and Chronicles*, pp. 115–16).

p. 196

(*Successive positions.*) Of the six logically possible variants involving all three characters on stage, Beckett only uses four: Flo, Vi and Ru (position numbered 1); Vi, Flo and Ru (3); Vi, Ru and Flo (5); and Ru, Vi and Flo (7).

(*Lighting. Soft, from above only and concentrated on playing area. Rest of stage as dark as possible.*) Katharine Worth points out the affinities with *Krapp's Last Tape* but remarks:

Here the ring of light is a soft and kindly thing: it holds the three women together and somehow upholds them. When each in turn goes out into the dark, the other two discuss with pity and horror the fate that threatens the absent one, but neither she nor we are allowed to know it: within the circle of light none of them is concerned with her own troubles, only with thoughts and memories of each other, sitting with clasped hands 'as in the old days', feeling invisible rings, seeming indissolubly joined in the gentle radiance of memory.

(*Beckett*, p. 205).

(*No rings apparent*.) Eugene Webb suggests that the women attempt to comfort themselves with the illusion that they are wearing engagement or wedding rings, the first 'promising the opportunity of a life to come', the second suggesting that 'they are widowed and have their wedding rings left as a testimony to the fullness of life that was once theirs' (*The Plays of Samuel Beckett*, p. 119).

EH JOE

Written in English in April–May 1965 for Jack MacGowran, the Irish actor.

First publication Faber and Faber, London, 1967, in a
    volume with 'other writings', *Act Without Words II* and
    Film
First broadcast   13 April 1966, SDR, in German, with Deryk
    Mendel and Nancy Illig, directed by Samuel Beckett
First broadcast in English 4 July 1966, BBC2. Samuel
    Beckett was one of the directors, along with Alan Gibson;
    Joe was played by Jack MacGowran and Voice by Sian
    Phillips.

RECEPTION

Once again there was little reaction from the critics, but in the
Listener J. C. Trewin described it as a 'lugubrious experience'
and criticized the scale of the work as 'almost excessively small'
(21 July 1966). Audience response was that it was 'dreary and
very dull to watch' (Zilliacus, *B & B*, p. 198). Since then, however, most people have congratulated Beckett on his success, at
first attempt, in exploiting the medium to the full.

DÉCOR

Exactly as specified on p. 201.

DRAMATIS PERSONAE

Joe, as described at the top of p. 201, hears in his head words
uttered by a woman from his past, who is both avenging and
vindictive. He, too, has similarities to Krapp; but Krapp's visi-
tation from the past is via his old tapes, whereas Joe's memories
are stored in his brain and rear up to haunt him. Beckett told a
German critic, Siegfried Melchinger, 'It is his passion to kill the
voices which he cannot kill.' The voice that haunts him is in fact
rather mechanical, like that of a tape recording.

STRUCTURE AND SITUATION

The play is punctuated by the nine moves of the camera. The situation is not only the simple one whereby the scrutinizing and inquisitorial camera represents the woman, it is also indicative of Joe's own introspection, and in this respect his preliminary precautions and his failure to appreciate the possibility of self-perception parallel the O/E dichotomy in *Film*. Of the movement of the camera, Martin Dodsworth remarks:

> The camera moves to follow Joe round the room as he locks himself into it but then confines itself to an ever more intense scrutiny of Joe's face, in ten basic movements viewing it in larger and larger close-up. Just as sound is used to emphasize the silence of *Film*, so in *Eh Joe* the mobility of the camera is used to draw attention to the way in which it is held by the sight of Joe.
>
> (In Worth, *Beckett*, pp. 170–1)

Clas Zilliacus comments for his part:

> As the camera, the viewers' eye, contents itself with merely observing, viewers are liable to put their minds to work in a similar manner. In this way we come to identify, in the course of the play, both with Joe and, via the camera, with the voice; the growing intensity both of the visual close-up and of the verbal pattern strengthens this tendency.
>
> (*B & B*, p. 191)

The fact that the camera moves only when the voice is silent has several parallels in Beckett's work. Cf. the separation of language and gesture in *Happy Days*; Mr Rooney in *All That Fall*, who cannot move and speak at the same time; and the separation of the various sounds in *Embers*. The camera could also be seen in part as representing Joe's masochism as well as his self-perception.

LANGUAGE AND DRAMATIC EXPRESSION

The voice's accusing statements resemble, formally at least, the confession in *Not I*. Notice that here the voice stops the camera and that the latter does not act as a goad like the bell in *Happy Days* and other such agents.

NOTES ON THE TEXT

p. 201

[*Directions 1–4.*] Closely paralleled by the measures taken by the protagonist of *Film*.

p. 202

Joe . . . In spite of all, his security measures have failed.

p. 203

Then your mother when her hour came . . . Like Krapp's, and Henry's in *Embers*, Joe's father has died before his mother.

That slut that comes on Saturday. Cf. Fanny in *Krapp's Last Tape*, p. 62.

Penny a hoist. Cf. 'Mrs Penny-a-hoist Pim . . . That old put' (*Watt*, p. 265).

Like those summer evenings in the Green. No doubt St Stephen's Green, Dublin's central park. Cf. 'the [*Irish*] *Independent*', p. 205.

p. 204

Your Lord.

> In early versions of *Eh Joe*, the phrase used was 'our Lord'; by changing 'our' to 'your', Beckett has allowed for the religious reference 'our Lord' unmistakably conveys as well as for the private and personal meaning of his *double entendre*.
> (Morrison, *Canters and Chronicles*, p. 103 n. 11)

The passion of our Joe . . .

> refers both to sexual arousal and to physical and spiritual suffering, with Joe here parodying the role of that God who does not love him. There is no 'Passion of Christ' in this play, no

God who gives his life out of love; only an exploitative sexual passion and painful sense of deprivation on Joe's part, and a fragile girl who commits suicide but whose death has not in any way redeemed Joe but damns him further to torment as he listens to the recital of her story.

(Morrison, Canters and Chronicles, p. 104)

'*Thou fool thy soul*'. See the parable of the rich fool (Luke 12: 13–21), which ends,

> But God said unto him, Thou fool, this night thy soul shall be required of thee: then whose shall those things be, which thou hast provided? So is he that layeth up treasure for himself, and is not rich toward God.

p. 205

The green one. Cf. *Krapp's Last Tape*, p. 58.

'*Mud thou art*'. Cf. 'For dust thou art, and unto dust shalt thou return' (Gen. 3: 19).

The importance of both the story element and the biblical associations in this play is suggested by Beckett's early notes. The word 'God' and the word 'story' are written large and each is circled, standing out alone, one above the other, toward the top of his notebook page. The biblical references to dust and to soul are also written out on this page.

(Morrison, Canters and Chronicles, p. 103 n. 10)

Sitting on the edge of her bed in her lavender slip. Note the macabre humour, mingled with pathos, of the failed attempts at suicide and its meticulous descriptions.

p. 206

Lies down in the end with her face a few feet from the tide. Another death by the seashore. Cf. *Embers*, p. 93. Note too that Joe, like Krapp, has rejected the possibility of happiness. According to Clas Zilliacus, in the Stuttgart SDR production, directed by Beckett himself,

205

A little sneer appeared on [Joe's] face, and it remained there for the fade-out. In this way, perhaps, the author created an opportunity to repudiate the undeniable sentimentality of his drama by insisting on the incurability of the old lecher . . . A more modest interpretation, and one more likely in the light of other Beckett works, would link Joe's grin to the fact that the voice seems to be relenting for the evening. He never hoped for more.

(*B & B*, p. 109)

Katharine Worth sees the end rather differently: 'The camera slowly moves in to leave the face of Joe a tragic clown's mask with a gash of mouth and pits of eyes' (*IDE*, p. 259).

BREATH

Written in English, about 1966. The piece was written (and laid aside) and only later sent to New York (rumour has it on the back of a postcard) in response to Kenneth Tynan's request for a contribution to his review *Oh! Calcutta!* in 1969; it was withdrawn at the London transfer because of Tynan's alleged failure either to respect Beckett's stage directions (which make no provision for the naked bodies that lent a rather different significance to the 'breath'), or to attribute the contribution to its author by name.

First publication   *Gambit*, vol. 4 no. 16 (1970), pp. 8–9. This was the first printing of Beckett's original text, since the previous New York publication included additions made by the producer.

First performance   16 June 1969, Eden Theater, New York, directed by Jacques Levy

First British production   October 1969, Close Theatre Club, Glasgow, directed by Geoffrey Gilham

RECEPTION

Although rumour flourished before that, the most attention was recorded after a performance at the Oxford Playhouse, 8 March 1970. Raymond Williams was not impressed, noting that he preferred to Beckett's respiratory shorthand 'one of the other life-sounds: a belly laugh' (*Listener*, 19 March 1970).

James Knowlson sums up the whole debate as follows:

Breath has either been treated too reverentially, surprising though this may seem, or has been considered a rather weak joke, unworthy of serious attention. Like most of Beckett's work it is a mixture of the comic and the serious. Beckett himself wittily described it in a version of the French translation, *Souffle*, as a 'farce in five acts'. Its humour stems largely from the way it deliberately fails to satisfy audience

expectations. It does this, of course, simply by being what it is, a 30-second play without characters and without words. Certainly, as written, it would have disappointed the audience of the erotic review, *Oh! Calcutta!*, for which it was composed ... The text is skeletal enough ... it is surely only memorable because of its *succès de scandale*. For ... however admirably shaped *Breath* may be, its dramatic interest and impact must be judged as severely limited.

If it was regarded at first by some critics as a logical terminal point in Beckett's writing for the theatre, it is now clear that its main interest is that, in the wake of *Play*, it points forward to the miniature dramas of the seventies. This is not so much because of its actual brevity, as because of its meticulous interplay of light, sound and silence, its balanced variations in lighting strength, its formal symmetry, and its use of amplified sound, adopted later in *Not I* and *Footfalls* (live) and in *That Time* (recorded).

If *Breath* has very little to add to what Beckett had already said with more resonance in his longer plays, it is worth remembering that it still has a modest part to play in the growing simplification and economy of his later drama.

(*Frescoes*, pp. 127–8)

DÉCOR AND STRUCTURE

Once again we find extreme simplicity. There are no visible characters nor audible dialogue, only recorded human sounds (cries and breaths). The changing light parallels the expanding and contracting diaphragm, suggesting a breath, a moment, a day, a life. The slow inhalation and exhalation of breath are akin to sighs.

NOTES ON THE TEXT

p. 211

Instant of recorded vagitus. The cry uttered by the human infant as it exhales its first breath haunts Beckett's mind. For him, it is a cry of pain, of lamentation, of grief, at being expelled from the warmth, safety and 'windowlessness' of the womb.

Barnard sees *Breath* as 'a stage presentation of the summary of life given by Pozzo's exit line in *Waiting for Godot*, Act II, p. 89 – "They give birth astride of a grave, the light gleams an instant, then it's night once more"' (*Samuel Beckett*, p. 100).

NOT I

Written in English, spring 1972.

First publication   Faber and Faber, London, 1973
First performance   November 1972, Forum Theater of the
    Lincoln Center, New York, as part of a Beckett Festival
First British production   16 January 1973, Royal Court
    Theatre, London, directed by Anthony Page. Beckett
    himself attended the rehearsals.

RECEPTION

The reviewers were generally very enthusiastic, greeting the
play as a new, exhilarating theatrical experience, but they were
in some doubt about why they responded so warmly to it. J. W.
Lambert described it as 'a small-hours nightmare such as we all
know' and laid stress on the importance of the listening figure
who seemed to him 'like Cro-Magnon man mourning across the
aeons' (*Sunday Times*, 21 January 1973). Harold Hobson writing in the same paper on 11 February 1973 congratulates his
colleague on emphasizing this and suggests 'that the dramatic
force of the play lies in this strange figure . . . even more than it
does in the attention-catching Mouth.' Jack Tinker spoke of
Not I as a 'new, harsh shriek of anguish' but warned that 'to
understand it and to absorb its shock one must first accept
Beckett as the poet of our modern despair'. This position is
wholeheartedly embraced by Martin Esslin, whose comment
sums up well the general enthusiasm and pious respect inspired
by these very Beckettian fifteen minutes:

> *Not I* is an immensely important work. It contains substance
> which lesser writers would have needed three or four hours
> on the stage or a 500-page novel (at least!) to encompass, and
> moulds that wealth of human suffering, a whole lifetime of
> human experience, into an image so telling, so graphic, into
> words so brilliantly meaningful, that a bare quarter of an
> hour suffices to communicate it all.
>
> (*Plays and Players*, March 1973, p. 39)

All this about a text that could not easily be followed when heard in the theatre!

DÉCOR

The tiny pinpoint of light that encircles Mouth contrasts with the less sharply lit figure of the Auditor. Both are set against total blackness so that nothing else is seen, not even the podium on which the Auditor stands. One visual effect of this is that Mouth and Auditor seem to hang in space, and it may increase the likely hallucinatory effects for a viewer concentrating on a small point of light, so that, for example, it seems to move sideways, or float, or change size and shape. The text suggests that Beckett was well aware of such effects: e.g. 'and the beam flickering on and off starting to move around' (p. 221). In performance at the Royal Court Theatre, Jack Lambert felt that the Auditor was difficult to make out at first but that the lighting gradually increased until he was visible and he congratulates the technicians and others for a 'beautifully handled lighting job'. It seems possible, however, that his eyes merely grew accustomed to the dark, because as Martin Esslin points out, the nature of the stage of the Royal Court made lighting of the Auditor difficult, if it was not to detract from the blackness surrounding Mouth.

DRAMATIS PERSONAE

There are at least three identities but only one character in *Not I*. The character is the dimly lit, mysterious, robed figure of the Auditor, so shadowy that even its sex is indeterminate. All we know of the Auditor is that he/she is 'compassionate' but 'helpless' and that his/her outward signs of this helpless compassion decrease to zero during the course of the play, but why this should be we do not know. Throughout the play Auditor is 'intent on Mouth' (p. 216), listening, we assume, and possibly fulfilling the Berkeleian role of proving Mouth's existence. In this respect, of course, he is also the cause of Mouth's existence and therefore of her anguish. In addition we may make random associations of the type noted under the section on *Language* below and see him as a religious figure, perhaps a priest at confessional (as maintained by Richard Roud in his review in the

Guardian, 24 November 1972), or perhaps a Dantean figure listening to the moanings of the Falsifiers of Words whose 'mouth is clogged with the filth that stuffs and sickens it' and who have 'the fever and a cankered brain' (*Inferno* XXX). But such allusions are strictly outside the situation of the play.

Mouth is not a character, not even a reduced one, but a manifold identity – physical mouth, brain that controls it, and as suggested by the title, a crisis of its own identity. A mouth is only the organ of speech: it is controlled by the mind. The Cartesian split between body and mind raises severe problems: the body has no feeling but the mind is still able to rave away on its own. This problem of identity therefore is not only the simple one of Mouth apparently refusing to acknowledge that the life and events described are her own. (Why should this in any way be the case? The details described by Mouth are not confessional: 'some sin or other' (p. 217) is hardly incriminating.) What is incriminating is having lived at all, having been born, having had a body and a mind, and the mind – which is producing the words that the mouth articulates – tries to avoid this burden, casting it all on to the body (the mouth) or any other third person available. The confusion of identities is most clearly seen in the pronouns of the text: not only the frequently repeated 'she' (which occurs more times than any other word except the definite article) but in the pronoun 'it'. 'It' is initially the brain: 'so it reasoned' (p. 218), 'raving away on its own' (p. 220), but also the voice: 'it was not hers at all' (p. 219), 'make it stop' (p. 220); but 'it' is also existence: 'how it was . . . how it had been' (p. 221) and the unknown solution: 'hit on it in the end' (p. 222), 'could that be it?' (p. 221). These are four of the shifting identities that issue from Mouth, and there are others implicit in the contradictions of narrative, of time, of ability, and sensibility. And by this means the text leads us to a similar situation that we are confronted with in a performance of the play: of grabbing at straws and fragments in order to establish an identity: but not our own identity, oh no: hers!

STRUCTURE

The narrative thread that study of the text reveals is briefly as follows: Mouth remembers birth of girl, deserted by parents.

Ordinary life until approaching 70. Wandering in a field, the lights went out; she could still hear buzzing and see a light. Unaware of her position. Thought she was being punished but realized she was not suffering. She felt numb but the brain was still functioning. She realized words were coming, and in time recognized her own voice, though previously she had been practically speechless, and avoided speech even when out shopping. She feared feeling was returning, but spared that. She cannot stop talking: her mouth raves, her brain reels with memories such as the occasion when she cried. She suddenly thinks she is being compelled to tell something: but what? The birth of the girl? No. How she had lived? No. Bits from her Protestant upbringing? No. No satisfactory explanation. She recalls how on occasions she would rush out to tell the nearest person, mad stuff which they could not comprehend. And now this ranting, quicker and quicker, babbling, babbling . . .

This is of course a gross simplification of the text: in effect its manifold backtracks, repetitions and variations make such narrative as there is much less obviously linear, and more a multi-dimensional process, with connections continually occurring in apparently random manner rather than logically. The dramatic structure into which this part of the process that we are permitted to see is fitted is essentially determined by the brief pauses during which the Auditor moves his arms 'in helpless compassion'. The opening section, to the first pause, lasts approximately one minute in stage time: beginning with unintelligible fragments, the Mouth is revealed to us talking about 'the typical affair' – few of these tales are ever repeated – 'till' . . . The second section, much longer (and lasting approximately 4 minutes in stage time), describes the basic situation. The length of this section is alleviated somewhat by internal division (occurring almost regularly every minute) of laughter (p. 217), laughter again (p. 217) and screams (p. 218). There is no alleviation in the third section, even longer (approximately 5 minutes), in which she realizes 'words were coming', is subjected to the continual stream, and begs it all to stop. The most desperate anguish is apparent in the next, shorter section ($1\frac{1}{2}$ minutes approximately) and continues into the fifth section of the same length which ends with the climactic 'SHE!' Thereafter only a few repeated fragments are heard and the voice fades again into unintelligibility.

It is interesting to note how this play turns a traditional notion of dramatic climax inside out. We are presented with the stark image and the rapid flow from the beginning, and the climaxes of 'what? ... who? ... no! ... she!' occur early, as do the variations in the aural fabric of laughter and screams. Thereafter (and we are only about one third of the way through the play at this point) there is no unforeseen item until 'SHE!': it is as if we were led into the situation and then totally abandoned to it. The events that Mouth relates are all in the past tense, but related in present real time. The raving brain and ranting mouth do not pause, do not even begin or end, but come into our view and pass beyond it. But in that time, and in the story that is related, the words move from past to present – from birth to 70 years of age and then to the beginning again. There is thus a tension between what we are told (in narrative form) is past and our experience of it in the present where we are plunged into the situation ourselves. As audience we mirror the same anguish as Mouth and pass through the same stages that she is describing. In this respect, and in the same manner as *Play*, perhaps even more successfully, the audience's experience of the situation that confronts them exactly parallels the situation itself. It is almost like a photographic plate: you can take the play away but it still seems to be there, because you are no longer a spectator of the anguish and dilemma, but a participant. And that, to say the least, is one reason why it is Beckett's most unforgettable play.

LANGUAGE

The total situation of *Not I* is an unchanging but hallucinatory visual image, plus language. And no more than language. Because of this there is even greater difference than usual between experiencing the play as a member of an audience and as a reader of the text. The broken syntax and descriptions issuing from Mouth, 'now this stream ... steady stream ... not catching the half of it ... not the quarter ... no idea ... what she was saying' (p. 219), reflect the situation of the member of the audience who vainly struggles to make something of the continual stream of fragments: the reader too may struggle but he has the advantage of his own pace rather than Mouth's enforced pace, as well as the advantages of referring back and rereading sequences – something denied to Mouth and audience alike. In this context it is interesting to note the comment of Billie Whitelaw, the actress who played Mouth at the Royal Court Theatre, when interviewed for the *Sunday Times* (14 January 1973):

> It goes at this tremendous pace. I've been practising saying words at a tenth of a second, I could see myself spelling them out like an Olympics clock. No one can possibly follow the text at that speed but Beckett insists that I speak it precisely. It's like music, a piece of Schoenberg in his head.

So, in production, language fulfils a purpose very different to textual study by the reader: Mouth, its referent the brain, and the audience, presented with a fabric of language, are left 'grabbing at straw ... the brain ... flickering away on its own ... quick grab and on ... nothing there ... on to the next ... bad as the voice ... worse ... as little sense ... all that together' (p. 221). Study of the text, however, reveals various narrative elements and linear threads, a process of continuing thought processes and sudden jumps heralded by the brain interrupting the flow. The speech of Mouth varies from objective sophistication: 'normally vented on', 'at any subsequent stage' (p. 216), 'insentient' (p. 217), to colloquial expressions like 'to the tick' (p. 216), 'not a twinge' (p. 218) (which is in contrast to the description of 'she' as a waif). It is also, of course, subject to a great deal of repetition, repetition of three major varieties: immediate repetition and variation, repetition of set phrases, and repetition of a concept but differently expressed. Exact repetition of phrases is surprisingly rare: the phrases are continually shifting and new words and information are almost continuously being introduced up to the final vehement 'SHE!'

NOTES ON THE TEXT

[Title.] This may derive, like so much else in Beckett, from

Schopenhauer, according to whom the bad moral character envisages the thought of other living creatures with a constant feeling of 'not I, not I, not I' (cf. the essay 'On Human Nature').

p. 215

(*a gesture of helpless compassion*.) Although, as suggested above, there are often problems associated with the staging of Auditor's part (in the Paris production where Madeleine Renaud played Mouth the character had to be omitted entirely due to the exiguity of the stage area), Beckett does attribute considerable importance to the role. It was suggested to him by Caravaggio's painting *The Decollation of St John* in Valletta Cathedral where a shadowy group in the background observes the beheading. In *Not I* Beckett similarly feels that a silent witness is necessary and that the play is incomplete without him, although he now believes the figure should stand elsewhere than is indicated in the script: perhaps behind and nearer to Mouth, although the facial features of Auditor must remain invisible if this position is adopted. In the BBC Television version, broadcast on 17 April 1977, there was no Auditor at all; Mouth was filmed in close-up (and incidentally came over as much more physical, even sensual, than in the carefully distanced stage performance): 'certainly Beckett displayed no trace of displeasure as, watching the BBC Television version, he realized that Mouth had the appearance of a large, gaping vagina' (Knowlson, *Frescoes*, p. 200).

MOUTH. Cf. 'Whispering it told, the mouth, a woman's, the thin lips sticking and unsticking...' (*Watt*, p. 258). The idea has thus been in Beckett's mind for some time.

p. 216

godforsaken hole called ... An ambiguous reference to the vagina and/or Croker's Acres (see p. 220)

before her time ... *eight months later*. 'She' was denied the safety of the womb for the natural span and was forced prematurely into the painful world.

p. 217

for she could still hear the buzzing. This could be the voice or the brain. 'Still' implies that it was with her in the normal situation before the event. It is impossible for a living person to find total silence. Even when people are placed in sensory deprivation boxes, experiments have shown that they can still hear their own heartbeat and possibly brain 'signals'.

brief laugh ... good laugh. Dramatically these usually mirror the staccato effect of the rhythm, i.e. they begin and end suddenly, rather than like a natural laugh, which wells up and simmers down. Cf. the screams on p. 218. On the religious significance of the laughter, James Acheson remarks that Beckett suggests two possibilities: 'either that there is no God, and that our suffering is purely a matter of chance; or that God exists and is inexplicably cruel to His creatures' (*AUMLA*, May 1981, p. 99).

p. 218

a distant bell. This description of her activities before the event does not tally completely with the earlier description (pp. 216–17). Here she is intent and hastening. Previously she was aimlessly wandering.

p. 220

what? ... tongue? ... yes ... The brain insists on the inclusion of all unimportant details. Cf. p. 217 where the brain insists on all possible positions being logically investigated.

Croker's Acres. This is, or at least was, a real place. Beckett comments: 'Adjacent to Leopardstown Race Course. Croker: American millionaire whose horse Joss won the Derby.' The specificity of the name is deliberately and painfully ironic, given the amorphousness of Mouth's situation.

p. 221

God is love. Fragments from a Protestant upbringing (in the orphanage). Cf. p. 222 and 'new every morning' which is the first line of a well-loved Protestant hymn. When all else fails these fragments momentarily fill the void. On the other hand, Irving Wardle points out that these 'automatic Christian pieties', interwoven with 'harsh satanic laughter' at the notion of the existence of a merciful God, stand in bitterly ironic contrast to the loneliness, distress and anguish of the life sketched in by Mouth (cf. Knowlson, *Frescoes*, p. 203).

p. 223

pick it up – At the end of the Paris production directed by Beckett in April 1978, 'Auditor covered his head with his hands in a gesture of increased helplessness and despair, as if unable to bear any longer the torrent of sound' (Knowlson, *Frescoes*, p. 198).

(*Voice continues behind curtain.*) In the introduction to the programme *Shades* (see p. 237 below) the suggestion was made that Mouth could be seen as a life-long deaf mute who had suddenly acquired uncontrollable speech.

THAT TIME

Written in English between June 1974 and August 1975.

First publication   Grove Press, New York, 1976
First performance   20 May 1976, Royal Court Theatre,
    London, directed by Donald McWhinnie and recorded
    and edited by John Delnero. Listener was played by
    Patrick Magee, for whom the play was written.

RECEPTION

This was on the whole respectful; The *Listener*'s critic John
Elsom described the bill, which also included *Play* and *Footfalls*, as 'a remarkable evening', adding that 'each play is a full
experience, distilled to its concentrated essence, requiring no
further development, no expansion or contraction, no other
form than that given to it by Beckett' (27 May). Frank Marcus
in the *Sunday Telegraph* (23 May) found the play 'deeply
moving' and praised the 'impeccable direction' of Donald
McWhinnie.

DÉCOR

(i) Aural. The only 'live' sounds made by the Listener during
the play are the 'slow and regular' sounds of breathing that
occur at the four moments indicated in the text. The words
spoken are entirely prerecorded and alternate between three
loudspeakers placed to the sides and above the Listener. In the
1984 Edinburgh Festival production, the speaker relaying the A
text was on the left, that for the B text in the middle, and that for
the C text on the right. With characteristic precision Beckett
demands that the switch from one to another must be 'clearly
faintly perceptible'; in the Royal Court production this was as-
sisted by slight tone modulation. Such techniques are more
commonly associated with stereo radio drama and constitute a
clever and unusual adaptation of that neglected form, providing
not only a novel solution to the problems of stage soliloquy, but

a theatrical realization of the plight of many previous Beckett narrators (from the Unnamable onwards) who claim that the thoughts, memories, images, fancies or whatever they relate are not created by them but simply exist (Beckett uses the word 'relay' to describe this in the note on p. 227). Krapp was clearly listening to recordings he had created himself, but the Listener exists quite apart from the recordings and has no control over them.

(ii) Visual. Krapp could move about, eat a banana, make a recording: the Listener can only listen. His exact situation is of course ill defined, but the initial and very arresting image of – quite simply and starkly – a head 10 feet above stage level with long flowing white hair 'as if seen from above outspread' is reminiscent of the narrator of *Texts for Nothing*, who at times believes he is buried deep down somewhere. An addition in the production to the directions as first published was an increase in the strength of the light on the head at each of the three pauses, of which Beckett writes, in a letter to the authors dated 5 August 1976:

> In *That Time* the light on face is brought up each time the memories flag (after B4, A8, C12) and faded back to normal as they resume. The effect at the end after C12 is no different from the preceding except that fade back is continued to fade out.

Stage dimensions are manipulated in an interesting manner. With only one head visible, and very little stage movement (four eye movements, one toothless smile) or stage sound (breathing heard four times), the dimensions of the play still seem substantial, the prerecorded sound encompassing the width and height of the stage, and the hair resulting in a contradiction of perspectives. While the image is both effective and disturbing, however, it is probably true to say that it is not as dramatically effective throughout the length of the piece (which lasts about 25 minutes) as the startling images in *Play* or *Not I*. We seem for once to have a Beckett play that is more interesting to read than to watch performed. Indeed, in writing it, 'Beckett was very much aware that *That Time* lay "on the very edge of what was possible in the theatre"' (Knowlson, *Frescoes*, p. 219).

DRAMATIS PERSONA

The character of the old man invites little comment beyond the fact that he is typical of many aged Beckett heroes who return, nostalgically or sardonically as the case may be, to their fragmented recollections of the past.

STRUCTURE

As Beckett's letter quoted above clearly indicates, the switching of the voice between A, B and C is specifically structured together with the pauses, and alternates 'without solution of continuity' in regular sequences, thus (reading down each column in succession):

```
         I             II                  III
      ⌒⌒⌒       ⌒⌒⌒⌒          ⌒⌒⌒⌒⌒

     A   A   A     C   C   C   C     B   B   B   B   B
     C   C   C     A   B   B   B     C   A   A   A   A
     B   B   B     B   A   A   A     A   C   C   C   C
    ——12——→  S——  12——→  S——  12——→     S
```

where S stands for 'silence'. It is of note that of the six possible combinations of the letters A, B and C Beckett does not use ABC itself, and BCA and CAB are used only once each, just before the second and first pauses respectively. These occur, as can be seen, after twelve passages (four sets of three) of which there are thirty-six in all. A further possible grouping, into one set of three, another of four and a third of five, determined by the lead letters A, C and B, is indicated by the Roman numerals I, II and III above. Apart from his characteristic concern for combinations, variations and symmetries, Beckett does not appear to have any particular kind of sequence (such as bell-ringing) in mind. His own comment to the authors was that the control is stylistic through the technique of association; he wished, he said, to make each passage verbally interesting and to provide it with some associative connection with the next.

The subject matter of the A passages is a return in middle age to a childhood landmark, Foley's Folly; the atmosphere is a grey morning with pale sun. The B passages treat of a young man's love affair and the note that dominates is that of bright sun and blue skies. In the C passages it is wintry and raining, and the hero seems to be an old man. In this respect the play roughly echoes the three ages of Krapp as seen on stage or heard about on tape.

LANGUAGE

This reflects a return to the aural beauty that marked plays of an earlier period, *Krapp's Last Tape* in particular. As in the novel *How It Is* the reader or speaker needs to supply for himself the breath pauses since there is no formal punctuation.

NOTES ON TEXT

p. 227

(*without solution of continuity*.) Fr., '*sans solution de continuité*' (without interruption, without a break).

p. 228

(LISTENER's *face about 10 feet above stage level*.) Cf. Winnie's situation in *Happy Days*, and also Mouth's in *Not I*.

the eleven. The number 11 tram, of course, as is made clear immediately after.

Portrait Gallery. Beckett had no particular gallery in mind, but says that it could be the London one. The hero is living in exile away from his home country (featured in the A passages).

straight off the ferry. From England to Ireland, no doubt.

p. 229

folly. In the sense of an architectural folly.

was your mother. ' . . . still alive then?' is perhaps the unspoken thought here.

green greatcoat. Beckett has in mind a long motoring coat of thick, felt-like cloth, such as was fashionable around 1900, when his own father, one of the first people in Dublin to buy a car, wore one. It clearly made quite an impression on his young son: the heroes of Beckett's novels habitually wear such coats.

felt shufflers. Beckett has in mind 'sloppy, loose carpet slippers'. The word is not defined in this sense in either the Oxford English Dictionary or Webster's Third New International Dictionary. Museums and galleries on the Continent often insist on visitors wearing them over their outdoor shoes in order to protect the parquet.

back on her the next. The ferry, not of course the girlfriend referred to as 'she' a couple of lines higher up.

p. 230

the womb. According to rumour Beckett claims to recall life in his mother's womb.

that old Chinaman. Lao Tse, born according to legend with long white hair and beard.

p. 231

no better than shades. In the sense of spirits.

Doric terminus of the Great Southern and Eastern. Sc. 'Railway'. The reference is to a familiar Dublin landmark, Harcourt Street Station, built in neo-Grecian style.

p. 232

pass by on the other side. An obvious reference to the story of the Good Samaritan (Luke 10: 30–5).

or the bent. In the sense (given in the COED) of reedy grass.

old green holeproof coat your father left you ... huddled on the doorstep in the old green greatcoat. An example of a link-up between two different strands of memory; cf. 'out on the stone' and 'child on the stone' in B and A on p. 233.

p. 235

(*Silence*.) The end of the B and C sequences is obscure. Is B telling of the end of the affair through the hero's inability to speak any more? In C the dust in the public library seems to say 'come and gone'.

(*Smile*.) In the Royal Court production the smile struck the spectator as a rather wicked, conniving one; cf. the grin at the end of the Stuttgart production of *Eh Joe* (see note to p. 206 of that play above). It struck a note rather at variance with the final sad words, thus effectively undercutting them.

> The pattern of sound in *That Time* seems in the end a triumphant 'weaving' of a life, an achievement. Though memory contains so much that is painful, confused, anxious, yet the relentless flood of time has been subdued, turned into 'that time', the jewels of memory.
>
> (Worth, *IDE*, p. 264)

FOOTFALLS

Written in English; begun March 1975 and substantially finished by November. It was written for Billy Whitelaw.

First publication   Grove Press, New York, 1976
First performance   20 May 1976, Royal Court Theatre, London, directed by Samuel Beckett. May was played by Billie Whitelaw and Woman's Voice by Rose Hill.

RECEPTION

See under *That Time* above. John Elsom made much of the play's meditation on 'endless childhood' and 'premature senility' ('never . . . so graphically and compellingly expressed') but Frank Marcus found the play's meaning 'impenetrable', a description that seems a trifle exaggerated.

DÉCOR, ETC.

The pace of delivery in Beckett's production can be gauged by the fact that a text totalling approximately 1,000 words took some 30 minutes to complete. The opening may serve as an example of the extraordinary contrast to the verbal torrent of a play such as *Not I*: the first line is not simply delivered as published but spoken in a low 'dead' voice as four distinct syllables, and it lasts the best part of 15 seconds: 'Muth . . .ther. (Pause) Muth . . . ther.' The delivery remains very slow and regular throughout, linked to the precise pacing of May which produces the clearly rhythmic tread of footfalls. Beckett told Billie Whitelaw, 'The words are only the excipient [i.e. the sugar on the pill]; the pacing is far more important.'

The appearance of a named, costumed (John Elsom wrote of 'a Miss Havisham film of folds') and identifiable character is something of a novelty in Beckett's recent work, as is the suggestion of a specific situation: an isolated daughter caring for a dying mother. But poignant though this undoubtedly is – and not to be disregarded because more specific than tradition expects – the play is starkly minimal in more than its situation, and is particularly interesting as a composition of sounds. The tread of May pacing the 'strip', the drag of her trailing wrap, the ploy of the chiming clock growing fainter and of the instruction 'pause for echoes', the slow delivery of words and syllables (e.g., 'Sequel' on p. 242 almost becomes 'seek well', and in production was repeated), the measured steps, which are carefully counted at first (p. 239) and on subsequent pacings form a subconscious counterpoint that the audience provides for itself, the build-up, comic in parts, of the story about Evensong, which resolves itself not in a joke but simply in 'I saw nothing, heard nothing ... I was not there', and later in the softly intoned words of the Christian blessing (not specifically indicated in the text as intoned): all these features of the play, to the last slow airy gasps of 'It all ... It all', create fascinating traces of minute and memorable sounds, a beautiful and minimal form of music.

There are of course problems with such a minimal form, not least of which is a cough in the audience or a creak in a seat. That Beckett's work is vulnerable in this respect is demonstrated by the problem surrounding a light that was visible high on the left at times during the Royal Court production. Many spectators associated it with the mother, some believed it must symbolize something between Mother and May (though exactly what is not clear) and others did not notice it. The answer is simpler; in the letter already referred to (see p. 220 above) Beckett writes:

> In *Footfalls* the purpose of the light is to forestall an end-of-play audience reaction in the blackout of all light but it precedes final fade up on empty strip and fade out of all light including it. I am not sure it is necessary.

NOTES ON THE TEXT

p. 239

MAY. Another in the long line of Beckett names beginning with M (or its inverted form W, as in Watt, Woburn, or 'Mrs Winter' below). In early drafts May was first named Mary and

Amy was named Emily; the change in both names was made in the same typescript and reinforces the similarity between the two women.

(*Strip.*) Note once again the concern for symmetry and balance, so characteristic of Beckett's drama.

(*Pacing.*) Beckett now requires nine steps, not seven as at the foot of p. 239, but 'seven or nine, the figure is uneven, as she paces out the days of the week, or the months of gestation, after which, in Beckett's stern vision, suffering is handed on from mother to daughter' (Knowlson, *Frescoes*, p. 228). 'If the play is full of repetitions,' said Beckett, 'then it is because of these life-long stretches of walking. That is the centre of the play, everything else is secondary' (quoted in Knowlson, *Frescoes*, p. 221).

p. 240
inject you again. With a pain-killer: cf. Hamm in *Endgame* or Bolton in *Embers*. Note too that the M/V situation is similar to that of Hamm and Clov, only a lot more tender.

forgive me again. Sc. 'for having you'. Note, once more, the guilt over avoidable procreation: V must have conceived M just before the menopause, since M is now in her forties and her mother nearly 90.

p. 241
She fancies she is alone. Unlike the situation in *Eh Joe*, V's words are not heard by M, who in the Berlin production (which Beckett directed after the London one) muttered to herself to make the point clear to the spectator.

lacrosse. Beckett says he chose this word because of the association with the shape of a church and its transepts, which represent the crucifixion.

p. 242
She began to walk . . . At nightfall.

Who is that 'she', the image of the mother (that painful memory) or, as the visual pattern strongly hints, the daughter herself, so like the semblance she describes, in her pale grey tatters? To be there is difficult; she seems to be seeking ways to project herself and the pain she is supporting. It is a comical and unsettling moment when this remote being confronts the audience directly, forcing them to collaborate as readers of fiction who will be able to help on the process by which characters acquire life. So the story is recast, with May as narrator and the shadowy mother given a presence as Mrs Winter going to Evensong with her daughter, Amy. That story too ends with the daughter's sense of not being fully there: 'I saw nothing, heard nothing, of any kind. I was not there.' She has never been anywhere but where we see her, pacing her strip, calling out to her mother and 'creating' her by speaking in her person.

(Worth, *IDE*, p. 255)

Professor Knowlson (*Frescoes*, pp. 222–3) links May with the 'poignant re-creation of a girl who had never really been born, isolated and permanently absent, distant and totally encapsulated within herself' evoked by the psychologist C. G. Jung in a lecture Beckett attended in the 1930s (see note to *All That Fall*, p. 36).

his poor arm. Christ's; at one stage in Beckett's drafts 'his' was written 'His'. She walks up the north transept. Beckett specifies the north door in the preceding line but one because, he says, it 'sounds colder'.

passing rack. In the sense of 'driving clouds' (see COED).

p. 243

Amy. This anagram of 'May' links the supposed fiction (for this is yet another 'story' in a Beckett play) with the situation on stage.

We realize, perhaps only *after* the play has ended, that we may have been watching a ghost telling a tale of a ghost (herself), who fails to be observed by someone else (her fictional *alter ego*) because she in turn was not really there ... Since even the mother's voice may simply be a voice in the mind of a ghost, everything may be regarded as illusion in this little play.

(Knowlson, *Frescoes*, p. 227)

GHOST TRIO

Written in English in 1975 for BBC Television.

First publication   Grove Press, New York, 1976, in *Ends and Odds*
First broadcast   17 April 1977, BBC2, in *The Lively Arts*; directed by Donald McWhinnie, produced by Tristram Powell. V was played by Billie Whitelaw, F by Ronald Pickup. Beckett attended rehearsals and closely supervised the filming, which the BBC says he 'relished' because of the tight control it gave him over movement, lighting, cutting, etc. He later directed the play himself for SDR, with Klaus Herm as F.

RECEPTION

Reviewing *Ghost Trio* and *... but the clouds ...* together in the *Guardian* (19 April), Michael Billington spoke enthusiastically of 'the concentrated beauty of the images: no naturalistic clutter, no fast cutting, no colour but simply a mesmeric piece of painting for TV'; he considered *Ghost Trio* 'particularly stunning'. On the other hand Richard North thought both plays 'brought on the yawns' (the *Listener*, 21 April), and Dennis Potter (of the *Sunday Times*) came out even more vehemently, on 24 April, against their 'affirmation of pointlessness', asking,

> Would Solzhenitsyn have understood? Would the Jews on the way to the gas chamber? Question: Is this the art which is the response to the despair and pity of our age, or is it made of the kind of deliberate futility which helped such desecrations of the spirit, such filth of ideologies come into being?

DÉCOR, ETC.

The setting is laid out on p. 247. The only puzzle is the door, described in I.13 as 'imperceptibly ajar'. Beckett explained to a BBC technician, who was understandably having difficulties with this, that 'imperceptibly ajar' meant 'closed'. Music is used more extensively than in *All That Fall*, the only precedent where it serves as accompaniment rather than as a character-element in its own right. The title first given to the play, *Tryst*, sums up the theme, that of a man waiting for a woman who does not come. This frustrated expectation, and the boy messenger, link the work with *Waiting for Godot* and the situation of F recalls certain aspects of *Film* and *Eh Joe*. In the BBC production, F was dressed in the familiar long overcoat one associates with other Beckett heroes. In the SDR production, the boy did not turn and go in III.32, but backed away, as in Beckett's STB production of *Godot* (see note to p. 92 of that play), as if to emphasize the sadness and finality of his message that the woman (like Godot) is not going to turn up after all.

NOTES ON THE TEXT

p. 248

stating the obvious. We shall avoid doing so here. Most of the printed text is made up of instructions for the director and producer; the spoken words contain no obscurities or recondite allusions. The following points, however, can usefully be made:

1. The 'trio' aspect of the play is important in several ways:
    a) structure of the play
       i Pre-action
       ii Action
       iii Re-action
    b) three positions of camera (A, B, C)
    c) three static positions of Figure (5, 6, 7)
2. The set is deliberately 'stagey': there is deliberate emphasis on the perspective sight lines, the door and window cut slits in the surface of the walls (rather than a door or a glass window as noted in the text). Everything is in shades of grey: walls, floor, pallet, figure, and this cell (a large 'cell', 6m × 5m) an arranged void.
3. The Voice calls attention to all these aspects in her opening

remarks. Perhaps the least well-executed aspect of the Voice's description in practice is the 'omnipresent lighting': while no lighting source is visible there is no sense of luminosity and the set is conventionally if skilfully lit.

4 The cuts to close-up of the floor (I. 3), wall (I. 5, I. 7), door (I. 13), window (I. 15), pallet (I. 17) and later of the cassette on the stool (III. 12) and of the mirror (III. 24) are a significant innovation. There is clearly an interest in concerns of abstract art (grey on grey, simple shape on simple shape); the most interesting line in the whole play follows a close-up of the floor: 'Having seen that specimen of floor you have seen it all' (p. 248).

5 While the script in Pre-action necessitates that as the camera goes nearer the music gets louder and vice versa, suggesting that F is the source point of the music, this convention changes (I. 33); the music ceases at B as the camera withdraws to A, is audible at A for the first time (II. 35) and then increases in volume there (III. 37). The music can be raised and lowered even if the voice cannot be (I. 2). The quality of this music is clearly not produced by the cassette; F makes no movement to manipulate the controls.

6 In keeping with the set, the actor's movements are theatrical ('tense pose', II. 2); he even leaps up, puppet-like, once or twice. The use of sound effects is also theatrical (creaking door, window, rain, steps and knocks).

7 Although the text opens with the voice giving explicit television directions ('kindly tune accordingly', etc., p. 248), so making explicit at once that this is consciously a TV script, the logic of television itself is emphasized by the voice's stress on its lack of inflexion: 'It will not be raised, nor lowered, whatever happens.' For, of course, the television camera is simply an expressionless eye, and Beckett goes out of his way to keep the viewer aware of this absence of inflexion, interpretation, and camera commentary. The camera angles have been planned with great care, and like the early cinema directors he restricts the camera movements and positions to three – though with some close-ups, withdrawals, etc. But the stress on greyness and the absence of shadows still further, and deliberately, underline Beckett's minimal use of

the television camera: for the camera just sees, and everything else (shadow, reflection, etc.) is interpretation and is consciously planned by the director as the artist. And in this play the *artist*'s role is always presented as the minimal figment that it is (i.e. Beckett is having no truck with the Romantic concept of the artist as 'creator', the 'divinely inspired', or even 'the marker': which takes him into a postmodernist aesthetic at once).

8 The stress on the *artist* leads us to one of the central secrets of this play, that Beckett is calling on the resources of all the arts, and presenting a critique of what they can and cannot achieve (the poet is represented by the presence of words; the novelist by the presence of plot and narrative; the dramatist by the presence of dramaturgical devices; the composer by the reliance on music; the television director by the very medium of *Ghost Trio*'s presentation; the painter by the handling of the visual devices; the photographer by the presence of the grey colouring and the still figure framed in the lens of the still-life picture). Each of these *artists* has the tools of his craft and the devices on which he has traditionally relied are analysed in this play into the most basic, and uninterpretative/non-communicative elements, i.e. no *artist* is the saviour, no artist presents the truth for we no longer can grant him this degree of presumption. Beckett is specifically interested in the painter and the composer, although of course the television director is omnipresent in the very presentation of the play.

The painter enters metaphorically in I. 2, for v's presentation of the scene is almost as if the description was of a seventeenth-century Dutch interior, with the window, 'the indispensable door', 'the light'. And yet this artistic presentation is at once dispossessed, for 'the willing suspension of disbelief' is quite literally undone by the sequence of camera close-ups which present the wall as only a 0.70 m × 1.50 m specimen, just as is the floor, and subsequently we are shown that the door leads nowhere, save down an endless, darkening corridor, and the window opens on to nothing. In a seventeenth-century interior such details are employed just because they are 'real', 'fictions of reality'; but in Beckett's world they are only what they literally signify, and as images they have no resonances beyond their verbal definition by the Female Voice. But this painting analogy is taken further by Beckett (and here there is a parallel with Velasquez, *Las Meniñas*, and Picasso's life-long series of pictorial meditations on that brilliantly provocative masterpiece) because by showing that there is nothing and no one beyond the door or the window, and by using the classic painter's device of the mirror on the wall (in Velasquez's painting it reflects the King and Queen, in Van Eyck's *Marriage* the painting's observer), he makes the analogy with the established painting convention even more explicit.

The very title, *Ghost Trio* (as with Strindberg's *Ghost Sonata*, or Tolstoy's *Kreutzer Sonata*) takes up the metaphor of the *artist* as musician, precisely punning on the 'Ghost' Trio by Beethoven, the tripartite division of the play, and the three 'ghostly' characters themselves. But what is especially significant, the text makes clear, is that there is no automatic linking of the music that we hear and the cassette that the man is holding (i.e. the Male Figure does not control what music is heard, nor is there any indication that he hears it, even though Beckett in several cases (I. 31–4; II. 26–9; III. 36–41) has the seated Figure holding what has become identified eventually (?I. 33) as a cassette. For the truth, according to the post-modernist aesthetic, is that music is the one art that can achieve perfection since it is the only art that is not informed, at any obvious level, by human verbal intervention, lying, as it does, beyond words and existing as 'sense'-defying sound. But in *Ghost Trio* Beckett takes this aesthetic one stage further: he demonstrates that music exists outside of human control (the sound appears whether ordered to appear, through manipulation of the cassette's controls, or not), and by its very structuring it has that very order (of beginning, build-up, middle, end, etc.) that no other art can be trusted now to aspire to, and, by sounding at the odd intervals when the Beethoven music is played in the play, by being turned on and off, increased or decreased in volume, started and stopped at any point, it has an existence which is outside of time, place and the human perspective.

Beckett's *Ghost Trio* is thus a profound reflection on the atmosphere and the potency of one particular motif from the second movement of Beethoven's trio, employing the music both to counterpoint the dramatic action and to crystallize his assumptions about the *artist* and especially the differing status of the individual arts.

9 The Beethoven Trio – nicknamed the 'Ghost' because of the mysterious nature of the slow movement – relies on two main themes, the second of which is the 'ghostly', haunting one: except for the final passage of music (in III. 36 to the end) all Beckett's musical passages are taken from passages that prominently utilize this second theme. And this final passage, which in fact is the concluding coda, serves like film or theatre background music, to wind the whole thing up. Thus the process of the play is the process of the musical examples that Beckett selects for inclusion. The most dramatic and powerful moment is in III. 30–3 when a ghost (the small boy) actually appears, and it is here that the music is totally silent because the action being presented physically now enacts what the 'Ghost' Trio music has hitherto been representing.

So it is hardly surprising to discover that the music is integrally associated with the play's movement itself. The following comments give the gist of this musical 'argument', as this is summarized in the notes to the Music on p. 254:

a) I. 13 *beginning bar 47*: musically this is the recapitulation of the second motif of the opening subject – which is the 'ghostly' haunting theme.

b) I. 23 *beginning bar 49*: this passage begins two bars after the point when the previous music started, and is, in fact, a more dissonant, highly charged version of the same musical 'ghostly' motif, with the main rising interval in the melodic line being greater, thus producing greater tension.

c) I. 31–4 *beginning bar 19*: the music here begins as at I. 13, but with an unrestful piano accompaniment. The gradual build-up in the music results from the *crescendo*, the increased harmonic tension, the rising pitch of the music, and the *stretto* (i.e. overlapping of motifs from bar 22).

d) II. 26–9 *beginning bar 64*: the music here (as the dramatic action) is the parallel passage in the recapitulation to that used in I. 31–4. This time the *stretto* effect starts earlier (after only one bar), i.e. this is similar to the previous piece of music, but with even greater tension.

e) II. 35–6 *beginning bar 71*: the music is like the previous passage, but instead of the two main themes overlapping, this time it is the 'ghostly' theme overlapping itself, with more movement in the piano part.

f) III. 1–2, 4–5 *beginning bar 26*: the music is again a recapitulation, the equivalent passage to bar 71 (used in II. 35–6). The music is marginally more restful since the rising intervals this time are all octaves.

g) III. 29 *beginning bar 64*: same music used as for II. 26. Dramatically on the screen one is expecting the same sequence to be followed. But of course it is now (III. 30) that footsteps are heard and the boy appears.

h) III. 36 to end *beginning bar 82*: the music grows as the camera shot moves in. Suitably for the play, the music does not start with the 'ghostly' theme, though the theme does appear later in the passage Beckett uses. This is the coda, the end of the movement.

. . . BUT THE CLOUDS . . .

Written in English in October–November 1976 for BBC Television.

First publication   Faber and Faber, London, 1977, *Ends and Odds*

First broadcast   17 April 1977, BBC2, in *The Lively Arts*; directed by Donald McWhinnie and produced by Tristram Powell. M was played by Ronald Pickup and W by Billie Whitelaw. The programme, which included *Not I* and *Ghost Trio*, was entitled (by Beckett himself) *Shades*. Beckett later directed the play himself for SDR, with Klaus Herm as M.

RECEPTION

See under *Ghost Trio* (p. 230, above).

DÉCOR, ETC.

This is clearly set out in the text. The circle of bright light through which the remembered image moves north, east and west works well, as do M's emergence from and disappearance into the darkness. Shot 'M' was (no doubt deliberately) ambiguous, and looked rather like a detail from a painting of limbs and drapery by La Tour or David. There was also – no doubt equally intentionally – a degree of distortion in the soundtrack that contrasted with the totally silent memory images; the voice sounded weak, even ghostly.

NOTES ON THE TEXT

p. 259

when I thought of her. Once again the subject matter is half-recalled memories; cf. *Eh Joe* and *Ghost Trio*. Note that in this play w never speaks audibly, not even in a whisper.

p. 260

(*Dissolve to* w). At no point in the film do w's eyes close or even blink. Of note too is that, unlike the earlier television plays, this involves no camera movements at all.

I so begged when alive. Beckett intends it to be ambiguous whether 'when I was alive' or 'when she was alive' is meant.

p. 261

that MINE. Beckett means by this 'an inexhaustible treasure house'.

p. 262

. . . but the clouds of the sky. The source of this quotation (which of course also gives the play its title) is W. B. Yeats's poem 'The Tower', which ends:

> Now shall I make my soul,
> Compelling it to study
> In a learned school
> Till the wreck of body,
> Slow decay of blood,
> Testy delirium
> Or dull decrepitude,
> Or what worse evil come –
> The death of friends, or death
> Of every brilliant eye
> That made a catch in the breath –
> Seem but the clouds of the sky
> When the horizon fades;
> Or a bird's sleepy cry
> Among the deepening shades.

The haunting beauty of the closing lines, which w utters inaudibly and v quotes, arouses in the spectator feelings similar to those provoked by Beethoven's equally moving music in *Ghost*

Trio. In both cases the quotation is carefully chosen to create maximum emotional and aesthetic impact and to reinforce the works' plangent lament on love and loss.

A PIECE OF MONOLOGUE

Written in English, about 1979, for and at the request of the British actor David Warrilow.

First publication   *Kenyon Review*, Summer 1979
First performance   14 December 1979, La Mama Theater, New York, by David Warrilow, in a production by David Warrilow and Rocky Greenberg
First British performance   19 August 1984, Edinburgh Festival

RECEPTION

Reviewing the play at the Edinburgh Festival, Mary Brennan praised Warrilow for delivering 'a lengthy and challenging text superbly without "performance" intruding upon communication' (*Glasgow Herald*, 20 August 1984), and in the *Scotsman* (same date) Hayden Murphy spoke of 'a Dickens of a narrative' but added that it was 'no mere word game; it is a gift to language'. Writing in *The Beckett Circle* (Spring 1980) on the original New York production, Dougald McMillan felt that the visual image of the speaker and his mode of delivery remain so static that there is little to sustain a performance lasting well over half an hour, but in his book on Beckett's theatre Charles R. Lyons praises the way, in this and other plays, Beckett uses the resources of the theatre to develop an image that dominates his writing: the figure of an ageing person who attempts to determine the authenticity of his or her existence by grappling with the details of a baffling environment and struggling to understand the enigmatic memories that possess the mind. Writing in the *Journal of Beckett Studies* (Spring 1982) Linda Ben-Zvi asserted that the form of this play

> is the most daring experiment that Beckett has yet adopted in an attempt to create what he has described repeatedly in his fiction, the schismatic nature of man ... the voice that

speaks and the figure that listens are one, the *me* and the *I* of the self ... man silent *and* man erecting bogeys of words. And both turned to the blackness without.

For Joyce McMillan, the play offered 'images of the brief glow of human consciousness snatched from the surrounding dark' (*Guardian*, 23 August 1984).

DÉCOR

As is usual with Beckett's later plays, this is prescribed clearly and in detail on p. 265. Soft white is the dominant colour. As in *Endgame*, there is a feeling of enclosure: a window facing west is referred to in the text but not featured in the décor, and the blank east wall is in fact the side where the audience sits.

DRAMATIS PERSONA

Speaker, like Krapp in *Krapp's Last Tape*, is an old man, and ruminates alone on stage throughout.

STRUCTURE

As befits a monologue read as if it were prose, this is simple. It is conveniently summarized by Dougald McMillan in the article mentioned above as follows:

> The subject of the monologue is 'this night', which is like all the other '30,000 nights' that intervene in the 'two and a half billion seconds' between the speaker's 'birth' (the first word of the piece) and the time when he and all his memories will be 'gone' (the last word of the piece). From the moment of his birth he has been 'dying on' through 'years of night', each of which 'dies on to dawn and never dies'. His nightly ritual is unvaried: 'Up at nightfall.' 'Gropes to window and stares out.' Gropes to lamp, lights it, backs away to edge of light and turns to face east. 'Blank wall' once covered by family pictures now gone. In the 'veil of black' beyond the wall, he sees memories from his past: the room of his birth, a moment of love, and a funeral.

There are obvious parallels with previous plays. The speaker here is like the protagonist in *Eh Joe*, who inhabits a similarly

241

sparse room with bed, lamp and windows, and tries without success at nightfall to evade memory in the form of a woman's hectoring voice in the head. Like O in *Film*, the speaker reveals attempts to wipe out the events of a past life by destroying the photographs that survive as a pictorial record of them. Physically, he appears to be a fuller embodiment of the white-haired head that dominates the stage in *That Time*, just as the patterned interplay of voices in that work is recalled by the carefully orchestrated musical structure of this monologue and the use of repeated phrases to blend layers of past and present. And finally, as McMillan points out, the voice here, as in *Not I*, is experienced as an 'involuntary effusion'.

The speaker is preoccupied with autobiographical reminiscences, almost certainly Beckett's own; his spring birth, like the author's, was heralded by the greening of larch trees outside a room facing west. 'This inclusion of specific, autobiographical details', McMillan comments, 'is reflected in the major structural motif of the piece.' The speaker repeats seven times the phrase 'he all but said', drawing attention to his close approach to the particular memories that haunt him, especially that of a coffin (his mother's?), which he sees being lowered into a dark hole in the pelting rain. 'Rain bubbling in the black mud' of the 'ditch . . . empty for the moment' (p. 268) is an especially graphic image that is almost certainly taken from Beckett's personal recollections of a family funeral.

On the other hand the piece frequently draws attention to itself as a work of theatrical illusion, with the motionless speaker's 'actions' being described in the spare present-tense style of stage directions: 'Stands facing wall after the various motions described' (p. 267), so that we are 'reminded immediately that whatever reality might lie behind the pronouns, the figure must be seen as part of an artificially ordered, theatrical perspective'. This kind of self-conscious theatricality goes back a long way: to Estragon and Vladimir's ironic awareness of the audience – or as Beckett expected when he wrote the dialogue, virtual non-audience – in *Waiting for Godot*.

LANGUAGE AND DRAMATIC EXPRESSION

Authentic as *Monologue*'s pedigree is, there is no denying that it presents real problems for the director and the performer. The problem of a static figure has already been referred to. The text, like most of Beckett's later writings, is of great aural beauty, hauntingly evocative and moving. Read as a monologue for radio, designed to come out of the dark, it would be a poignant elegy to 'the dead and gone', to 'the dying and the going' (p. 269). Beckett's works – but few more explicitly than this, with the exception of the superb novella of 1980, *Company* – are peopled with, and animated by, 'ghost loved ones' (p. 269). Like his speaker, Beckett almost reveals which ones, but in this play stops just short of it, to 'suspend them', as Dougald McMillan puts it, 'in the distanced world of his fictions'. Even if, in responding to Warrilow's request for a stage play on the theme of death, Beckett failed to give proper weight to his normally sure instinct about the appropriateness of material to a particular genre, and composed a text that might work better as a radio play or as a short prose work, he certainly provided the British actor with a magnificent speech, and Warrilow responded by delivering it perfectly. Speaking slowly and clearly, he used an old, hoarse voice and long, painful, gasping hesitations. As Nicholas Zurbrugg observes, in this 'carefully censored fragmentary monologue ... every effort is made either to avoid the expression of autobiographical data, or at least to minimize the anguish accompanying its expression by repetitive and circumambulatory narration' (in *Samuel Beckett: Humanistic Perspectives*, ed. Morris Beja *et al.*, p. 182).

NOTES ON THE TEXT

p. 265

(*Speaker stands well off centre.*) Warrilow stood motionless, facing the audience, 'describing a character in the third person – "he" – who moves in a setting that we do not see, but can only imagine with the eye of the mind' (Martha Fehsenfeld, *Modern Drama*, September 1982, p. 356).

up at the lid to come. The lid of his future coffin.

p. 266
dropping gentle on the place beneath. Cf. *The Merchant of Venice*, IV, i, 185–6; Portia is talking of the 'quality of mercy' falling as 'gentle rain' to bless those who give it as well as those on whom it falls.

p. 267
Holding aloft a lighted spill. A spill is a 'thin strip of wood, spiral tube etc. of paper for lighting candles etc.' (COED).

That nevoid smile. 'Nevoid' means 'resembling a nevus' or 'accompanied by nevi or similar superficial lesions'. A nevus is a congenital pigmented area on the skin, such as a birthmark or a mole.

Thirty thousand nights. At this point, and at 'Fade. Gone' (p. 269, l. 10), Warrilow raised his left hand slowly, a gesture expressive of great pain. These embellishments of an otherwise static performance were his idea, not Beckett's.

p. 268
Parts lips . . . Birth. Parts the dark. Malone in *Malone Dies* sees himself as 'being given birth to into death', 'far already from the world that parts at last its labia and lets me go' (*Three Novels*, pp. 285 and 190). Kristin Morrison comments:

> By a nice tautology, the 'first word' is 'birth', which like a foetus gathers itself in his mouth and then like an infant emerging from the womb parts the darkness and thrusts itself forward. Words, speech, expression are thus a kind of parturition, which here and elsewhere in Beckett's work is an unfortunate not a blessed event.
>
> (*Canters and Chronicles*, p. 110)

Stifled by nasal. The nasal consonant in 'gone', Beckett informs us.

p. 269
his way. Her way. Note the revealing, if belated, correction.

head haught. Head held high (SOED). The term is archaic.

Waiting on the rip word. The RIP ('Rest in peace') word, the magic word that rends the darkness.

'Rip word' condenses, in this highly condensed play, every-thing that 'story' has meant in Beckett's other drama.

'Rip tide' is an ordinary phrase; 'rip word', a surprise that yields its meaning by comparison with the more familiar. The Oxford English Dictionary in its definition of the noun 'rip' as 'a disturbed state of the sea' makes reference to the verb form, which includes after the more immediate mean-ings of violent slashing or tearing the figurative meanings 'to open up, lay bare, disclose, make known' and 'to open *up*, rake *up*, bring *up* again into notice or discussion (esp. some-thing unpleasant or which is to a person's discredit)'. Thus just as one 'waits on the tide' for an appropriate flow, so here the speaker waits on the rip word, that word which will lay bare what is at the critical centre of his monologue. The rip word is that disturbance in the flow of language which reveals what is hidden, the unpleasant or discreditable truth which may be disguised or submerged but never completely evaded. The rip word is sometimes just a single word, as it is in this play, but elsewhere it has been whole narratives, the stories and anecdotes that burst forth, breaks in the surface of the drama that reveal the truth of motives, feelings, themes.

The rip word in *A Piece of Monologue* is 'begone', that word by which the speaker dismisses from his life what he has always really wanted.

(Kristin Morrison, *Canters and Chronicles*, pp. 104–5)

It could also have connections with 'rip cord', the cord that opens a parachute. The 'rip word' would thus be the word that brings release.

Unutterably faint. After the final fade, the figure of Speaker shone luminously on the darkened stage.

ROCKABY

Written in English between autumn 1979 and June 1980 at the request of Daniel Labeille, who wanted a play to put on during the Beckett 75th birthday celebrations held at the Buffalo campus of the State University of New York.

First publication   Grove Press, New York, 1981 in *Rockaby and Other Short Pieces*
First performance   8 April 1981, Buffalo (New York State), with Billie Whitelaw, directed by Alan Schneider
First British performance   9 December 1982, National Theatre, London

RECEPTION

The first American reviewers found Billie Whitelaw in perfect sympathy with the text, and the play a surprisingly tender piece.

> Beckett has stripped theatre to essential images and words, and few performers have found sympathy for that style to compare with hers. Her own rich vocal authority is a commanding dramatic technique which seeks and finds the ironies and various humours of Beckett's carefully pared words.
>
> (Ned Chaillet, *The Times*, 4 December 1982)

'The play's interest', Henry Popkin wrote,

> is not primarily in the fragmentary story it tells but in the expression of loss it conveys, its images ... On the tape, Miss Whitelaw speaks musically, conveying both the pathos and the repetitiousness of the life she describes. In person before us, she is a rapt but despairing listener who galvanises us with her four plangent interventions. The form of *Rockaby* is precise: Mr Schneider and Miss Whitelaw are faithful to its precision.
>
> (*Listener*, 30 April 1981)

Reviewing the London transfer, Ned Chaillet was equally impressed:

> Billie Whitelaw, probably the theatre's most accomplished surviving explorer of Beckett's dramatic intentions, sets up a contrapuntal melody to the meeting of the words through the sweet, lulling rhythms of her voice.
>
> (*The Times*, 11 December 1982)

The significance of that 'silken, incantatory, amplified voice' was well perceived by Lawrence Graver when he wrote that when memory speaks through it,

> we get not only the simultaneous desire to live and die, but enough of the woman's history to give her dilemma its strong claim on our feelings and attention. The skeletal story, the chiselled poetic lines, the continual repetition of pregnant phrases, re-create in minutes the hours, days and decades of frustrated longing; and yet – despite the sterile fatigue – a sense of the pathos and enormous resistance of the effort.
>
> (*The Beckett Circle*, vol. iii no. 2)

DÉCOR, ETC.

w, a prematurely old woman with drawn features and hollow eyes in a black, lacy, sequined gown and gaudy, tilted hat, sways in a rocking chair that holds her in a kind of embrace, and sustains a 15-minute dialogue with herself by four times triggering the voice of memory with the passionate (or desperate) word 'More'. This recorded voice (v) is doubled by the voice of the live performer at intervals, but only on the enigmatic phrase 'time she stopped'.

While it is not possible in Beckett's later theatre style to talk about scenery in the usual sense, Enoch Brater notes how

> *Rockaby* makes us conscious of the fact that darkness, greys and blacks, shades, and other gradations of sheerly theatrical light can be 'scenery' too. What initially appears to be monochromatic is, on closer inspection, not really monochromatic at all. For light and colour in *Rockaby* appear soft and faded

but never dull. A 'Subdued' light uncovers the chair. The rest of this stage is 'dark'. A 'Subdued spot' rests on the face 'constant throughout, unaffected by successive fades'. Beckett in fact makes us see the same figure in different artificial lights, offering us an ever-shifting series of perspectives from which to encounter the image anew. At the opening fade-up the stage directions are 'first spot on face alone. Long pause. Then light on chair.' At the close of the play the movement is reversed. For his final fade-out Beckett specifies 'first chair. Long pause with spot on face alone.' Throughout the play other gradations of light are similarly meant to shift and vary, sometimes even to sparkle and gleam as the rocking chair is made to sway 'to and fro'. So insistent was this rocking in the original production that the actress, Billie Whitelaw, never had her feet rest on the stage floor for one moment during the entire production.

(*Modern Drama*, September 1982, p. 344)

There are four sections – Brater goes so far as to designate them 'acts' – each of which begins with the stage direction '*Long pause*'. These sections consist mostly of short phrases or lines similar to those in the poems in *Words and Music*. In the first act or movement the voice recalls, in this quasi-poetic form, the day she abandoned the search outside for 'another living soul', 'another creature like herself' (pp. 275–6). In the second and third sections, she remembers continuing the quest 'inside', sitting by her window, still looking for the 'famished eyes/like hers/to see/be seen/no . . .' (p. 279). But there is an unexpected development at the end. The recorded voice describes having gone down to sit in the chair her mother sat in for years, in which she had gone harmlessly 'off her head' and eventually died. In her 'mother rocker' – the word Beckett uses, perhaps to capitalize on the overtones of the colloquial phrase 'off her rocker' – v had recapitulated the quest outside and in, and she became, at the 'close of a long day', her 'own other living soul', encaged in loneliness, embraced by the arms of the chair her mother had inhabited, longing for death: that is, precisely the situation in which we see w now to be (pp. 280–1). The surprise that Beckett springs on the spectator is that v's voice grows progressively softer as her words become more vicious and violent: 'rock her off/stop her eyes/fuck life' (p. 282). Lawrence Graver calls this phrase a 'last eerie, unnervingly comic stab of defiance'; but the director, Alan Schneider, considered that it was about accepting death, coming to terms with the mother's passing, and that the phrase 'fuck life' was not vicious but resigned and rueful. To the present writers it sounds like cruelty to the dead mother's image, something not alien to Beckett's world; cf. Molloy's attitude to the 'poor old uniparous whore' to whom he owed his calamitous existence (*Three Novels*, p. 19). As we saw in *Krapp's Last Tape*, attitudes to the death of mothers are not unambivalent (see *Krapp's Last Tape*, p. 59).

Nevertheless, Graver is right to single out for praise *Rockaby*'s 'dazzling synchronization of visual and aural images', the hallmark of Beckett's later plays. 'Coming out of the dark', he writes, 'a whey-faced woman with huge eyes, unkempt silver hair, glistening hat and dress, moves lullingly back and forth, intermittently crying for "More" from the voice of memory.' Such an image, he says, evokes 'panic, skewed dignity, a need for pacification and an unappeasable hunger: a wish to look again into the past for a clue to the futility of her life'.

Once again there are some obvious parallels with other Beckett plays. The use of a tape recording to contrast past aspiration with present despair was inaugurated to great effect in *Krapp's Last Tape*; v's, like Joe's woman in *Eh Joe*, is yet another hectoring voice in the head, although this time the protagonist's own; and the mother–daughter relationship recalls *Footfalls*. As Henry Popkin points out, 'the daughter is worse off, more isolated, more forlorn than the mother' in both plays. And Ned Chaillet's description of *Rockaby* as 'a sonata for an actress's voice' would apply equally well to *Not I*, the other play that Billie Whitelaw has made her own. Finally, the exploitation of resonant verbal ambiguities in *Rockaby* is quintessential Beckett. Susan Brienza draws attention (in *The Beckett Circle*, Fall 1982) to the four uses of 'down' in the play: (1) down into the rocking chair (an idea that goes back to the novel *Murphy*); (2) down into the other self; (3) down the stairs; and (4) let down the blind, to signify death (see *Krapp's Last Tape*, p. 60). Moreover 'down' in the last section harks back to 'up' in the previous one.

NOTES ON THE TEXT

p. 273

(*Rounded inward curving arms to suggest embrace.*) This connects with 'those arms at last' on p. 281, and with the title's pun on the well-known lullaby 'Rock-a-bye baby'.

p. 274

(*Towards end of 4.*) The sections or 'acts' are not numbered in the text. Professor Knowlson thinks they may have been numbered in an earlier version, in line with the instructions here and under 'Eyes', p. 273.

(*Lines in italics spoken by* w *with* v.) This occurs only with the phrase 'time she stopped'. The phenomenon occurs in *Krapp's Last Tape* as well (cf. old Krapp joining in his younger self's brief laughter, p. 58). Note that the last 'time she stopped' on p. 281 is not said by w, as if the latter has become too weak to utter it.

p. 276

(*echo of 'time she stopped'.*) This was a sort of echo-chamber echo, electronically done.

p. 280

More. This final 'More' sounded like 'Please, no more' to Susan Brienza, who noted 'growing dread, compulsion, ambivalence' in w's use of her 'trigger' to restart the voice.

best black. Note that the sequins on w's dress are made of jet, a black stone associated with mourning.

p. 282

(*slow fade out.*) Susan Brienza thinks that this 'ageing, bitter woman in her glittering black lowers her head and dies' at the end of the play. Actually the ending is more ambiguous; Professor Knowlson suggests that she might simply have fallen asleep. Enoch Brater comments:

> This denouement needs no punctuation. The words have stopped. The rocking chair comes to rest. There is stage silence. There is also stage stillness. In the slow fade-out of the chair, the lights of a spot, like sudden stigmata, momentarily isolate the head, now 'slowly inclined' (p. 273) to resemble – if not become – the narrative's "head fallen" (p. 280). The poem's performance is at an end.

OHIO IMPROMPTU

Written in English in 1980 for the Samuel Beckett Symposium and 75th birthday celebrations held at the Columbus campus of Ohio State University.

First publication   Grove Press, New York, 1981, in *Rockaby and Other Short Pieces*

First performance   9 May 1981, Columbus (Ohio), directed by Alan Schneider, with David Warrilow as R and Rand Mitchell as L

First British performance   13 August 1984, Edinburgh Festival

RECEPTION

In *Samuel Beckett: Humanistic Perspectives* (ed. Morris Beja *et al.*), the published version of the Ohio Symposium proceedings, Yasunari Takahashi points out that what Reader reads from the book in front of him is clearly a story from Listener's life, forcing upon the latter a realization of that life as a failure. Henry Popkin agrees:

> One man reads to the other of a broken romance, telling him how a beloved woman sent to her desolate, forsaken lover a messenger, who read to him from a book; obviously, it is this message, this book, and this reading which we observe on stage.

(*Listener*, 30 April 1981)

Lawrence Graver, however, finds the piece more complicated, more ironic about itself and its occasion. For him it is a 'cryptic, provocative mirror play' which used the traditional form of the impromptu to address the assembled Ohio symposiasts in a 'wry, unsettling fable'. Listener (L) seems to be the 'he' of the story and Reader (R) the person who comforts him, but R may be the author of the sad tale and L its audience, 'as Beckett is the author and we the audience'. R's final words, 'Nothing is left to tell', are deliberately ambiguous in Graver's view: '*Nothing*, as ever in Beckett, is still left to tell,' he points out (*The Beckett Circle*, vol. iii no. 2).

Theatrically, then, this was seen as a dazzling piece, wrily self-aware, and scenically dazzling, too: the black coats and white table made a stark visual contrast in line with the mirrored costumes (trousers matching the other's jacket) in Beckett's Berlin production of *Warten auf Godot*. But, as so often in Beckett, the premièred version is not the only possible, or even the most convincing, interpretation available. Susan Brienza pointed out (in *The Beckett Circle*, Fall 1982) that a later Los Angeles production, in which Alan Mandell played Reader, 'had more realism and humour, less other-worldly atmosphere' than the Ohio version, with R amusingly impatient at L's interruptions and requests to repeat sentences already read, an attitude calculated to enlist the audience's sympathy (as indeed happened). Could it be that the rather literary ironies Graver noted at Columbus were not necessarily in the text as written, but in the text as perceived by the learned Beckettians there assembled? In other words, did the occasion influence the interpretation rather than the other way round? Whatever it was, the two productions, separated in space, time, and circumstance, vindicated (paradoxically) the richness of Beckett's writing in these highly compressed works of his old age.

Writing of the Columbus production, S. E. Gontarski stressed how the 'power of the play swelled in the unsaid: Warrilow's voice was fragile, cracking, unhurried, always on the edge of cessation'; the final impression was 'balletic, precarious' and the production the work of a 'deft miniaturist' (*Journal of Beckett Studies*, Autumn 1982). Reviewing the Edinburgh transfer, Jack Tinker spoke of 'a hypnotic repetitive rhythm with the words and the occasional movement of a hand' combining to 'weave a strange and sepulchred theatrical spell' (*Daily Mail*, 15 August 1984). In the *Guardian* Michael Billington was impressed by 'Beckett's ability to combine a potent, Rembrandtesque puritan image with language that is concrete and allusive at the same time' and by Warrilow's 'gravelly' voice which seemed 'to contain its own death rattle'. In *The Times* (15 August 1984) Irving Wardle wrote: 'Consisting of spiralling and recurring images of farewell and death, the piece sustains its vitality through highly disciplined slow-motion timing and a rasping undertone delivery of a dried-up old pedant.'

DÉCOR

This is clearly prescribed on p. 285. Detailed points about the set will be found in the notes on the text below.

DRAMATIS PERSONAE

Two bowed, black-coated old men with long white hair – 'as alike in appearance as possible' – are seated at a table, Listener facing the audience, Reader in profile. Despite their separate identities they are halves of a split self that Beckett has by now made us familiar with (Vladimir/Estragon, old Krapp/young Krapp, for example).

STRUCTURE, ETC.

This play, like *Rockaby*, runs for about 15 minutes. Although the structure looks complicated on the page, it is simple when experienced in performance. 'Who, in the audience,' Francis King asked, 'will ever forget the scene in which an ancient, black-garbed man, seated at a plain deal table, rehearses yet again to his *alter ego*, a figure exactly like himself, the story of an irremediable loss?' (*Sunday Telegraph*, 19 August 1984). Little is, indeed, left to tell, once this sad tale of inconsolable bereavement has been a last time told.

NOTES ON THE TEXT

[Title.] The play acknowledges, in its title, its adherence to a long tradition of impromptus in French theatre history, from Molière's *Impromptu de Versailles* (1663) through Giraudoux's *Impromptu de Paris* (1937) to Ionesco's *Impromptu de l'Alma* (1955). In theory an impromptu is improvised, played without rehearsal, and used by the playwright to explore the paradoxes of theatricality by drawing attention to his own activity as a writer for the stage. In line with this tradition, while characteristically modifying it, Beckett invites the spectator to ponder the mysterious relationship between a reader and his audience in what Ruby Cohn wittily refers to as 'a tale within a tale within a play'; in her view, *Ohio Impromptu* 'almost drains a story *of* experience in order to theatricalize the reading/writing itself *as* experience' (in *Samuel Beckett: Humanistic Perspectives*, ed. Morris Beja *et al.*, pp. 14–15). Comparing Beckett's 'impromptu' to the three others mentioned above, Pierre Astier writes:

Through its very title, *Ohio Impromptu* shares a feature with the other three dramatic impromptus: the name of the location where it was first performed. It also shares two other characteristics (notwithstanding that these appear also in most of Beckett's latest plays): it is short, very short indeed; and it is, up to a point, comical. Finally, all previous impromptus have in common two other features, one apparently lacking in Beckett's play, while the other is most certainly there, although perhaps not as obvious. First, the missing link: whereas Molière, Giraudoux and Ionesco used their respective impromptus to defend their own theatre aesthetics through explicit and virulently satirical attacks against their respective critics, Beckett does not seem to defend anything or attack anyone in his impromptu. Second, the metatheatrical dimension: previous impromptus all deal to a large extent with problems of play-acting or play-writing through the acting or the writing of a play that turns out to be the very one performed before our eyes. So it is with *Ohio Impromptu*, but with two marked differences. The work within the play is not a play, but a story read from a book. Moreover, this story ends with events which the audience can witness on stage at the end of the play, yet it also seems timeless. Read aloud now by a character in the play, it is concerned with a certain 'sad tale' once before read aloud by another character (the visitor in the book story), a 'sad tale' of which we know nothing except that it is a repetition of the repetition of a repetition, and so on *ad infinitum*, of the same old 'sad tale'. While the story we hear might refer to the relatively recent past of the characters in the play, the 'sad tale' to which it is linked refers to a past so absolutely remote that it might well go back to the very origin of time itself.

(*Modern Drama*, September 1982, p. 332)

p. 285

(*Light on table midstage.*) Deal is a common cheap wood for furniture. In the Paris production in French the author's instructions were followed strictly: only the table surface was lit up. In Edinburgh, the table legs and the chairs were visible.

(R *seated at table in profile.*) Beckett suggested to the director Alan Schneider that the table be angled slightly so that the audience could see R's face.

(*Book on table before him.*) Beckett sees this as 'an old quartotype thing'; in Paris it was small, like a missal, and in Edinburgh large, like a register. R should read from it, Beckett says, calmly and soothingly, as if telling a child a bedtime story (Martha Fehsenfeld, *Modern Drama*, September 1982, p. 357).

(*Black wide-brimmed hat.*) An 'old world Latin Quarter hat' (p. 286) such as students and artists used to wear in Paris in the heyday of bohemia.

(*Knock.*) L uses the knock to get R to go back a little in his reading (somewhat like Krapp winding the tape back to hear a section again), and then to order him to go on. Beckett uses the device once more of the voice; disembodied in *Rockaby*, it is embodied in this play in R, 'and treats, as always, the themes of separation and communion, of presence vs. absence, and of the past haunting the present' (Pierre Astier).

the Isle of Swans. On the Seine in Paris near the Eiffel Tower (the bereaved lover moves across the river after living with the loved one on the opposite bank, i.e. he moves from his home on the left bank to the right bank, where he sees from his strange room the Ile (or Allée) des Cygnes). In an elaborate exegesis of this topographical allusion, Pierre Astier notes that although few Parisians have ever set foot on it, they have all seen – especially from the windows of the *métro aérien* (elevated subway) that passes over its upstream tip – its one and only tourist attraction standing high at the end of the 'allée', at the *downstream* extremity of the islet: a much reduced but still quite imposing replica of one of Frédéric Auguste Bartholdi's most famous works, the Statue of Liberty.

(*Modern Drama*, September 1982, p. 337)

p. 286

my shade will comfort you. She (it is clear that the loved one is female) is dead, of course. Note the much gentler theme of this play as compared with, say, *Eh Joe*, where the returning 'shade' is a tormentor, not a comforter.

White nights. Sleepless nights (cf. French *nuits blanches*).

p. 287

and here he named the dear name. For the discretion in this demure concealment, cf. the refrain of *A Piece of Monologue*, 'he all but said'.

p. 288

(R *closes book.*) In Paris, with the left hand, from left to right; in Edinburgh, with the left hand, from right to left (i.e. across the body); the former seems more natural.

(*Knock.*) This last knock, like all the 'acquiescing' knocks, was soft in Edinburgh, much lighter than the peremptory knocks ordering R to backtrack; in Paris all the knocks were equally light.

(*Fade out.*) A moment of intense emotion, strongly felt by the audience, follows the last, quietly emphatic 'nothing is left to tell'; compare the end of *Godot* ('Yes, let's go.' – *They do not move*) and of *Krapp's Last Tape* (Krapp staring before him as the tape confesses that there is no longer any chance of happiness).

QUAD

Written in English, about 1980, for the Stuttgart Preparatory Ballet School.

First publication   Faber and Faber, London, 1984, in *Collected Shorter Plays*

First broadcast   8 October 1981, SDR, directed by Samuel Beckett and produced by Reinhart Müller-Freienfels, under the title *Quadrat 1 + 2*. The same production, entitled *Quad*, was first transmitted by BBC2 on 16 December 1982

RECEPTION

In a talk at the Edinburgh Festival in August 1984 Martin Esslin described the play as 'a dynamic, witty yet terrifying attempt to compress eternity as endless recurrence into a single dramatic image, a poem without words'. On the day of the BBC transmission, the *Radio Times* commented:

> It is a kind of canon or catch – a mysterious square dance. Four hooded figures move along the sides of the square. Each has his own particular itinerary. A pattern emerges and collisions are just avoided. From these permutations, Beckett, as writer and director, creates an image of life that is both highly charged and strangely funny.

DÉCOR, ETC.

Beckett sees this play as a mime for four players, with colour, percussion instruments, the sound of footsteps and no spoken words. Mime has of course attracted Beckett from the beginning; cf. not only the *Acts Without Words* but also the 'balletic' movements in *Waiting for Godot*. But, as Martha Fehsenfeld points out,

> the harmonious chamber orchestration of sound and echo, light and darkness, and measured movement with its accom-

panying sound, evolves most specifically from their previous syntheses in *Footfalls*, *Ghost Trio* and . . . *but the clouds* . . . . And the picture of a square ABCD enclosing two diagonals crossing at a central point E is a continuation of the same picture and pattern that defined the circuits of movement included in the notes for *J. M. Mime*, conceived about 1963 and now in the Beckett Collection in the Trinity College manuscript room in Dublin.

Beckett related that the actual filming of *Quad* at the Süddeutscher Rundfunk in Stuttgart as it evolved from the first rough text required alteration resulting in several innovations. The coloured lights simply 'did not work' so that the colour was only in the costumes. Beckett's cameraman, Jim Lewis, who had worked with him since 1966 on *Eh Joe*, *Ghost Trio* and . . . *but the clouds* . . ., gave this account: 'We couldn't use the coloured lights. First the combination of white plus blue plus red plus yellow produced an effect of an indefinite shade of orange. I worked on it and got a closer delineation but then the frequency of light going on and off with the entrance and exit of each player proved too distracting and had to be abandoned.' The original idea for the placement of the percussionists on a raised platform behind the players was altered – they were placed at the point of each right-angle outside the square and were hardly visible. The instruments used were two Javanese gongs (Beckett himself had played the gong during the recording of *MacGowran Speaking Beckett* made for Claddaugh Records in 1966), an African wood block and an African talking drum, and 'a wonderful wastebasket – from Rathmines' (Beckett added whimsically). The players – 'mimes not dancers' – were young, slight, all the same size, and wore floor-length coloured gowns with cowls which covered headphones by means of which they could hear the percussion sounds and time their movements. They held themselves in the same position Billie Whitelaw had used for *Footfalls*, 'crossing their arms tightly against themselves' under the loose gowns, 'in a bent shape which they kept throughout', as if, Lewis said, 'they were resisting a cold wind'. The running time originally envisioned by Beckett as 'approximately 25 minutes' became 'about a quarter of an hour. They did it twice.' The first time included the original complete cycle of four series without interruption, but the timing was '164 beats a minute', according to Lewis, 'about 9 minutes' according to Beckett's calculation. 'It was feverish. Feverish monotony.' The second time they played at 'about 160 beats a minute – about 4 minutes, in black and white, white costumes, same grey square, no percussion, just a metronome and shuffling footsteps'. The problem of 'the negotiation of E without rupture of rhythm when three or four players cross paths at this point . . .' was resolved inventively. As each player arrived at a point close to the centre, he made a 'jerky turn to his left as a diversion away from it'. At first it seemed 'they were merely avoiding one another, but gradually one realized they were avoiding the centre. There was something terrifying about it . . . it was danger.'

The overall effect of this most recent Beckett dramatic work is unbearable and unrelieved tension strained almost to the breaking point. He has painted a picture, deliberately choosing colour for the first time in using film. One sees through the eye of the camera fixed above, a group of figures moving in a tightly prescribed pattern in relation to one another but not necessarily aware (or unaware) of one another as individuals (as the distinct colours of costumes, sounds of footsteps, and instruments establish them). Beckett has exchanged the sound of the word for other sounds – the percussion instruments and the footsteps – which are the extensions of the movement. One hears something very close to a musical composition. Or perhaps that is precisely what one hears. Each figure comes out of darkness into dim neutral light, goes through its 'course', returns to darkness. Darkness is the only relief, and like all relief in Beckett it is only temporary. The only cessation perhaps lurks in the black centre that is to be avoided at any cost, even at the risk of perpetual motion. This pattern is clearly infernal; the players, like Dante's damned, are committed to an endless unyielding punishment – continuous movement of excruciating sameness.

(*Modern Drama*, September 1982, pp. 360–1)

NOTES ON THE TEXT

[Title.] Self-explanatory, given the 'square dance' referred to above. There should be a footnote (1) against the title. (The note itself is 1. on p. 293.)

p. 291

(*each following his particular course*.) The centre is taboo; when they meet in the centre they avoid it by moving in a clockwise direction (see the diagram on p. 293).

p. 292

(*Footsteps.*) The players shuffled along, making a swishing sound with their feet. They all moved with great rapidity.

(*Costumes.*) The gowns were sleeveless and so sealed in their arms.

p. 293

(*As alike in build as possible.*) Cp. the characters in *What Where*, p. 309.

(*Sex indifferent.*) Although it was impossible to tell this, there were in fact two women and two men in the SDR production.

(*Both players and percussionists in frame.*) Not in the SDR production; only the players and their square were visible, so that the music had a 'ghostly' source.

(*E.g. series 1.*) E was marked by a sort of golf hole. Eventually the footmarks drew lines, very similar to those in this diagram, by natural wear of the floor covering.

p. 294

(*5. No colour.*) Müller-Freienfels's suggestion on playing back the tapes that it would look equally good in black and white led Beckett to add this, saying that 5 is 'one hundred thousand years later'. It was a masterly idea, creating much the same feeling as the second acts of *Godot* and *Happy Days* and the *da capo* of *Play*, that is repetition-with-a-difference offering an ironic comment of its own on the principal movement.

CATASTROPHE

Written in French, about 1982, for *Une Nuit pour Vaclav Havel*, sponsored by the organization 'Artistes en Défense d'autres Artistes' at the Avignon Festival, 1982.

First publication   Faber and Faber, London, 1984, in *Collected Shorter Plays*; it also appears in the February 1984 issue of *Index on Censorship*

First performance   21 July 1982, Avignon, directed by Stephan Meldbegg

First Paris production   15 September 1983, Théâtre du Rond-Point, directed by Pierre Chabert, who was advised by Samuel Beckett, with Michel Lonsdale as D, Catherine Sellers as A, Jean-Louis Barrault as P, and Dominique Elhanger as L

First British production   13 August 1984, Edinburgh Festival, directed by Alan Schneider, with Donald Davis as D, Leigh Taylor-Young as A, David Warrilow as P, and Rand Mitchell as L, in a triple bill with *Ohio Impromptu* and *What Where*

RECEPTION

Reviewing the Avignon Festival première, Martha Fehsenfeld was impressed by the way Beckett made 'a metaphor of Havel's humiliation' by using 'both the framework and context of the theatre', with P 'the image of suffering under ruthless spotlight' (*Theatre Journal*, March 1983, pp. 110–11). The reaction in Edinburgh was equally enthusiastic. In the *Daily Telegraph* John Barber noted that *Catastrophe* 'expresses pity for the cadaverous victims of Death, or a god as cruel', and John Peter that Beckett elevates 'a metaphor of our time by telling us that the harassed artist suffers like a prisoner of conscience: solitary, pitiable, unloved and shabbily heroic' (*Sunday Times*, 26 August 1984). In *The Times* (15 August) Irving Wardle praised the play's 'immediacy of focus and indignation expressed in its reflection of all kinds of manipulated feeling from theatrical performance to show trials'. Putting it another way, Michael Billington of the *Guardian* perceived 'a study of power and terror using the theatre as a metaphor ... the tyranny of the state is combined with the inherent autocracy of the theatre. Thus, Beckett implies, dictatorships venerate and persecute artists at the same time.'

DÉCOR

Once again this is clearly prescribed, and once again directors tend to depart from their instructions (see notes on the text below). In line with the whole tone of the play, the setting and costumes are more familiar or 'everyday' than we have come to expect in Beckett's later works.

DRAMATIS PERSONAE

The same remark applies here too. But all that the Avignon, Paris and Edinburgh directors seemed agreed on is that the characters should be played fairly 'straight', as if they were more or less real people, with the obvious exception of the (deliberately) unsettling figure of P, who reminds one very much of the tormented slave Lucky in *Waiting for Godot*.

STRUCTURE

Again, straightforward; the narrative can easily be followed even in the reading text. Rather like a serious revue sketch (the oxymoron is appropriate) it builds up economically to its punch line, 'There's our catastrophe' (p. 300).

LANGUAGE AND DRAMATIC EXPRESSION

'The text, in Beckett's translation from his French original, has a slight American flavour and odd, ungrammatical locutions: the great master of language as a precision instrument is hinting that his theme is universal' (John Peter). An example of Americanisms is 'step on it' (p. 298) and of odd locutions 'I make a note' (ibid.).

NOTES ON THE TEXT

[Title.] Enigmatic, but partially explained by D's use of the word on p. 300.

[Dedication.] Vaclav Havel (b. 1936) is a well-known Czech playwright (author of *The Memorandum*, a political comedy that satirizes bureaucracy and offers an Ionesco-style critique of language) and dissident. He has been held as a political prisoner since 1979 and the publication and performance of his work is of course banned in his own country. Although Beckett's play is not a direct satire on the situation in Czechoslovakia, the tormenting of P (who could be a *p*olitical *p*risoner) holds out a direct analogy with the bullying of Havel and other dissidents in totalitarian countries. It is written, as were others by famous authors, for Havel's benefit night at Avignon; once again Beckett has done a play almost to order, only this time the solicitation was more political than artistic. He would not normally accede to such a request, but he is known to feel deeply about human cruelty and injustice, no doubt because he thinks that something can be done about it (unlike the cosmic variety for which, as Hamm might say, there's no cure; cf. *Endgame*, p. 37).

p. 297

(*Director*.) Dressed opulently in thick furs in Paris; less extravagantly so in Edinburgh.

(*female assistant*.) A revealed that she was very much on P's side in Paris, by (for instance) blowing smoke from the large matches with which she lit D's cigar over D as she extinguished them. Catherine Sellers was dressed in a rather severe linen suit, the austerity of the costume intended as an allusion by Pierre Chabert to the holy women who attended Jesus at Golgotha. In Edinburgh the role was played quite differently, with marked sexiness: Miss Taylor-Young's skirt was slit a long way up the front, and as she bent forward to light D's cigar she revealed a beautiful stockinged leg and a glimpse of thigh to the

265

audience. This was not lost on reviewers; Jack Tinker noted in the *Daily Mail* that 'Miss Leigh Taylor-Young (she of a thousand soap operas) clip-clops around the stage on disturbingly erotic stiletto heels – sex in Beckett!' Although the assistant must be soft and feminine in order to contrast with the *machismo* of the bullying director, she should perhaps not be so distractingly attractive as Miss Taylor-Young played her.

(A *standing beside him.*) In Edinburgh she always moved in front of him to address him. Her overall was greyish or bluish, not white as prescribed. As for the armchair, this was bright red in Edinburgh, white in Paris.

p. 298
I have a caucus. An American word for a 'local political usu. elective party committee for fighting elections, defining policy, etc.' (COED). The political overtones would not have been lost on the audience at Havel's benefit night.

p. 299
He's shivering. Like Lucky, in some productions of *Waiting for Godot.* At Avignon, quite contrary to the author's indications, P was bound, seated on a wheeled-in stool.

(*Exit* D, *not to appear again.*) Pierre Chabert took this to mean, surely rightly, that his voice is heard from somewhere in the theatre but that he should not be seen again. In Edinburgh he re-entered the auditorium after a brief eclipse (during which A wiped his chair, etc.) and could clearly be seen standing by the right exit facing the stage. Since he *says* he is in the front row of the stalls this was distinctly confusing to the audience.

(*discards rag.*) In Edinburgh she stuffed it hurriedly under the cushion of the chair.

p. 300
(A *transmits in technical terms.*) A rare occasion on which Beckett invites the performer to improvise (cf. the exchange of insults in the French version of Godot; set out in full in the English text

p. 75, it is left up to the French players to fill in); in Edinburgh, A called out spot numbers, etc.

In Patagonia? The southernmost part of Argentina, apart from Tierra del Fuego itself at the very tip of the continent; cf. 'alive and well . . . in the Argentine', *Embers*, p. 94. In both plays the names are obviously chosen because of the remoteness from Europe of the places concerned.

There's our catastrophe. This play is similar in tone to some of the 'Roughs' for theatre and radio (cf. especially p. 115 of the *Collected Shorter Plays*), but is more self-conscious about theatre, even self-ironic (in that P is almost a caricature of a Beckettian hero in his appearance). It is decidedly 'jokey' despite the seriousness of its dedication, and a good production would bring this out without (and here is the difficulty) going quite 'over the top'. Only the Paris production seems to have achieved this to date. But if anyone doubts that Beckett has a sense of humour and can enjoy a joke at his own expense, this play should convince them. On the other hand, like the ending of *Godot*, this play should close on a serious note; as Irving Wardle noted, the figure raises his head at the end in defiance of all instructions from D and fixes the (real) audience with 'a gaze to freeze all words on the lips' as the (stage) audience's applause falters and dies away. It is an accusatory gaze, and impresses the (live) audience as such; it is a sobering and chastening moment in the theatre, and one that makes its political point far more effectively than overt propaganda against oppression could do.

NACHT UND TRÄUME

Written in English, about 1983, for SDR.

First publication   Faber and Faber, London, 1984, in *Collected Shorter Plays*
First broadcast   19 May 1983, SDR, directed by Samuel Beckett, with Helfrid Foron, Dirk Morgner and Stephan Pritz

This slight work (felt by Martin Esslin to be 'a bit too sentimental an image') is, like *Quad*, a play without spoken words. The music is Schubert's, hummed and sung by a male voice; the song, or *Lied*, in question, 'Nacht und Träume', which gives the play its title, is a late (1827) setting of words by a minor Austrian poet, Heinrich Josef von Collin (1771–1811), and the line we hear is 'Holde Träume, kehret wieder', or 'Lovely dreams, return again', the desire of an old man to recall the love of his youth (a theme with obvious parallels to *Krapp's Last Tape*). In a letter to us Beckett states 'text of song of course in German and to be left so in eventual translations', like the title, which means 'Night and Dreams'.

The only points calling for comment are that the cup mentioned in 9 at the bottom of p. 305 is a chalice of solace, and that 27 on p. 306 specifies repetition-with-a-difference as in *Quad* (and indeed before that as in the second act of *Waiting for Godot*). The lighting was greyish, indeed it gave the impression of being shot in black and white, which reduced the visual interest; this, together with the difficulty of containing the images of both the dreamer and his dreamt self within the small frame of a television screen leads one to doubt whether this script makes for a successful or effective use of the medium.

WHAT WHERE

Written in French, about 1983.

First publication   Faber and Faber, London, 1984, in *Collected Shorter Plays*

First performance   Graz Festival, 1983, in Elmar Tophoven's German translation

First British production   13 August 1984, Edinburgh Festival, directed by Alan Schneider, with Donald Davis as Bam (and Voice of Bam), David Warrilow as Bom, Rand Mitchell as Bim and Daniel Wirth as Bem, in a triple bill with *Ohio Impromptu* and *Catastrophe*

RECEPTION

This slight work, which harks back to *Cascando* and *Rough for Radio II* and their dramatization of what Beckett calls in 'Text for Nothing XIII' the probing of 'no's knife in yes's wound', was generally felt by critics at Edinburgh to be the weakest technically of the three plays on the triple bill. Irving Wardle in *The Times* asserted that 'the spring-to-winter ceremony of a "last tribe" torturing its last members to death' was 'Beckett at his most rigid and repetitious', while in the *Guardian* Michael Billington agreed that 'for once Beckett's constant themes of mortality and time and his more recent preoccupation with political brutality don't find an image of matching resonance'. Other reviewers were content to sum up the theme of the play as being that of authoritarian violence, political torture, or the cyclical repetitive nature of persecution; John Peter in the *Sunday Times* summarized the plot as being 'about a godlike tormentor whose victims perish one by one and leave him still without the secret he sought'.

STRUCTURE, ETC.

This is clearly set out and calls for little comment. For 'head haught', p. 310, see note to *A Piece of Monologue*, p. 269. The names have been used by Beckett before, notably in *Murphy* and *How It Is*; here, Bam is obviously the boss or overlord. The similarity of the players' costumes recalls *Quad*. The play might have been called 'The Four Seasons' since these are run through in order, but in fact takes its title, as usual, from words ('what' and 'where') occurring at strategic points in the text. The last spoken sentence but one, 'Make sense who may', provoked many spectators to sigh, 'Yes, indeed', which perhaps was just what the author intended.

SELECT BIBLIOGRAPHY

Abel, Lionel, *Metatheatre: A New View of Dramatic Form*, New York, Hill & Wang, 1963

Adorno, Theodor W., *Noten zur Literatur, II*, Frankfurt, Suhrkamp, 1969

Alvarez, A., *Beckett*, London, Fontana/Collins, 1973

Anders, Günther, *Die Antiquiertheit des Menschen*, Munich, Beck, 1968

Anon., *Materialien zu Becketts 'Endspiel' [Endgame]*, Frankfurt, Suhrkamp, 1968

Bair, Deirdre, *Samuel Beckett: A Biography*, London, Cape, 1978

Barnard, G. C., *Samuel Beckett: A New Approach*, London, Dent, 1970

Beckett, Samuel, *'Das letzte Band' [Krapp's Last Tape]: Regiebuch der Berliner Inszenierung*, Frankfurt, Suhrkamp, 1970

Beja, Morris, S. E. Gontarski and Pierre Astier (eds.), *Samuel Beckett: Humanistic Perspectives*, Columbus, Ohio State University Press, 1983

Birkenhauer, Klaus, *Samuel Beckett in Selbstzeugnissen und Bilddokumenten*, Reinbek, Rowohlt, 1971

Chevigny, Bell Gale (ed.), *Twentieth Century Interpretations of Endgame*, Englewood Cliffs, NJ, Prentice-Hall, 1969

Coe, Richard N., *Beckett*, Edinburgh and London, Oliver & Boyd, 1964

Cohn, Ruby, *Just Play: Beckett's Theater*, Princeton, NJ, Princeton University Press, 1980

Cohn, Ruby, *Samuel Beckett: The Comic Gamut*, New Brunswick, NJ, Rutgers University Press, 1962

Descartes, René, *Discourse on Method*, London, Dent, 1965

Doherty, Francis, *Samuel Beckett*, London, Hutchinson, 1971

Duckworth, Colin (ed.), *Samuel Beckett, En attendant Godot*, London, Harrap, 1966

Esslin, Martin (ed.), *Samuel Beckett: A Collection of Critical Essays*, Englewood Cliffs, NJ, Prentice-Hall, 1965

Esslin, Martin, *The Theatre of the Absurd*, Harmondsworth, Penguin Books, rev. ed., 1968

Federman, Raymond, and John Fletcher, *Samuel Beckett: His Works and His Critics*, Berkeley and Los Angeles, University of California Press, 1970

Select Bibliography

Fletcher, John, and John Spurling, *Beckett: A Study of His Plays*, London, Eyre Methuen, 1972

Friedman, Melvin J. (ed.), *Samuel Beckett Now*, Chicago and London, University of Chicago Press, 1970

Gessner, Niklaus, *Die Unzulänglichkeit der Sprache*, Zurich, Juris, 1957

Gontarski, S. E., *Beckett's 'Happy Days': A Manuscript Study*, Columbus, Ohio State University Libraries Publications Committee, 1977

Harvey, Lawrence E., *Samuel Beckett, Poet and Critic*, Princeton, NJ, Princeton University Press, 1970

Hayman, Ronald, *Samuel Beckett*, London, Heinemann, 1968

Hensel, Georg, *Samuel Beckett*, Velber, Friedrich, 1968

Kenner, Hugh, *A Reader's Guide to Samuel Beckett*, London, Thames & Hudson, 1973

Kenner, Hugh, *Samuel Beckett: A Critical Study*, New York, Grove Press, 1961

Knowlson, James (ed.), *Light and Darkness in the Theatre of Samuel Beckett*, London, Turret Books, 1972

Knowlson, James, *Samuel Beckett: An Exhibition*, London, Turret Books, 1971

Knowlson, James, *Samuel Beckett, 'Krapp's Last Tape': A Theatre Workbook*, London, Brutus Books, 1980

Knowlson, James, and John Pilling, *Frescoes of the Skull: The Later Prose and Drama of Samuel Beckett*, London, John Calder, 1979

Lyons, Charles R., *Samuel Beckett*, London, Macmillan, 1983

Melchinger, Siegfried, *Geschichte des politischen Theaters*, Velber, Friedrich, 1971

Morrison, Kristin, *Canters and Chronicles: The Use of Narrative in the Plays of Samuel Beckett and Harold Pinter*, Chicago and London, University of Chicago Press, 1983

Reid, Alec, *All I Can Manage, More Than I Could: An Approach to Samuel Beckett*, Dublin, Dolmen Press, 1968

Robinson, Michael, *The Long Sonata of the Dead: A Study of Samuel Beckett*, London, Hart-Davis, 1969

Schoell, Konrad, *Das Theater Samuel Becketts*, Munich, Fink, 1967

Schramm, Ulf, *Fiktion und Reflexion: Überlegungen zu Musil und Beckett*, Frankfurt, Suhrkamp, 1967

Seipel, Hildegard, *Untersuchungen zum experimentellen Theater von Beckett und Ionesco*, Bonn, dissertation, 1963

Webb, Eugene, *The Plays of Samuel Beckett*, London, Peter Owen, 1972

Select Bibliography

Winkler, Elizabeth Hale, *The Clown in Modern Anglo-Irish Drama*, Frankfurt, Peter Lang, and Bern, Herbert Lang, 1977

Worth, Katharine (ed.), *Beckett the Shape Changer*, London, Routledge & Kegan Paul, 1975

Worth, Katharine, *The Irish Drama of Europe from Yeats to Beckett*, London, Athlone Press, 1978

Zilliacus, Clas, *Beckett and Broadcasting: A Study of the Works of Samuel Beckett for and in Radio and Television*, Åbo, Åbo Akademi, 1976

INDEX